Raise the Banners High!

Making and Using Processional Banners

Making and Using Processional Banners

Pamela T. Hardiman
Josephine Niemann, SSND

Visit our website at www.ltp.org.

This book was edited by David Philippart and designed by Lucy Smith. Audrey Novak Riley was the production editor. The typesetting was done by Kari Nicholls in Galliard and Ludovico. The illustrations are by Pamela T. Hardiman. The authors are grateful to those whose photographs appear in this book; please see page 180 for more information. Printed in China by Palace Press International.

Library of Congress Control Number: 2001099486

ISBN 1-56854-368-9

RAISE

One never writes a book in isolation. We are first of all grateful that life allowed us to meet and be enriched by one another. We appreciate all those who supported and encouraged us through the extended process of writing this book. In particular,

I, Josephine, would like to thank
my mother, Cecilia Niemann, for teaching me to sew and transferring to me her love of quilts,
my college art teacher, Mary Luke Jordan, SSND, for modeling for me inspired creativity,
the sisters in Liturgical Fabric Arts for their patience and willingness to work through my artistic schemes,
and Monsignor James Telthorst, for nourishing my love for liturgy.

I, Pam, deeply appreciate
my mother, Jean Thibodeau, who taught me how to sew, how to dream, and the importance of acting on dreams,
my husband, Chris, for urging me to develop my talents and allowing me the time to do so,
my children, Gregory, Nicholas, and Daniel, for the light in their eyes and for giving me "just another minute,"
Len Kraus, SJ, and Mary Nagel, for sharing their love of sustaining sacrament, liturgy, and art.

Contents

Preface

It is exciting when one can experience the coming together of artistic grace, wisdom, and creativity with practical, down-to-earth planning of the liturgical year. Most often, it seems, artists go off and create their work (in this case processional banners) and then come back to the other members of the community who are planning the liturgy or celebration and say, "Here it is!" What a gift it is to have a book that unites creative ideas and directions with a basic exposition of the liturgical cycle.

For a pastor, this book is a godsend: It integrates an overview of the liturgical seasons with wonderful suggestions pertaining to a powerful way to bring the seasons to life through the use of processional banners. It offers the opportunity for both those who prepare the liturgy and those who create the environment literally to be on "the same page." For that reason, this book will be a catalyst for parishes and other communities who strive to bring together the disparate elements out of which all hope to make an integrated celebration.

The authors compare a liturgical procession to a parade in which all participate. This is an apt comparison when the procession unites the assembly and helps to focus the energies and attention on the celebration of the event. For one just beginning to study how to bring beauty and order to the liturgical celebration, as well as for the experienced artist or liturgy planner, this book is a welcome resource and a stimulating aid to the work of providing dancing color for celebrations ordinary and extraordinary.

Len Kraus, SJ
Saint Francis Xavier Church
St. Louis, Missouri

Foreword

I live and minister in a unique place: a cathedral. So much of what happens here is on a grand scale, but similar things happen at parish churches, too, on a different, smaller scale. At almost any time of the day, individuals pause in quiet prayer, some sitting peacefully, some bent over in almost desperate petition. On the weekends and special occasions, countless numbers of people gather to celebrate with song, procession, instruments, and warm greetings. The personal dimension and the communal dimension: We are called to follow Christ and to live the gospel as individuals and in community.

The personal and the quiet have long been associated with religious experience and, in some ways, are perhaps the easier expectation for those who prepare the liturgy and the things that the liturgy uses. These are not only familiar but also, in our culture of individualism, perhaps more appealing. Yet, if anything is certain, it is that liturgy is a communal enterprise and experience.

Unfortunately, the model of communal gatherings in our society is one of superficial and passing excitement. We are held together for a moment at a political rally or an enthusiastic parade or in the joy of rooting for a winning team or a favorite performer. Our communal gathering as a church, however, while it builds on these experiences, is essentially different. For we experience the mystery of God's presence within that community. Our Christian experience says boldly that this God has become and remained incarnated, revealed in the flesh.

Sacramentally, we borrow from our world the water, oil, bread, wine, the love of marriage, and even our sinfulness as the "stuff" of life in which to encounter the divine. We do so by using these ingredients in ways that allow us to meet and experience God profoundly and passionately. But how do we use the rest of human experience, the world of music and movement, color and shape, sound, and silence in our worship? This has long been discussed, if not debated.

Josephine Niemann and Pamela Hardiman, in this extensive work, provide insight into one way: the use of processional banners in liturgy. As they remind us, banners have long been used in history, from the pennants of marching armies to the now popular and ever-present seasonal banners flying from porches and patios alerting us to spring, winter, Saint Patrick's Day, and all such special times.

How might we use this same dynamic to celebrate the liturgy in its seasons? How might we walk in procession in ways that acknowledge not passing fashion or fad but touch and hold eternal life? How shall we invite the participation of all and not leave others only watching from the sidelines? This book goes a long way in guiding us in the use of banners not only by providing details of their history and their practical creation, but also by offering a scholarly review of the liturgical seasons and sacramental celebrations of our church.

Those who seek to bring a sense of life, color, and movement to parish communities will find much help in the chapters that follow. The promise this work holds out, however, also comes with a caution. It is the hope and caution that Romano Guardini expressed some years ago in a letter to fellow liturgical scholars. He reminded them that the goal of the liturgical renewal was not simply that the procession went well, but rather that we rediscover a deeper way of doing things, a way in which even walking can be an epiphany of the Lord.

Msgr. James T. Telthorst
Cathedral of St. Louis
St. Louis, Missouri

Chapter 1

USING PROCESSIONAL BANNERS

It never fails. Every time processional banners are used in a liturgy, people seem a bit more alert, more attentive. And they never fail to make comments afterward. "Oh, those are great. I wish we could use those at . . ." What makes people respond in this way to a well-made banner? Is it just a bit of excitement and color, a bit of fluff? Or do processional banners speak to us in some deeper, more fundamental way? Do they help us do liturgy better? Do they add something that other works of art do not?

A good set of banners actually helps people celebrate the liturgy in ways that other works of art do not. They help us participate with more of our senses. Their movements draw our eyes, whose path sweeps across the faces of others in the assembly, further uniting us as Christians; banners call us to follow! Their use makes it immediately clear that our gathering is a celebration, thus helping to set the tone. They can help focus our attention on certain actions, especially in churches where it can be hard to see over others' heads. If you choose to use *processional* banners, you will be drawn to consider when and why processions occur in liturgy. You may find yourself restructuring wedding processions, highlighting movement in the rites of baptism, or sending the newly confirmed forth in a burst of flame-colored ribbons.

Before settling down to the details of how you can use banners in your liturgies, we invite you to consider parades, then to reflect on how processional banners function in general and how these functions might apply to liturgy in particular. Have you been to a parade lately? Recall it for a few minutes before reading further. Is there one scheduled soon that you can experience? Go and participate in it, then come back and read or reread this chapter.

Identifying with the Group

Everybody loves a parade. Even the humble town parade of Farmington, Connecticut, draws people of all ages out of their houses and onto the sidewalks to watch neighbors marching in the parade. Somehow, the magic of the parade transforms the little girls up the street, Susan's husband, and the guy next door who mows his lawn every weekend. The people you know as scattered individuals now step forth in unison with others, marching with a sense of purpose. They have been transformed into members of a group. The little girls are Girl Scouts, Susan's husband represents the board of education, and the guy next door is the chief of the local fire department. We celebrate their dignity as members of these groups and delight in the special joy this identification brings.

How did that transformation from individuals to members of a group happen? It started when a number of individuals gathered together at a specific time and place. They stood in ordered rows to form a marching unit and henceforth move as one. Sometimes the individuals have uniforms or other special clothes that mark and identify group members. Band instruments, flags, and tiny zooming cars can also help identify individuals as members of a group. The grouping, the spacing, the clothing, and the instruments all help spectators recognize that this is a marching group. The first thing most marching groups want to share with the flag-waving crowd is their name, prominently displayed at the head of the group on a banner carried by two or more group members.

Normally, marching banners have a horizontal format, with the name of the group and its locality in prominent lettering on it. Colors often indicate ties to a school or other organization, further identifying the group. Although the banner is seemingly just an informational device, its very existence at the head of a group defines this event as a parade. It declares this event to be a celebration. Without the group identification, without the banner, the group could be just a group of people walking together—or an angry mob.

The entrance or gathering rites of a liturgy can be likened to a parade: a coming together of a diverse group of individuals, each with his or her own worries and cares. Somehow, in that coming together, they become something more than a collection of individuals. They become the primary symbol of the presence of Christ. They are the people of God. They are a group with an identity. Appreciation for this identity allows us to "respond with a faith and love that will transform us."[1]

One of the ways that we can choose to proclaim our identity, as well as express our joy in that identity, is to carry a banner in procession. (In this sense, the primary "processional banner" is the cross!) The banner simultaneously identifies us as belonging to Christ and evokes a feeling of celebration. This dual nature of banners is further developed in a story Gertrud Mueller Nelson tells about her then-young daughter:

> *Some years ago, I spent an afternoon caught up in a piece of sewing I was doing. The wastebasket near my sewing machine was filled with scraps of fabric cut away from my project. This basket of discards was a fascination to my daughter, Annika, who, at the time, was not yet four years old. She rooted through the scraps searching out the long bright strips, collected them to herself, and went off. When I took a moment to check on her, I tracked her whereabouts to the back garden, where I found her, sitting in the grass with a long pole. She was fixing the scraps to the top of the pole with great sticky wads of tape. "I'm making a banner for a procession," she said. "I need a procession so that God will come down and dance with us." With that she solemnly lifted her banner to flutter in the wind and slowly began to dance.*[2]

Intellectually, we know that God is present and interacts with us when we come together and lift our voices in prayer. Jesus himself told us so. But the child, through her heart, clearly sees God dancing with us. For too many of us, the reality remains too cerebral. We need heart; we need soul. We need to find our dancing feet. How do we do that? We can do it by remembering who we are as a people and the purpose for our gathering, in ways other than words. Music is the tool most commonly used for that purpose. But we can engage other senses as well. As we lift our hearts in song, we can lift our eyes to follow colorful swaying banners, awakening our souls to the spirit of the present moment. What works in a parade also works in a liturgical entrance procession, helping us more truly to "dance with God."

As in a parade where the banner precedes the group, a liturgical gathering can begin with a banner at or near the head of the procession. With few exceptions, liturgical celebrations always begin with a gathering rite whose purpose is to bring individuals together as a community of believers and to prepare them to hear the word of God. The focus of this rite is the entrance procession, in which at least a portion of the group assembled moves from the church door to the altar, transitioning from daily routine to sacred space in a pilgrimage to the table, the banquet of love. The movement itself is symbolic of the journey through life, from birth to death to resurrection. We do not travel alone, for God precedes us, simultaneously leading and calling us forward, inviting us onward in our pilgrimage. A processional banner can serve to focus attention on this movement and remind us of the God who goes before us.

All present participate in a good entrance procession, even though practicality may dictate that a sampling of ministers actually move down the aisle. Unlike a parade, there are no spectators. We are all the people of God. Making this statement clearly sets a tone for the rites that follow. Much rests on an inclusive and all-encompassing entrance procession.

But the feeling of participation is easily diminished or lost if the entrance procession is minimized, particularly if it is not visible. Too often, the entrance procession seems merely a functional way of moving the ministers from one place to another, with our attention being optional. Including as many people as possible in the procession helps to indicate the importance of all parts of the assembly, as does using the full length of aisles and walkways. In some churches, it is logistically possible to spread the procession over multiple aisles, increasing the possibility that everyone can see. But even then, sight lines may prevent visual participation. By including one or more banners in the procession, the movement becomes visible to all.

But like the parade banner, processional banners can do much more. They can help inspire as well as reflect our joy in praising

God. Because many Christian churches link color and time in the liturgical year, the color and form of banners, as well as what they depict or the design they bear, can highlight the celebration of a specific feast or season. We are a people of God at a particular place in time. In addition, elements of ethnic heritages can be incorporated in a banner's design through fabric or design choices so that it more truly belongs to those who gather behind it.

The flowing liveliness of banners is appropriate for ending as well as beginning the liturgy. When our liturgy is ended, we are to "go in peace, to love and serve the Lord." We are sent forth to serve Christ in the world. The Latin origin of the word "Mass," *"Missa,"* actually means "to send." We don't come to liturgy only to receive, but also to go forth and to give Christ to others. We are challenged to live what we have celebrated, "to live our Christianity [so] that we make a qualitative difference in the world around us."[3] What better way to go forth accepting this challenge than behind billowing, streaming colors!

Celebrating as a Group

The processional banner of the parade not only identifies the group, but it proclaims that the event is a time of celebration. Human beings need to celebrate important life events. It's part of what makes us human. We celebrate the gift of life and the joy of growing in birthdays, the life well-lived of loved ones in funerals, the gift of love in ceremonies and anniversaries of commitment. Celebrating these days deepens the joy in our lives. Ignoring them may indicate dissatisfaction with life—or even cause it! Celebrations are vital to living a full life in community with others. This is true for the spiritual life of a community as well as for the ordinary lives of individuals. Celebration is vital to the life of a community.

What a rich heritage of celebration the church provides for us! Every liturgy celebrates the death and resurrection of Jesus Christ, each through a different prism. The prism might be an earlier event in Christ's life, or the life of a saint. That these celebrations provide something fundamental to human life is attested to by the swelling of congregations on the major Christian feasts of the year. The human heart longs for real celebration.

Each kind of celebration evokes different moods and feelings. Birthdays are loud and cheerful, with balloons, cake, and ice cream. Weddings are at once more festive and more serious; flowers, fine clothes, promises, and rich foods. Funerals draw the dark clothes from the closet, potluck dishes from the stove, and time from the schedule to share stories of our loved one. Like all major life events, Sunday liturgies and weekday feasts also evoke particular moods or feelings. While it is true that every liturgy celebrates the joy of resurrection, the tone of the celebration modulates from penitential, to hopeful waiting, to exuberant joy.

How might elements of a liturgical environment change to support the mood? In family celebrations, the kinds of food we serve and their presentation help to set the atmosphere. The mood may be reinforced with other environmental elements, such as balloons, streamers, and flowers. Banners provide yet another device for setting the stage of a celebration.

By their very nature, banners are celebratory. The image on the banner tells something about the reason for the celebration. Three attributes of that image assist in setting the tone or mood of a celebration: color, symbolism, and shape.

Color strongly influences mood, making it a primary tool of the artist and banner-maker. Emotion naturally takes expression in the form of color. Bright warm colors like yellow, red, and orange express joy and excitement. Blue is calming and gentle. Green is refreshing, suggesting life and growth. The traditional color of royalty, purple is dignified and somber. Each of these colors can take on a range of nuance by altering its hue, value, and intensity.

Certain kinds of banners depend on color to communicate specific messages, like the white flag of truce or the red flag warning of danger. In the liturgical year, color is used to communicate the season or the nature of the feast. In the Roman Catholic tradition, violet is used for Advent and Lent (lately, blue-violet is often used for Advent and red-violet for Lent); white for Christmas, Holy Thursday, Easter, and other feasts of the Lord, the Virgin Mary, or the saints; red for Passion Sunday, Good Friday, Pentecost, and the memorials of martyrs; and green for Ordinary Time, whose name might have been better translated from the Latin as "ordinal" or "counted" time. Ordinary Time is not the opposite of "extraordinary" time, but rather those Sundays and weekdays that are counted (the Twenty-second Sunday in Ordinary Time, the Twenty-third Sunday in Ordinary Time, and so on) because they are not of the seasons of Advent, Christmas, Lent, or Easter.

The color contains the message. Since liturgical colors are not arbitrary, but linked to their symbolic and emotional connotations, they reflect the mood of the season as well. In this sense, colors interact between the intellect and the emotions.

Mood can also be developed through the use of symbols or the pictorial representations of ideas or things. For example, a dove bearing an olive branch symbolizes peace, a stork indicates a new baby, and a skull and crossbones today signals danger. Symbols can identify a season or feast by using images strongly associated with a season, like a star for Christmas or flames for Pentecost. Mood can be expressed through symbol as well. In any pictorial image, vertical lines are active, expressing force and inspiration, while horizontal lines are passive, stable, and calming. Diagonal lines are active and dynamic, capable of drawing mood up or down. Curved lines are more graceful and rhythmic than straight lines; bold lines, more forceful and dynamic than thin lines.

Richness and variety characterize the multitude of symbols used in the service of the church, the primary and most obvious of which is the cross. In its most basic form, the cross is made of two unadorned lines, one horizontal and the other vertical. The passive horizontal line is an old symbol of one human being reaching out to another, while the active vertical line symbolizes the human search for God, a link between heaven and earth. The lines crossing in the center show graphically the primary relationship of God with God's people.

The meaning of symbols can change over time, and our ability to interpret and appreciate symbols changes with literacy. So we no longer understand many Christian symbols that were once commonly used. One example is the peacock. We ordinarily associate peacocks with pride, as in "proud as a peacock." This might lead to questioning its appropriateness for use in church, or a mistaken interpretation that a peacock in the adornment of a church refers to pride in one's faith or religion. In fact, in the language of symbols, "the peacock is the symbol of immortality, originating in the legend that its flesh is so hard that it does not decay. The haunting wail of the peacock in the night was likened to Christians' crying out to God for help. The 'hundred eyes' of the peacock's splendid tail are likened to the all-seeing Church. The feathers of the peacock's tail renew themselves with ever-increasing brilliance—an allusion to resurrection."[4]

Although the meaning of many Christian symbols is no longer common knowledge, artists can expand our symbolic vocabulary by drawing on this great store of symbols. If particular symbols are used often enough and in specific contexts, people will come to recognize them. This is particularly true if the symbol is well chosen to harmonize with the mood of the season, so that it helps to place or reveal the context of the occasion. Then whether everyone is able to define its meaning fully is not critical.

Some people might find background information about such symbols valuable. *A Handbook of Symbols in Christian Art* by Gertrude Grace Sill is a comprehensive source of such information.[5] However, explanation is not required to appreciate a symbol. So, for example, the brilliant colors of the peacock and its allusion to resurrection make it an appropriate symbol for Easter.

Given the importance of evoking a mood of celebration at liturgy and the value of modulating that mood throughout the year, how does one decide which days and events call for banners? There are so many possibilities—feast days of the church, particular seasons of the liturgical year, special events. But every liturgy is worthy of what banners can bring to it. So processional banners are appropriate for every Sunday and each major feast of the year. Certainly baptisms, weddings, and funerals are all events worthy of celebrating with banners as well.

One particular event in the life of a church almost demands processional banners: the dedication of a church building. A principal part of this rite is the procession—for the first time—of the whole parish, together with the bishop, into the new space. This procession begins either at the previous place of worship, or at least outside the doors of the new building. The use of multiple brightly colored, free-flowing banners seems not only fitting but even in a sense necessary, given the importance of this occasion and the opportunity to give witness to the event to the whole neighborhood.

A church already comfortably at home in its building will initially want to invest its resources in the days and events in the church year that lend themselves to a greater feeling of festivity and importance, such as Easter, Christmas, and Pentecost. Over time, the banner collection can be increased to include more special days, such as Holy Thursday and All Saints, celebrations of that particular community, for example, the feast day of its patron, and feasts in Ordinary Time.

The church's store of liturgies includes other sacramental and non-sacramental rites of fundamental importance to a community, some of which may be celebrated within Mass, such as baptism, marriage, and funeral rites; and others that are always within Mass, such as first communion, confirmation, ordination, and religious profession. These celebrations differ in character, but in each we celebrate the resurrection of Jesus Christ and thus might fittingly use processional banners.

Often, these rites are thought of as private celebrations for the families and friends of those receiving the sacraments. There may be no prior public announcement of the event. But all sacramental celebrations are celebrations of the whole community. "Each sacrament is actually a meeting with the risen, living Lord Jesus, a meeting with Christ within his mystical body—the Church."[6] When a sacrament can be celebrated in the context of a community gathering, such as at a Sunday liturgy, the public and communal nature of the event is more obvious. However, for various reasons it may not always be possible to celebrate this way. In that case the processional banner can serve as a two-way communication device. By using a banner that belongs to and represents the community, we can communicate the symbolic presence and support of the community at the liturgy.

Reciprocally, if that banner was placed in a public space for the next Sunday gathering of the assembly, it would communicate that the event had taken place and allow people to offer prayer and support to those receiving the sacrament. To be effective, different banners should be used for each sacrament.

Setting and Use

The design and construction of processional banners for a liturgy requires consideration of not only the type of celebration, but also of the setting. Will the banners be used inside or outside? How many do we need? Who will carry them? How large should they be? What shape? These practical details flow out of a more fundamental question: What is the nature of this particular community, and what kind of processional banners will help it enter more deeply into this particular liturgy?

Consideration of these issues will suggest different possibilities for design and construction. For example, it might be desirable for a funeral banner to accompany the procession to the place of interment, which would mean both indoor and outdoor use. Inclement weather would spell a quick demise for a banner made of silk, so durable materials should be chosen.

While most banners will only be used inside a church, certain outdoor celebrations other than funerals call for the use of banners, such as when the whole assembly walks in procession outside. The rite of dedication calls for just such a procession, and the joyful exuberance of the day almost demands the use of banners. Wouldn't it be right and fitting on Pentecost to invite the whole assembly to join the exiting procession as it sails down the aisle and out the doors behind streaming red, yellow, and orange ribbons? Some places keep alive the custom of processing around the church building on the solemn feast of the Body and Blood of Christ, accentuating the procession with new modern banners. When a family lives close enough to the church building, a procession to the church for a baptism is possible—a sign of faith to all the neighbors.

Processional banners can also be arranged outside to create a space for celebration on occasions when the assembly is quite large or the out-of-doors is a more appropriate venue. For example, on the memorial of Saint Francis (October 4), Pam's parish held an outdoors blessing of animals in an area demarcated by six simple banners depicting images from the Canticle of the Sun, a hymn of praise attributed to Saint Francis. Large-scale events often utilize an outside setting and may be enhanced by a series of banners outlining the space. To ensure that you will be able to use your banners despite the weather, use nylon flag material, weather-resistant ribbons, and other similarly weather-resistant fabrics.

Different factors influence banners used only indoors, including the interior architecture of the church. First, consider the number of aisles or walkways. A church with a single central aisle requires only one banner for most liturgies, although more may be used.

Churches with multiple radiating aisles suggest placing multiple processional banners in the aisles, in order to provide a stronger sense of inclusion and encourage participation. On special occasions the same effect might be gained in a church with one main aisle by setting banners in the smaller side aisles to surround the assembly with color.

The number of people moving in the entrance procession also influences the number of banners needed. At an event like an ordination, an anniversary or a large diocesan event, the entrance procession can be quite lengthy. Multiple processional banners can break the monotony of this long line, and help sustain the heightened sense of festivity throughout the procession. (See the photo on page 181, top.)

The interior of the church can also influence the shape, color and design of the banners. If the church architecture is neo-Gothic, then an inverted arch shape would be fitting. Curves or scrollwork might also suggest a basic shape for the design. Stained-glass windows may provide a source of color inspiration and suggest shapes and symbols. Although the artist should not strive to match the windows, sensitivity to the palette will enhance the overall environment.

Ultimately a person will carry the banner, so the design and scale must be sensitive to that person. If children are to carry a banner, the size should be appropriate to the scale of a child and what they can comfortably carry. The pole should not be overly long, or the banner itself too large. It's possible for a seven-year-old to carry a two-foot-square banner on a six- or seven-foot pole fairly easily and with a modicum of grace. Anything much larger requires an older child or adult.

A further source of inspiration can be the assembly itself, depending upon the composition and heritage of the community. Regional plants and animals, as well as striking local land formations might suggest design elements. The ethnic heritage of church members can be reflected in the use of certain types of fabrics or symbols. With some research, fabrics can be obtained from different parts of the world reflective of the cultures that produced them. Using these fabrics can add depth and diversity to a design, and help to underline the fact that we are all one in Christ. Banners that are strongly reflective of a single specific heritage should be considered thoughtfully, in order to avoid divisiveness. Multiple banners representing different heritages yet used all together may be a better choice than one alone.

At some time before your event, the person designated to carry a banner should practice walking with it. Confident, sure, fluid movements enhance the impact of the banner and help it be used to its fullest potential in expressing a celebratory and awe-filled mood. To hold a banner surely and securely, use one hand to grasp the bottom of the pole, and the other to hold the pole at least two feet above the bottom. The carrier then has sufficient leverage and control to move the banner rhythmically from side to side while walking at a slow to moderate pace. A slight sway will allow for fluid movement of ribbons or streamers, without being exaggerated. If the banner is to be placed in a visibly located stand during the liturgy, practice putting it in the stand as well. Practiced motions will help the assembly to focus on the celebration without being distracted by an individual.

Notes

1. Bernier, Paul, *Eucharist: Celebrating its Rhythms in Our Lives* (Notre Dame, Ind.: Ave Maria Press, 1993), p. 155.
2. Nelson, Gertrud Mueller, *To Dance with God* (Mahwah, N.J.: Paulist Press, 1986), p. 3.
3. Walsh, Eugene A., *Celebration: Theology, Ministry, and Practice* (Portland, Ore.: OCP Publications, 1994), p. 11.
4. Bernier, p. 13.
5. Sill, Gertrude Grace, *A Handbook of Symbols in Christian Art* (New York: Collier Books, MacMillan Publishing Co., 1975), p. 24.
6. Ibid.
7. David Q. Liptak, (1998) "Sacraments are really 'meetings'," *The Catholic Transcript* 2, no. 3 (1998): p. 35.

Chapter 2

THE LITURGICAL YEAR

The church's life revolves around the weekly gathering on the Lord's Day. The Sunday liturgy provides both the locus of organization and the reason for the existence of the community. So it is right and proper that considerable care and effort be expended on celebrating Sunday liturgies.

As a gathering of Sundays into seasons, the liturgical year shades the weekly gathering with different moods. Clearly, the joyous mood of Christmas is quite different from the sorrowful mood of Passion Sunday, which again differs from the glorious mood of Easter. The environment is clearly important in developing the atmosphere for these liturgies. The pure white trumpet of the Easter lily is so synonymous with Easter that it even contains the word "Easter" in its name. And what would Passion Sunday be without palm branches, or Christmas without poinsettias? The banner maker can easily build on the feel of these major celebrations and further develop mood and atmosphere for these special days.

The church offers us many days to celebrate in a special way. Christmas is not just a day, but a season, with a whole season before it, Advent, for preparation. Easter takes forty days of preparation, three days of experience, and fifty days of celebration. Yet, many people think that the Easter lilies are still there the next week simply because they haven't wilted yet.

It's not an easy thing to keep up that gloriously buoyant mood for seven weeks. By the third week, most of the lilies are in the compost pile. What's a church to do if it's unwilling to resort to artificial flowers? Call in the banner makers! Using the same banners for the whole season not only helps to maintain a mood of celebration, but makes clear the continuity of these days.

Besides the seasons of the liturgical year, we have a wealth of special days to celebrate—dates that we celebrate as though they were Sunday, no matter on which day of the week they fall. These include the solemnity of All Saints (November 1) and the commemoration of All Souls (November 2), the solemnities of Mary (January 1, March 25, August 15, December 8), the solemnity of Saint Joseph (March 19), the solemnity of the birth of Saint John the Baptist (June 24), the solemnity of Saints Peter and Paul (June 29), the day dedicated to the patron saint of the diocese, the day dedicated to the saint or event after which the parish is named, and the anniversary date of the dedication of the parish church. (These last three dates are not widely observed in the United States.)

And we can't forget to express our gratefulness for the gift of the gospel, which we celebrate and read through almost continuously during the long segments of the year that we name Ordinary Time.

The Liturgical Year

There are five seasons in the liturgical year: Advent, Christmastime, Lent, the Paschal Triduum (only three days, but the three most important days of the whole year), and Eastertime. These five seasons are the two poles around which the whole year revolves: the Winter Passover (Advent and Christmastime) and the Spring Passover (Lent, Triduum, and Eastertime.) Historically, the Spring Passover came first. It was the privileged time of the year to celebrate the sacraments of initiation (baptism, confirmation, and first eucharist). Eventually, the need to celebrate baptism at other times of the year (in January, either on the solemnity of the Epiphany or the feast of the Lord's baptism), as well as deepening reflection on the events in the life of Christ recorded in the gospels (such as his nativity and revelation to the Gentiles), gave birth to the Winter Passover (Advent and Christmastime). Today, the liturgical year begins with the seasons of Advent and Christmastime.

Apart from these seasons, the rest of the year is called Ordinary Time, of which there are two blocks. One block is the period in winter after Christmastime and before Lent, and the other is the period in summer and fall between Eastertime and Advent. Ordinary Time isn't a liturgical season, but a way to describe the weeks between the seasons. In this sense, the word "ordinary" means "counted." Ordinal numbers are counted numbers. We count the weeks of Ordinary Time to keep track of which scriptures to read during the liturgy on Sunday.

The Winter Passover

Christmastime is the first of the two defining poles of the church year, celebrated always shortly after the winter solstice on the same date each year, December 25. We celebrate the birth of the "sun of justice" at the time when the sun begins to return in the Northern Hemisphere—not a coincidence. It is significant that the birth of Christ is celebrated at the darkest time of the year. The church recognizes and ritualizes the period of waiting in the celebration of Advent, and the period of rejoicing in the celebration of Christmas.

Advent. In the Northern Hemisphere, Advent is a time of long dark nights, beginning on the eve of the fourth Sunday before Christmas and culminating on Christmas Eve, once thought to be the longest night of the year. (We now know that December 21 is actually the longest night of the year.)

This is the season in which we await the coming of the Lord, the Son of God, the Sun of Righteousness. Advent means "coming." We remember the coming of Jesus Christ in the incarnation, and we await his coming at the end of time. We consciously take this time to wait and to watch for God.

Waiting can try the soul, especially when we cannot be sure of the outcome. Will I ever find meaningful work? Will my baby be all right? How will the operation turn out? Will the hurricane hit our home? Will this gift be the right one at the right time? How long before this injustice is righted? We have so many fears, so many longings. Advent is a time to name our fears, to name that which we await, and to join together as a church in our waiting. The only way to make it through these times of trial safely is to join together. "Advent is the church linking arms to get it safely to eternity."[1]

Our primary models and helpers during Advent are Mary, the Mother of God, and John the Baptist. During Advent, we remember Mary's time of waiting for the birth of her child. Anyone who has experienced the birth of a child knows that the last month must be endured day by day. There is joy in the hope that the child will be born soon and join the family that has waited for so long. But there are the difficulties of sleeping at night, getting up from chairs and couches, making it through the day, and enduring the beginning stages of labor. Imagine adding to all that having to travel to your ancestral home because of a government census (see the gospel of Luke) and fleeing for your child's safety and living as a refugee (see the gospel of Matthew). Through it all, Mary kept faith in God. She heard God's word and she kept it.

The word of God comes to us during Advent also through the fiery preaching and example of the last of the great biblical prophets, John the Baptist. During the first part of the season especially, the selected scriptures are full of apocalyptic visions of the end of time and the culmination of God's justice that Christ's second coming will bring. John spent his life demanding justice in his day, and only caught a glimpse of it in Jesus before dying in Herod's prison. Through it all, John kept faith in God's promises as he waited for them to be fulfilled.

For us also, the wait for the second coming is fraught with difficulty, filled with tests of faith, of love, of hope. That is why we need so much to keep this time, this season of Advent, truly and well, to embrace life by emulating the saints who thrived spiritually in their struggles with life. It is practice for all the other times in our lives that we must wait with patient endurance, knowing that we are not alone. And it is a time to make ready for the coming of Christ.

The one thing Advent is not is an early celebration of Christmas. The readings are full of the voices of the prophets exhorting us to "prepare the way of the Lord." They speak to a people at risk of falling into despair, overwhelmed by the work of their time, of our time. We desperately need to hear their voices. If we imitate the culture of commerce and begin our decorating and celebrating too early, we lose the gifts and joys of Advent, of waiting, of preparing in quiet expectation, of experiencing darkness. We must let Advent be Advent.

TIMING. Although the timing of Christmas is constant—Christmas Day is always December 25—the date on which Advent begins is variable because it depends on what day of the week Christmas falls. Advent begins at sunset on the Saturday before the fourth Sunday before Christmas, which can vary from November 27 to December 3. So the fourth week of Advent is rarely a full week, and can be as short as one day. Advent begins about three weeks before the winter solstice, when night is longest, and ends just after the sun begins to reassert itself.

The four Sundays of Advent are particularly significant as markers of time. A domestic custom imported into the church is the Advent wreath, an evergreen wreath with four candles marking each of the four weeks of Advent. On the eve of the first Sunday of Advent, one candle is lit. A second added the second week, and so on until all four candles are lit for the fourth week. The third Sunday is Gaudete (*gow-DAY-tay*) Sunday. Gaudete is Latin for "rejoice." The antiphon for this Sunday is: "Rejoice in the Lord always. Again I say, rejoice! The Lord is near." This Sunday reminds us that joy is also a part of our waiting and preparation.

As we reach the middle of Advent, the anticipation becomes more intense. Beginning on December 17, the church chants the O antiphons at Evening Prayer. There is one antiphon for each of these last seven days, each one a biblical title of Christ: O Wisdom, O Ruler of Israel, O Root of Jesse, O Key of David, O Dawn of the East, O King of the Gentiles, O Emmanuel. "If Advent is like the night, now are the last moments before dawn."[2]

COLORS. The appropriate color for liturgical vestments in Advent has been a topic of considerable discussion in recent years in the Roman church. Officially, the color of the season is violet, the same as in Lent. Violet is the color of sorrow and penitence, but also of royalty, love, and truth. Often, a single set of vestments is used for both seasons. Unfortunately, this can lead to a perception that the seasons are the same, that both are seasons of penance. Yet, the seasons are not the same; Advent, according to the *General Norms for the Liturgical Year and the Calendar*, is "a period for devout and joyful expectation" (#39). It is not a season of penance as Lent is, and thus the alleluia is sung during Advent but not during Lent.

For vestments, a solution is to use different shades of violet for Advent and Lent: a blue-violet for Advent, suggesting the midnight sky, and a red-violet for Lent, signifying the passion. Since banners are not restricted to the use of the official colors, ranges of color can and should be used to great effect. Along with violet and blue-violet, blues of many shades can be used to further develop the sense of mystery of night and winter.

IMAGES OF THE SEASON. The most recognizable symbol of the Advent season is the Advent wreath, with its four candles, three purple and one rose. The wreath itself should not be literally illustrated on a banner to avoid duplication of symbols. Why have a picture of the wreath when you have the wreath itself? But many aspects of the wreath are highly symbolic and could be used to great advantage in banner design development. The number four is related to earth and the material world, while the circle symbolizes eternity, the perfection of God, and heaven. Candles evoke the image of the "light of the world." So the Advent wreath speaks of heaven wedded to earth in the coming of the light of the world.

The task of banner design is made easier during Advent by the wealth of quilting patterns available containing fourfold symmetry. Some of these even include circular images. The impression of light can be evoked through the judicious use of bright or light fabrics.

Another source of Advent images are the O antiphons: O Wisdom—the lighted lamp; O ruler of Israel—the two tablets of the ten commandments; O root of Jesse—a tree or a root; O key of David—key and scepter; O dawn of the east—rising sun; O king of the Gentiles—crown; O Emmanuel—the figure of a child or of the manger. A striking banner could be designed by overlaying one or more of these images on a background of fourfold symmetry.

But pay attention as well to the wealth of images in the scriptures, set out for us as a banquet: the Lord's mountain; swords into plowshares, spears into pruning hooks; withered leaves carried away on the wind; the heavens rent apart; signs in the sun, the moon, and the stars; roaring seas and waves; the wolf lying down with the lamb, the leopard with the kid, the lion with the calf, the bear with the cow, the baby playing with the cobra unharmed; clothing of camel's hair; locusts and wild honey; every tree that does not bear good fruit will be cut down; like a shepherd feeds the flock; the desert blooms; a virgin shall conceive; the angel of the Lord; house of David. Look at the lectionary—the church's book of readings—and see what other images you discover.

SPECIAL DAYS WITHIN THE SEASON. Although the season of Advent is fairly short, it contains a number of days worthy of special consideration. While you probably would not make special banners for each of these days, you might wish to use simple ribbon banners to celebrate certain days or consider making a Mary banner to use at all the feasts of Mary during the year.

The first of the feasts and memorials within Advent is the memorial of Saint Nicholas, falling on December 6. Next to Mary and Joseph, Nicholas of Myra is probably the best-known saint in popular culture. His charity was legendary; he saved three impoverished noblewomen from a life of prostitution by supplying them with dowries and restored to life three little boys who had been killed. The custom of giving presents to children on his feast day evolved into the present-day custom of gifts from Santa Claus on Christmas. In art, Nicholas appears as a bishop with three purses of gold, three gold balls, or three boys. A simple ribbon banner containing the red of bishops and three prominent gold stripes would help remember Nicholas on his day.

The solemnity of the Immaculate Conception is December 8. On this day, we celebrate the freedom of Mary from sin from the moment she was conceived. Mary did not earn this special grace; it was bestowed on her by God to prepare her to be the Mother of God. The art depicting the Immaculate Conception shows Mary as a young woman wearing blue and white, bathed in the sun, floating on clouds, surrounded by cherubim, with her feet on a new moon, one foot crushing a serpent or snake, symbolizing sin.

On December 12, another of Mary's feasts is the feast of Our Lady of Guadalupe. In 1531, an image of the Virgin Mary dressed as a pregnant Aztec princess miraculously appeared on a simple *tilma* (coat) made of cactus cloth belonging to an indigenous farmer named Juan Diego. In a vision, she gave him a message for the local bishop to build her a church where she stood. When the bishop failed to believe Juan Diego, Mary took Juan to gather wild roses blooming in winter. As the roses spilled from his *tilma*, a more amazing sign appeared—the image of Mary as she had appeared to Juan.

Elements of these two feasts of Mary could be combined for a single banner that might be used for other Marian feasts as well. Roses, cherubim, the sun and moon, and the colors of blue and white could be used singly or together.

December 13 is the day for celebrating the memorial of Saint Lucy. The name "Lucy" means light, and her feast day comes in the middle of Advent, guiding us toward the coming of the Light of the World. Lucy was engaged to marry a pagan during the reign of the Roman emperor Diocletian, before his conversion to Christianity. When she told her fiancé that she wished to devote her life to the service of the poor, he turned her in as a traitor to the state. Although she was tortured and martyred, nothing could dim the light of Christ in her eyes.

On Saint Lucy's Day, in Swedish families, the eldest daughter dresses in a white dress with a red sash, commemorating the martyrdom of Lucy. She rises before dawn and, wearing a crown of lighted candles, carries a special breakfast to the parents in bed. Younger girls carry candles and boys wear caps with stars, both Advent symbols.

Christmastime. What is it we celebrate at Christmas? And how long do we celebrate? The culture of commerce and the culture of faith provide us with two very different answers to each of these questions. The culture of commerce says we celebrate Christmas all through December, and what we celebrate is the arrival of Santa Claus and the "shopping season." When Santa has come and gone and the presents are unwrapped, Christmas is over, and stores can go on to after-Christmas sales and business as usual.

The church makes an entirely different proposition about the meaning of these days. The birth of the Lord Jesus is not a birthday in the historical sense of the word, in that we're celebrating the two-thousandth-and-something birthday of Jesus. More than that, we celebrate that God has become one of us. Because Christ shares in us, we share in Christ. Christ is born today. The Glory of God is revealed. Heaven appears on earth. The Light of the World shines forth. On the night of Christmas Eve, we are welcomed back into paradise and led to the tree. Lights blaze and flowers bloom. The entire world rejoices.

One of the most ancient customs of Christmas is the giving of gifts, inherited from the custom of exchanging gifts on New Year's Day in pagan Rome. When Christians give gifts and send greetings at Christmastime, it is with a different purpose. It honors "the 'holy exchange,' in which 'the divine becomes human that humans might become divine.'"[3] We honor the birth of Christ in each other. We give gifts that we hope will help each other become more the person we were meant to be. Santa Claus is the friend of Jesus and of children and helps to mediate the "holy exchange." His arrival helps to begin the celebration in a burst of glory and light. The church then continues to celebrate long after the decorations are gone from the mall.

TIMING. The Christmas season always begins at the same time, at sunset on December 24. It continues through the feast of the Baptism of the Lord, which is celebrated on the Sunday after Epiphany (or in the United States, on Monday if Epiphany is kept on January 7 or 8). Epiphany is January 6, but in the United States, it is celebrated on the first Sunday after January 1. This means that, like the season of Advent, the length of the Christmas season is variable and can end anytime between January 8 and January 13.

The timing of Epiphany and the length of the season have not always been variable as they are now. In fact, the celebration of Christmas has evolved considerably over time, being originally celebrated as just a single feast day. In 567, the Council of Tours declared the days between Christmas and Epiphany a festival season, making it the second of the festival seasons of the year, after Easter. From ancient times, Epiphany had been celebrated on January 6, as is still true in most of the world. The number of days was a constant—the twelve days of Christmas. Twelfth Night had many special customs associated with it, including gift-giving. In many countries today, Epiphany is the primary feast of the Christmas season and the day for exchanging gifts.

The current practice in the United States is to celebrate Epiphany on a Sunday, thus ensuring that the whole assembly can participate in the celebration of the first revelation of Christ to the Gentiles, that is, to those people not born into God's holy people, the Jews. Fixing that celebration on Sunday makes the length of the whole season variable.

COLORS. The basic liturgical color for Christmas is white. White suggests light, innocence, purity, joy, virginity, faith, and glory. Gold and the family of yellows are appropriate as well, and can provide a rich, shimmering, radiant effect for the celebration. Yellows indicate solar light, divine intelligence and illuminated truth. All colors of the rainbow can be added to help celebrate this glorious season in the liturgical year. In fact, the rainbow is pure white light refracted into the spectrum of colors. Clearly, light and bright are the two key properties to consider when designing banners for the Christmas season.

IMAGES OF THE SEASON. Symbols of light are a primary image of Christmas; the Light has come into the world. The Prince of Peace is born. In particular, the eight- or twelve-pointed star and the sun help symbolize the Light of the World. The theme of starlight can be carried over from Advent, emphasizing the exuberance of the light over the mystery of the night.

The wreath is a symbol of eternity, both in its unending shape and in its green color. It is preferable to simply hang evergreen wreaths on the doors or windows than to depict a realistic-looking wreath on a banner, but circular imagery could be used to great effect in Christmas banners.

The triangular shape of the tree points to the Trinity, and symbolizes hope and growth. Again, the abstract shape of the tree, rather than a realistic-looking evergreen, is how this image would be utilized most successfully on a banner.

For Epiphany, three crowns can suggest the three kings. The star they followed speaks resoundingly of Christmas. The gifts they bore and the camels they rode can all evoke the feeling of Epiphany.

Other images from the scriptures that are read during this season include: bride and groom rejoicing; the angel of the Lord; an infant wrapped in swaddling clothes; shepherds in the field; a multitude of angels; elderly prophets and newborn babies; Jerusalem, the city of peace, radiant and restored and open to all; the star; the spirit of God descending like a dove. Look in the lectionary—the church's book of scripture readings—for other images.

SPECIAL DAYS WITHIN THE SEASON. The season of Christmas is full of feast days to celebrate, some of which are always celebrated on Sundays so that the whole community can participate. You need not have special banners for each of these days. Anything extra should coordinate with the overall seasonal décor.

When not falling on a Sunday, December 26 is the memorial of Saint Stephen, the first Christian martyr, whose story is told in the Acts of the Apostles. He was the first person chosen by the apostles when they needed seven people to help them. He was called a deacon, or servant, and his job was to distribute funds to the needy. In honor of his life's service, many people save money throughout Advent to give to the needy on this day. Stephen's name is the Greek word for "wreath," here referring to the laurel wreath given to the winner of a competition or an athletic event. If your parish is named after Saint Stephen, meditate on his story before beginning banner design.

The first Sunday after Christmas (or December 30 if Christmas falls on a Sunday) is the feast of the Holy Family. If your Christmas banner is other than an image of the Holy Family, you might consider making a banner with a simple representation of a nuclear family for this day: father, mother, child. Notice that this family is a trinity that mirrors on earth the inner life of God-as-Trinity. See the discussion of the Epiphany below. Maybe a banner or set of banners that is designed to be used on this day can also be used on Epiphany and then again on Trinity Sunday.

January 1 is the Octave of Christmas and the solemnity of Mary, Mother of God. Eight days after his birth, Jesus was circumcised and named. This solemnity celebrates the fulfillment of the promise made by the angel to Mary: God's child is her child. She is the mother of God. On this day, the banners used on solemnities and feasts of Mary could be integrated into the Christmas environment already in place.

The crown of the Christmas season is the solemnity of the Epiphany of the Lord. Epiphany means "an appearance or revelatory manifestation of God." It is also a "perception of the essential nature or meaning of something." In the Western church, we celebrate Epiphany as the day the magi arrived, guided by a star. While the scriptures do not tell how many magi come in search of Christ, since three gifts are mentioned (gold, frankincense, and myrrh), tradition has assumed there were three magi. The number three, of course, is significant, pointing to the very mystery of God. A triplet of regal-looking tapestries carried in procession on this day can communicate something of this mystery.

The magi represent all of us who were not born Jewish, the peoples from all lands and times and cultures that go looking for God. So any depictions of the three mysterious seekers should be multicultural.

The feast of the Baptism of the Lord officially ends the Christmas season. On Christmas, we celebrate the fact that his mother gives Jesus to us all, while on this closing feast of Christmas, it is God's Spirit who comes and gives us Jesus in a new way, as "my beloved." A pair of banners representing the Holy Spirit (for example, red ribbons, or perhaps an image evoking the coming of the Spirit as a dove alighting) and water (for example, blue and green ribbons) would help to celebrate this day and signify a transition into Ordinary Time. These banners could then be used throughout the year when the rite of baptism of children is celebrated.

The Spring Passover

Easter is the Sunday of all Sundays, the most important day of the Christian year. At Easter, we celebrate the death and resurrection of Jesus Christ. We celebrate that we have become sharers in the passover of Christ through baptism. We renew our baptismal vows and thus God renews the covenant with us that makes us God's own people.

The Easter cycle has three parts: Lent, the Paschal Triduum, and Eastertime. Lent is the period of preparation. In the Triduum, we celebrate the passover of the Lord in a connected set of liturgies celebrated over a period of three days. Eastertime is the overflowing exuberance of celebration of the resurrection of Jesus Christ.

The timing of these three seasons is centered on the cycles of the moon: Easter Sunday is always the first Sunday after the first full moon after the vernal or spring equinox. This method of establishing the date might seem to be a mere curiosity related to the ancient Jewish calendar. Truly, it makes little sense to those who dwell in houses with artificial light and heat. But on this day of the first full moon in spring, the daylight is finally stronger than the night, and the moon rises in the east as the sun sets in the west.

There is never a time in these twenty-four hours not illuminated by the sun or the full moon.

Lent. Lent is a forty-day season of preparation for the Paschal Triduum. The number forty is significant in that it recalls several periods of cleansing in scripture. Noah experienced forty days of rain, the Israelites wandered forty years in the desert, and Moses, Elijah, and Jesus each fasted forty days in the wilderness to prepare them for their work. The stories we hear in Lent often involve a journey. We travel and end in a different place from where we began. Forty days is long enough to require dedication to the task of preparation and to the journey, yet not so long that we lose heart.

Lent comes at the right time of the year in the Northern Hemisphere. In days past, stored food would be nearly running out. The house has been closed up tight all winter. It's good to turn that time of scarcity into a time of spiritual and physical cleansing. Our bodies need the fast as much as our souls need the spiritual preparation. The physical cleansing of our homes and churches is not only in the spirit of the season, but an essential aspect of caring for our world.

Since at Easter we celebrate baptism, Lent is a time when we scrutinize what it means to be baptized. What do our promises mean and how can we live them more deeply? Lent is the time when the catechumens seeking to join the church are making their final preparations for baptism, so we redouble our support for them through prayer, fasting, and almsgiving. We also pray for estranged members who are returning to the church. Preparation for baptism is clearly a central theme of Lent that can be considered in making banners for Lent.

TIMING. The beginning of Lent, Ash Wednesday, is tied to the date of Easter. Easter Sunday occurs on the first Sunday after the first full moon after the vernal equinox, that is, the first full moon of spring. Ash Wednesday is the seventh Wednesday before Easter. Because Lent and Easter are both tied to specific days of the week, the timing is variable but the length is not. Lent ends with the fading of the daylight on Holy Thursday.

The Easter cycle is timed so that in the Northern Hemisphere, Lent begins at the end of winter. The earth is damp, muddy, and cold. Winter may be losing its grip, but not without a fight.

COLOR. Violet is the official liturgical color for Lent. Violet is the color of sorrow and penitence, but also the color of royalty. The violet of Lent tends toward red, the color of passion. Black and gray may be used with red-violet, black being a color of earth and night, and gray the color of humility. Combinations of these colors, such as lavender and mauve, also help express the penitential feeling of the season.

On Passion Sunday, the color of the vestments worn is red, the red of the Passion, not of Pentecost. With the change in color, the mood of the liturgy shifts recognizably from the previous days of Lent. It begins on a triumphal, victorious note with the blessing of the palms and the entrance procession of the assembly singing, "Hosanna to the Son of David," and waving palms—a procession that needs banners! With the reading of the Passion, the mood shifts again, becoming quite somber and sorrowful, but not despairing. We already know this is not the end of the story. The challenge in making any banners for this day is to highlight the initial triumphal mood, while also pointing to the Passion. Therefore, colors used should combine red, dark red, and red-violet, not the fiery colors of the Holy Spirit.

IMAGES OF THE SEASON. Relatively few symbols are connected with Lent; the major "symbol" of the season is the person entering the final phases of preparation for baptism, confirmation, and eucharist. This person—these people—remind us of where we have come on our own spiritual journeys, and who we are becoming as God's people. Otherwise, Lent is more characterized by the absence of familiar symbols than by the presence of particular symbols. Although we are meditating on baptism, we do not surround ourselves with candles and water, but consider their effect on our lives by their absence. The cross may be shrouded during Lent. The baptismal font and holy water stoups may be emptied and shrouded, too. Flowers are absent. We begin Lent by considering what happens to our bodies when the life force is no longer present—we become ashes or dust. If banners are used in Lent, perhaps it is best that they have no images, but evoke a sense of journey or of penitence and humility. Color, texture, and form do this best.

On Passion Sunday, the red vestments used should not carry images of the Holy Spirit. Likewise, any banners used on Passion Sunday should use images appropriate to that day, such as the phoenix, the rooster, the olive tree, crowns, the lamb, and the holy city of Jerusalem. The paradox of joy and sadness, of triumph and servitude, is seen especially well in the humble "foal of an ass" that Jesus rode.

SPECIAL DAYS WITHIN THE SEASON. Ash Wednesday is the day the lenten fast begins, a day for plainness and emptiness. The First Sunday of Lent begins the actual counting of the forty days, and may be marked by a penitential procession that includes banners or a decorated processional cross.

The Third, Fourth and Fifth Sundays of Lent are of particular importance for those catechumens chosen for baptism, now called "the elect," who celebrate the rites of scrutiny and exorcism on these days. Simple banners may lead the elect in procession and flank them during these rites.

The memorial of Saint Patrick on March 17 always occurs during Lent. Although not a major feast day in the church and still a day for lenten vesture, many Catholics celebrate Saint Patrick's Day with great gusto. Since Patrick found his role in life as a missionary and evangelizer, he can be of particular importance to the catechumens. We remember Patrick through his use of the shamrock to explain the Trinity. The Celtic cross, both Irish and Christian, also evokes the memory of Saint Patrick.

Likewise, the solemnity of Saint Joseph on March 19 always falls during Lent. White is worn on this day and flowers may be used. Joseph was a "just man" and is considered to be the patron saint of the poor. One custom is to hold a special banquet for the poor on Saint Joseph's Day, where meatless dishes, fruit, and wine are served. Perhaps a banner bearing an icon-like image of Saint Joseph could grace this "Saint Joseph's table" as well as being used in the processions at Mass or the Liturgy of the Hours this day. Another opportunity to use this banner would be on May 1, the memorial of Saint Joseph the Worker, or even Labor Day.

The solemnity of the Annunciation of the Lord is celebrated on March 25. Again, there is a break in the severity of Lent with white vesture and flowers. Because we celebrate the first moment of Jesus' incarnation, a mystery achieved through the power of God and the consent of Mary, symbols of the Holy Spirit, such as wind and fire, are appropriate for this day. Or if you have a good banner or set of banners to celebrate Mary, these could be brought out this day, but returned to storage after vespers or evening Mass.

Passion or Palm Sunday is when we hear the gospel account of the triumphal entrance into Jerusalem, a time for marching in procession and waving palm branches. A large, fine banner of palms would enhance the festal feeling that begins this day's liturgy, and could possibly be used for the entrance rite in Holy Thursday's liturgy as well. Alternatively, a simple ribbon banner of red, dark red, and red-violet ribbons would help the assembly to feel both the exuberance of the crowd on the journey into Jerusalem, and the darkness of the time to come. Peter Mazar in *To Crown the Year* suggests a unique three-dimensional kind of processional banner for Passion Sunday—a donkey piñata hoisted high on a pole. The donkey is a sign of humility and service, and may be part of our celebration of Christ's presence among us.

The Paschal Triduum. The Paschal Triduum is the shortest of our liturgical seasons, a mere three days long, hardly long enough to be called a season. But into these three days are packed the celebrations of the defining events of Christianity: the institution of the eucharist, and the death and resurrection of the Lord. We celebrate these liturgies not as remembrances of events that took place two thousand years ago, but as if we were actually present. The church exists in eternity, not bound by time or space. Although we may not comprehend with our whole being, when we celebrate these and all other liturgies we join together with Jesus Christ and the whole world. It is the role of the liturgical artist and banner maker, among others, to help the assembly experience this reality at an emotional or bodily level, not just a cerebral level. At no other time in the year is this role more important than during these three days. To truly experience the joy of the resurrection, we must fall to the depths of sorrow on Good Friday.

The three days of the Triduum are reckoned from sunset to sunset, rather than midnight to midnight. The Triduum begins on Thursday evening with the Holy Thursday liturgy, continues through Good Friday and Holy Saturday, and ends with the fading of daylight on Easter Sunday. The three liturgies celebrated on Holy Thursday, Good Friday, and Holy Saturday (Easter Eve) form a continuum, with the assumption that we never leave the church, at least mentally. On Holy Thursday, there is an entrance procession, but no final dismissal. We remember and do again the washing of the feet, collect gifts for the poor, celebrate the eucharist with utmost solemnity, carry the eucharist for tomorrow in procession, and begin to keep watch with Christ.

In Good Friday's liturgy, there is neither an entrance rite nor a dismissal. We have been keeping watch all night, fasting all day, and now we follow Christ to his death and burial. We pray for the world and all its people, living and dead. We honor the wood of the cross.

Holy Saturday's Vigil begins with no entrance rite, but does end with a final dismissal. This day also begins with fasting. We come into a darkened church, and light the new holy fire of Easter, which we pass on to each other so that the whole church is illuminated by its flame. We listen to stories of our faith, stories of our people from the time of creation. We bless the new holy water, renew our baptismal promises, and baptize the catechumens. We celebrate the Passover of the Lord. It is the night of all nights. The liturgy ends with a glorious final procession.

Because these liturgies are connected, with only one entrance rite and one dismissal in the three days, we have to be careful to use banners in procession only at the very beginning and the very end. A single set of banners could be used for the three days. Use them to process in on Holy Thursday, to accompany the collected gifts for the poor, to accompany the eucharist on its procession around the church at the end of the liturgy, and to decorate the alternative place of reservation. On Good Friday, these banners *might* accompany the cross as it is carried in procession, but *only* if they do not overshadow it. They might form a backdrop for the cross, either as it is held while the people venerate it, or after the veneration, when it is set up until Saturday afternoon. At the Easter Vigil, these banners might accompany the gospel procession to the ambo, the procession of the catechumens to the font, the procession of the gifts of bread and wine to the altar, and then the dismissal and final procession.

Easter Sunday is the final day of the Triduum, the Sunday of all Sundays. On this day, we celebrate the resurrection as if we were there. It is a day of great joy, a liturgy overflowing with story, song, and joy. It takes up at the point where Holy Saturday left off and continues. "This is the day the Lord has made. Let us rejoice and be glad in it!" On this day of all days, a cascade of flowing color undeniably proclaims the Good News that Christ is risen indeed. Banners would well serve the entrance procession, the gospel procession, the procession with gifts, and the final procession as well. When vespers are celebrated on Easter Sunday, the banners can be used to accompany the candle in the entrance procession, as well as accompany the assembly in its procession to the font.

TIMING. Easter is always the Sunday after the first full moon of spring, when the day is finally longer than the night. The Paschal Triduum begins on the evening of the Thursday before Easter, or Holy Thursday. It continues through Good Friday, Holy Saturday, and the daylight hours of Easter Sunday. At sundown, the Triduum concludes and the season of Easter begins.

COLORS. At the Vigil and on Easter Sunday, the best white vestments are worn. Gold or other metallic fabrics may substitute for the white, as long as the total effect is as glorious as possible. In banners, white may be used in profusion, with golds and yellows and all colors of the rainbow. All color can sing on Easter Sunday. Because it is just early spring, Easter colors are light and bright, rather than rich and deep; tints rather than tones or shades. But choose carefully: Pale colors are hard to distinguish from a distance.

IMAGES OF THE TRIDUUM. To create a set of processional banners for all the Triduum liturgies as discussed above suggests that—as with banners for Lent—design, color, and texture be employed rather than specific representational or realistic images.

At the Vigil, however, the nine readings abound with imagery that might well be employed. There is the story of the creation, Noah's ark, Abraham's ram, the paschal lamb, dry bones coming back to life. Perhaps a banner for each scripture reading from the Old Testament could be carried in at the time of each reading and placed in position to remain for the rest of the liturgy. The gospel procession would use the banners that have been used for all three days of the Triduum. All the banners could be carried out in procession at the end. Or they could form part of the Easter season environment. Think about placing them all around the church, not necessarily grouping them all around the ambo. See the sidebar for the list of Easter Vigil scriptures.

Easter Vigil Old Testament Scriptures

Genesis 1:1—2:2
Genesis 22:1–18
Exodus 14:15—15:1
Isaiah 54:5–14
Isaiah 55:1–11
Baruch 3:9–15, 32—4:4
Ezekiel 36:16–17a, 18–28

Eastertime. Flowing from the Triduum is the fifty-day celebration of the resurrection of our Lord. The joy resulting from our experience of the Triduum cannot be contained in a mere week or two, but spreads out over a week of weeks, seven times seven, plus one day, Pentecost. In the Northern Hemisphere, this is the time when the earth bursts forth in blossom, echoing and intensifying our appreciation for new life. Indeed, we celebrate many different kinds of transitions into new life in the spring: first communions, confirmations, graduations, weddings, Mother's Day. It is the time when new growth leaps forth from the earth, from our minds, from our hearts, and from our spirits. Easter springs from deep roots within us all. We know from the depths of our being that we must keep Easter and celebrate it well.

However, it can be hard to sustain this feeling of joy for such a long period of time. The lilies fade after a couple of weeks. The leaves come out, and life doesn't seem quite so new anymore. Many people don't realize that we're still celebrating Easter a month later. Here's where processional banners can help. While the great splash of color used at the Vigil and on Easter Sunday is not needed every Sunday, you might consider using at least one processional banner on each Sunday of Easter, perhaps bringing back the banners used at the Vigil and on Easter Sunday for Pentecost.

TIMING. The season of Eastertime begins with sunset on Easter Sunday and continues for seven weeks. The fiftieth day is called Pentecost (from the Greek word for fifty). On Pentecost, we celebrate the coming of the Holy Spirit and the birth of the church. After Pentecost, we return to Ordinary Time.

COLORS. The liturgical color for Eastertime, as for Easter Sunday, is white. If there is more than one set, the best vestments would probably be reserved for the Vigil and Easter Sunday, and the usual white set used for the season of Eastertime. All colors of the rainbow may be used with white, a lovely concept, since white light is composed of all colors. For Pentecost, the liturgical color is red. Since Pentecost celebrates the coming of the Holy Spirit, fiery colors like orange, yellow, and fuschia can be used in banners.

IMAGES OF THE SEASON. The images from the scripture readings for the Easter Vigil would work well throughout the Easter season. The scripture readings for the season also provide other rich images: the empty grave; the Good Shepherd; Jesus on the road to

Emmaus with two disciples (another triplet or trinity—see the discussion of this on page 23, pertaining to the Holy Family); many angels surrounding the throne of God at the end of time; the four living creatures (symbols of the four gospels: the human being for Matthew, the lion for Mark, the ox for Luke, and the eagle for John, used together); the victorious Lamb on the throne holding the victor's pennant; the huge catch of fish; the sheepfold, the Eden-like garden; the mansion with many rooms; the vine and the branches; the holy city, the new Jerusalem, coming down out of heaven like a bride in a wedding procession; the holy city, the new Jerusalem, with twelve gates and twelve foundation stones, with the Lamb as its light.

At Pentecost, we celebrate the gift of the Holy Spirit to the church, so imagery may be related to the Holy Spirit or the church. Biblical images of the Holy Spirit include the dove, the wind, the tongues of fire. Representations of the church may include many faces, a large ship, or the new Jerusalem, as described above. If the banners focus on the Holy Spirit, they can be used for confirmations and other celebrations of the Spirit. A number of simple ribbon banners used together can help convey both the imagery of flame (in color) and wind (in the movement of the ribbons).

SPECIAL DAYS WITHIN THE SEASON. All days within Eastertime are special, but the days of the first week, or the octave of Easter, are ranked as solemnities, the highest ranking in the liturgical calendar. All through this time, we tell gospel stories of resurrection. Daily Mass participants may be delighted by the use of a ribbon banner this week. Alternatively, you could keep all the Easter processional banners in place all week.

Ascension Day, depending on where you live, is either the Thursday after the Sixth Sunday of Easter (thus being the fortieth day of Eastertime) or the Seventh Sunday of Easter. The solemnity of the Lord's Ascension recalls that Christ ascended to heaven and returned to his Father. In ascending to heaven, he rescued the human race from the grip of death. The use of the Easter banners on this day is most appropriate. If the Easter banners do not have ribbons, consider adding them, to float in the air during the procession and remind us that Christ fills the universe.

Pentecost is the Eighth Sunday after Easter, or the fiftieth day of Eastertime. The word itself simply means fiftieth day. On this day, often called the birthday of the church, we celebrate the descent of the Holy Spirit. It is one of the greatest days of the church year, along with Easter, Christmas, and Epiphany, so it should be celebrated to its fullest. The liturgical color of the day is red, for the Holy Spirit. Red is the color of fire, of love, of power and action. The banner may contain images of the Holy Spirit as a dove or fire, of Mary and the apostles gathered in the upper room, or other images of Spirit or church. Certainly, the banner should have an abundance of bright red, fuchsia, yellow, and orange ribbons. In fact, the ribbons alone would be sufficient to call to mind the Holy Spirit, with the colors of flame and the movement of the wind when the banners are in procession. Multiple ribbon banners provide a fine and festive effect.

Earth Day, celebrated on April 22, is a day that almost always falls during Eastertime. Although it is not a liturgical day, we read in the Easter Vigil that God created the earth and called it good. We are to be the stewards and caretakers of that earth. So on this day, we celebrate our first and most basic vocation, as stewards of life and the earth. If a banner was made to accompany the first reading at the Easter Vigil (see page 30), then perhaps it could be re-employed this day.

May 1 is Labor Day in many countries. The memorial of Saint Joseph the Worker may be kept on this day. When designing or commissioning a banner of Saint Joseph, keep in mind the overall Easter season décor. Design the banner of Saint Joseph to fit in with Easter, and then you will be able to use it both on May 1, in the context of the Easter season, as well as on March 19, the solemnity of Saint Joseph.

A feast of Mary that recalls her visit to her cousin Elizabeth, who was also with child, is kept on May 31. May is associated with Mary in piety and devotion, but any use of the Mary banners on this day must complement the Eastertime décor in place for the fifty days, and not suddenly change the focus from the season. The same is true of first communion celebrations, weddings, and other rites, which will be discussed in the next chapter.

Some saints whose feasts or memorials usually fall within Easter include Mark the Evangelist, whose sign is the lion; Philip and James, apostles; Matthias, apostle; Catherine of Siena, mystic, virgin, and doctor of the church ("doctor" here meaning scholar);

Athanasius, bishop and doctor of the church; Philip Neri, priest; Justin, martyr; Charles Lwanga and companions, the martyrs of Uganda; Boniface, bishop and martyr. Unless your parish is named after one of these saints, it is probably best to allow the Eastertime décor to remain without additions. If you create a parish patron banner for one of these saints, however, design it with the Easter season in mind.

ORDINARY TIME

Ordinary Time is not actually a liturgical season, but all of time that is not encompassed by Advent, Christmas, Lent, Paschal Triduum, and Easter. Approximately 32 weeks of the year fall outside the seasons. Each of these weeks is counted and numbered with an ordinal number. So Ordinary Time simply means "counted time." This is the time of culmination and fulfillment, when we live out the mysteries celebrated in the liturgical seasons. The church tells stories of the days of Christ's ministry, of his parables and miracles, and tales of his interchanges with the people he met. Since there is no overriding theme to the weeks of Ordinary Time, we can look to the natural seasons, to saint's days, and to the changing themes of the gospel to provide inspiration for banners.

TIMING. There are two periods of Ordinary Time, the first falling in winter, between Christmastime and Lent, and the second between Eastertime and Advent. The lengths of time for each are variable, depending on what day of the week Christmas falls and the date of Easter. The first, or winter, period is relatively short, lasting for a month or two, while the second period spans summer and autumn, or over half the year. For this reason, some have suggested that this second, longer period of Ordinary Time actually be divided into two: "Summer" Ordinary Time, from immediately after the Easter season until either the civil holiday of Labor Day or the Feast of the Holy Cross (September 14), and "Autumn" Ordinary Time, from Labor Day or Holy Cross Day until the First Sunday of Advent.

COLORS. The liturgical color for Ordinary Time is green. However, for the worship environment and processional banners, seasonal variations in the greens may be chosen. In the Ordinary Time winter weeks in the north, consider deep forest green with hints of silvery white and darker browns, russets, and plums, evoking the feeling of an evergreen forest dappled with snow and ice. Combinations of darker shades, as in Amish quilts, can be put to good use in this time period. More southern areas where spring is beginning in this time might consider color schemes based on the natural environment, involving lighter greens and accents.

The second, longer span of Ordinary Time can be divided into two approximately equal periods, summer and autumn. Summer's colors include rich, bright greens, accented by the bright colors of summer flowers and vegetables: bright yellows, oranges, reds, blues, and purples. Autumn, which can begin with the Feast of the Holy Cross on September 14, might emphasize a more muted, olive green with muted tones of gold, russet, and plum as accents.

IMAGES OF THE SEASON. Because Ordinary Time is not a liturgical season with an overriding theme, there are no symbols specifically for Ordinary Time. However, basic Christian symbols, like the cross and the fish, can be the basis of banners designed for use during Ordinary Time. The anchor is especially appropriate as a symbol of hope, playing off our associations with green as the color of life and hope. The special days within the season provide varied themes for banners used only once or twice a year. For example, a set of banners made to illustrate Saint Francis' Canticle of the Sun could be used to celebrate both Earth Day in April and the memorial of Saint Francis in October.

SPECIAL DAYS WITHIN THE SEASON. Ordinary Time has many special days to celebrate. We focus on a small number here, but you can find information on many others that may be important to your parish or neighborhood in Mary Ellen Hynes' *Companion to the Calendar.*

The first major celebration in Ordinary Time is the solemnity of the Holy Trinity celebrated on the first Sunday after Pentecost. The concept of one God in three persons is central to Christianity. In all that we say and do as Christians, we begin and end "in the name of the Father, and of the Son, and of the Holy Spirit." In particular, we celebrate that the Holy Spirit has been sent by the risen Christ to be God's presence in us and in all God's creation.

The liturgical color of this Sunday and the next is white, which can make it seem as though the church is still celebrating Easter. In a way, we are.

The Trinity can be symbolized either by a triangle, three overlapping circles, or three overlapping fish. At times, two human figures and a dove, or even three human figures have been used to symbolize the Trinity, but it is probably best to avoid depicting any member of the Trinity as human, except Jesus Christ. White, yellow, and gold are appropriate colors for ribbons.

In the United States and Canada, the solemnity of the Body and Blood of Christ is celebrated on the next Sunday. When the feast was created, people wanted a joyful way to celebrate the gift of the eucharist. They chose early summer as a time when they could process through the streets with the consecrated bread. These processions are still seen in many parts of Latin America and Europe. While you might not choose to carry the blessed sacrament in procession, it still might be nice to use banners created for use on Holy Thursday and at first communions.

On August 15, we celebrate the solemnity of the Assumption of the Virgin Mary into Heaven. It is Mary's greatest feast, her passover. This holy day is a relatively recent addition to the liturgical calendar, a response to the horrors of World War II. Catholics had long believed that after Mary's death, God raised her and that she lives with God forever. Thus, we rejoice on Assumption Day that all will be made new again, the lowly, the poor, the dead, raised to a glorious new life. A Queen of Heaven banner would help celebrate this day appropriately.

The memorial of Saint Francis of Assisi is October 4. Francis had a great devotion and respect for the beauty and unity of all of creation. He took the words of the gospel literally, followed Christ's example, and served the poor. His generosity of spirit continues to shine in our age, and we do well to remember him in a special way on his feast day. On or around his day, many churches hold a blessing of the animals. Banners could be made to help celebrate both the animal blessing and the feast, and could also be used in April to celebrate Earth Day or one of the Rogation Days, the three days in spring when people pray to God to protect crops, orchards, and flocks. For Pam's church, we made six simple banners illustrating Saint Francis' Canticle of the Sun. These were used to create an outdoor space for the blessing of the animals on the Saturday morning closest to October 4, and then on the memorial itself.

November 1 is the solemnity of All Saints. On this day we celebrate the gift of all God's saints, known and unknown, remembered and forgotten. We remember that all lived the Good News and helped announce the dominion of God. In this autumn season, we appreciate God's harvest of all who have helped build the kingdom. We also rejoice in our part of it, realizing that the church lives in eternity and we link arms across time and space. White is the traditional color of those who have lived pure and holy lives. Appropriate today would be a mostly white, silver, or gold banner. Another, more complex representation would be the church as many people—historical and modern. Perhaps some are easily recognized saints—Peter with his keys, Paul with his sword, Mary Magdalene with her jar of ointment, Cecilia with her reed organ. And perhaps some are "anonymous" saints.

On the next day, November 2, we celebrate the commemoration of All Souls. On this day, we pray for all who have gone before us marked by the sign of faith. We may remember the dead in a special way, by decorating graves or giving alms or service to the poor. This remembrance of the dead continues through the end of November until the beginning of Advent. Therefore, it would be appropriate to continue using the banner of All Souls until Advent.

The liturgical year concludes with the solemnity of Christ the King, celebrated on the last Sunday before Advent. This is the culmination of November's remembrance of all the saints and all the souls. Through baptism, we have become a royal people, called to share in the crown of Jesus along with all the saints. It is a kingdom not of earthly splendor, but of justice, self-sacrifice, peace, and freedom. Here, the dignity of the poorest of the poor proclaims itself without fear. Therefore, we who follow Christ and call him king are to bear witness to the priceless value of his whole kingdom and all its royal people, and seek to build up that kingdom in whatever ways we are called.

White is the color of the day and an obvious symbol would be the crown—whether the crown of thorns or the crown of glory. If designed thoughtfully, the same banner could serve for All Saints, All Souls, and Christ the King. Using the same banner draws a connection between the inhabitants of heaven and Christ.

Thanksgiving Day (the fourth Thursday in November in the United States, third Monday in October in Canada), while not a liturgical day, has become a major family holiday in the United States and Canada. The popularity of Thanksgiving church services, particularly ecumenical ones, points to a greater recognition that all that we have is a gift of God. We thank God for all the blessings of the year, and may include fruits of the harvest or other symbols of God's blessings in our lives in the procession with gifts. A processional banner might help ritualize our gratitude for all we have been given as we offer to God the bread and the wine of the eucharist. For ecumenical liturgies, perhaps each parish or church could carry in procession a banner that somehow symbolizes what its community means to the larger neighborhood, and these could be set up around the room to testify to this gathering of churches.

Thanksgiving and the November feast days are naturally linked more strongly than might first appear. All Saints and All Souls celebrate, in a certain sense, a harvest of souls for a kingdom of the royal people whose high king is Christ the King. In this month, we express our gratitude for the gifts of their lives and their example, as well as gratitude for the gifts of our own lives and all that sustains us in the holiday of Thanksgiving. One parish (Holy Infant in Ballwin, Missouri) chose to express the natural relationship between the November feast days and Thanksgiving by commissioning a set of banners to use through the whole month of November, one with a crown and the other with fruits of the harvest.

Conclusion

The church year is a cyclical calendar that spirals around the same two poles year after year. Like nature's seasons, liturgical seasons recur periodically throughout our lives. Processional banners made for the seasons and for special days, used year after year, become recognizable signals of the season, like the lights at Christmas and the lilies at Easter. As an assembly of praying people, we become more aware of the richness of our celebrations and the shades of difference among them. Our own lives are enriched by this deeper knowledge of the seasons and the possibilities for enrichment in living more closely to the days and seasons. We become one people, united in our rhythmic remembrance of God's presence in our lives.

Notes

1. Mazar, Peter, *To Crown the Year: Decorating the Church through the Seasons* (Chicago: Liturgy Training Publications, 1995), p. 201.

2. Mazar, p. 203.

3. Mazar, p. 232, quoting Augustine.

Chapter 3

CELEBRATING SACRAMENTS AND OTHER RITES

Sacraments are encounters with the divine through the use of human signs. We are human beings with bodies. We cannot experience spiritual realities directly; they must be mediated through our senses. This is why ritual is so important. In ritual, by means of signs perceptible to the senses, God communicates with us—gives us grace—as a church and as individuals within that church. When Jesus walked this earth, he was truly one of us. He touched others, cried with them, laughed with them, and went to their weddings and wakes. Although we no longer experience Jesus in this way, he transcends time and space as we become his Body. "He uses us to make the human signs through which he continues to reach all people and transform them, to make them his new people and bring them to God's realm."[1]

Sacraments are God's actions in which we participate, not "things" that we passively receive. As the Body of Christ, the assembly's role is primary. Sacraments "are actions of Christ, actions of the church, and actions of those who celebrate them."[2] We are all baptized in the blood shed from the cross. We are all members of a royal priesthood. We all celebrate the sacraments and minister God's healing love to one another, in ways that differ. This creates an opportunity for the artist to provide images that allow the visual to become another way to involve the assembly, another path to mystery in our liturgies.

Processional banners contribute to active participation, if in no other way than by simply focusing all eyes on the liturgical action. Because sacraments communicate the divine, the liturgy must be celebrated with attentive dignity. When done poorly, a liturgical ritual can bore or even repel us, instead of drawing us closer to God and to each other. To give life to the human signs of the sacraments, the active participation of all is vital.

Including banners in the environment can enhance sacramental or liturgical celebrations in several ways. They can evoke and form the mood of the celebration. They help unify the assembly by focusing attention on the action of the liturgy. Likewise, they can further unite the assembly by proclaiming something of the nature of the mystery being celebrated. And banners can be a means of communication to the wider parish beyond the particular assembly gathered. All sacraments are celebrations of the whole church, even though not everyone is present for every celebration.

When parishes were smaller and communities more stable, the communal nature of sacramental celebrations was more obvious. The whole community would have gathered to celebrate a marriage or a baptism. Parishes today are far different kinds of communities, composed of more people than could possibly fit in the church building at one time and composed of families whose members often live far apart from one another. We tend to think of sacraments as private events more than as public, ecclesial events: Jason and Cathy's wedding or Gilbert's ordination. While celebrations of baptism or the anointing of the sick during the Sunday liturgy are becoming more common, communal penance services are often the only liturgy other than eucharist thought of as belonging to the whole parish. Yet, as members of one body, no individual acts without affecting the whole body.

Even though we cannot invite the entire parish to a wedding, or find that only the relatives of those to be confirmed come to the celebration of confirmation, we can still communicate that a sacrament has been celebrated. Banners used at the sacramental celebration could be used at Sunday Mass to communicate to the parish in a colorful, vibrant, but subtle way that God's grace works among us. The effectiveness of this mode of communication would be facilitated by permanent and prominent spaces in church buildings for these banners, perhaps in the gathering space or near the font. And of course, someone needs to have responsibility for the proper hanging, storage, cleaning, maintanence, and repair of the parish's collection of banners.

The Roman, Anglican, and Orthodox churches define seven sacraments: baptism, confirmation, eucharist, penance, the anointing of the sick, holy orders, and matrimony. Baptism and confirmation, together with eucharist, are the sacraments of initiation, initiating us into the Body of Christ. We can divide the remaining four into the sacraments of healing—penance and the anointing of the sick—and the sacraments of service—holy orders and matrimony.

Certain other celebrations occur within liturgical rites, often followed by a celebration of eucharist, and bear a resemblance to the sacraments. These include the profession of religious vows by women and men, funeral rites, and the dedication of a church.

The Sacraments of Initiation

The sacraments of initiation are baptism, confirmation, and eucharist (sometimes in this instance called first communion). It is through these three sacraments that a person enters into the full life of the church. Baptism is our initial assent to God's invitation to a life of faith, and joins us to the body of believers we call the church. Confirmation provides us with the gift of the Spirit and a call to live by that Spirit. Baptism and confirmation are only celebrated once in the life of an individual. Eucharist, though, is the ongoing (weekly or even daily) sacrament of initiation. Eating and drinking the spiritual food given to us by Christ continually nourishes us in our commitment to live as followers of Christ and strengthens us as a body. These three sacraments form a kind of whole, and are, in fact, celebrated together for infants in the Orthodox churches, as well as for adults who undergo the Rite of Christian Initiation of Adults (RCIA) in the Roman Catholic church.

Baptism

There are many layers of meaning to the sacrament of baptism. The three principal ones are: death to sin and rebirth to holiness, adoption as sons and daughters of God, initiation into the church.

In baptism, we die to sin and rise to new life in Christ. The original Greek word meant plunge. In baptism we are plunged into water, symbolizing death, and we rise to this new life. The Jewish people are the sons and daughters of God. How do we who are not born Jewish enter into the covenant that God made with Abraham and Sarah and their descendants forever? In baptism, we are adopted by God as brothers and sisters of Jesus, sons and daughters of the Father, born of a new mother, the church. We say that the font is the church's watery womb, from which we are reborn. Now as children of the same parents, brothers and sisters to Jesus, we are brothers and sisters to each other and to all—initiated into the church.

The symbol of water contains many layers of meaning: water is required to sustain all created life; human life begins in the womb inside a watery sac; water is required for cleanliness. Yet too much water can bring death and destruction. There are many references to water in the Bible, including the stories of creation, the great flood, the parting of the Red Sea, and the crossing of the River Jordan into the promised land. Jesus was baptized in the Jordan at the beginning of his public life, but his ultimate baptism was his death on the cross—when blood and water flowed from his side—and his resurrection. But remember that before that, Jesus changed water into wine at the wedding in Cana, walked on the water, and commanded the waters of the stormy sea to be calm. In our baptism, we are wedded to the cross and united to Christ in eternity. We become one with Christ in his church. Baptism changes us for life.

The Bible really says little *about* baptism, but instead tells stories of the baptism *of* Jesus. (There is a lesson here for banner design: Tell of, not about!)

> *Then Jesus came from Galilee to John at the Jordan to be baptized by him. John tried to prevent him, saying, "I need to be baptized by you, yet you are coming to me?" Jesus said to him in reply, "Allow it for now, for thus it is fitting for us to fulfill all righteousness." Then he allowed him. After Jesus was baptized, he came up from the water and behold, the heavens were opened, and he saw the Spirit of God descending like a dove coming upon him. And a voice came from the heavens saying; "This is my beloved Son, with whom I am well pleased."*[3]

The images that we associate with baptism are all here: the one being baptized, the baptizer, the water, the dove hovering over the waters, and the voice from the heavens. These are the signs through which God identified Jesus as his beloved Son. Likewise, baptism allows us to be identified as God's own. We are made God's children. And no sin on our part can ever change that seal of identification.

The mystery of baptism is beautiful, and its liturgy powerfully touching, but what does it mean to become the child of someone you will never see or hear or touch with your physical senses in this life? In J. K. Rowling's novel, *Harry Potter and the Sorcerer's Stone,* the infant Harry Potter is attacked by the evil Lord Voldemort. Harry's mother dies protecting the life of her infant son. Years later, the villain is unable to touch Harry without great pain to himself, and Harry wonders why. His mentor, Albus Dumbledore, responds: "Your mother died to save you. If there is one thing Voldemort cannot understand, it is love. He didn't realize that love as powerful as your mother's for you leaves its own mark. Not a scar, no visible sign . . . to have been loved so deeply, even though the person who loved us is gone, will give us some protection forever. It is in your very skin. Quirrell, full of hatred, greed, ambition, sharing his soul with Voldemort, could not touch you for this reason. It was agony to touch a person marked by something so good."[4]

The image of a mother loving her son enough to die for him can lead us toward understanding what it means to be so loved by God. Although he no longer shares his mother's physical presence, Harry's being is forever changed by his mother's love unto death. He is forever marked and protected by her act of love. It is in his very skin, his whole body. Harry did nothing to earn this love, except be his mother's son.

Through faith, we know that Jesus lived on earth, loved us unto death, and changes us forever through his love. We have done nothing to earn that love or deserve that he should die for us. But he did die for us, each of us, so that we might live. Each of us becomes a child of the God who would die for us. It is the gathering of these precious individuals that makes the people of God. And it is together that we become much more than the sum of our parts. The story of Harry and his mother can help us see more clearly the One who died for us, who marks and protects all who would accept baptism and be called Christian. Clearly, this baptism changes us forever in a way that is unrepeatable.

The *Catechism of the Catholic Church* says, "Baptism seals the Christian with an indelible spiritual mark *(character)* of his belonging to Christ. No sin can erase this mark, even if sin prevents Baptism from bearing the fruits of salvation. Given once and for all, Baptism cannot be repeated."[5]

While we can only speculate on the nature of this indelible mark, clearly baptism radically changes us, removing any obstacles to the love of God, and in some way protecting us forever. While subsequent sins may prevent us from becoming the persons we were truly meant to be, they cannot dissolve this fundamental relationship. Baptism is a necessary requirement for admittance to the eucharistic banquet, and that banquet nourishes and strengthens our baptism.

Colors and Symbols of Baptism. The traditional color for baptism is white, the color of all joyous celebrations of the church, including the Christmas and Easter seasons. In Christian art, white represents light, innocence, purity, joy, virginity, faith, and glory. Pure white, "white as snow," also carries images of cleanliness, of being washed clean with the water of salvation. For all these reasons, it is appropriate that the baptized wear white. Robing the child within the ceremony itself, after the pouring of the water, helps to suggest the power of the change the child has undergone. A new name is taken as part of this symbolic change.

Baptism has many symbols; the most primary is water. As the words of the baptismal formula are spoken, "I baptize you in the name of the Father, and of the Son, and of the Holy Spirit," water is poured or the one being baptized is lowered into the water three times, at the mention of each member of the Trinity. In paintings, the pouring of water most clearly conveys the action of baptizing. Sometimes three fish symbolize baptism, three being symbolic of the Trinity, and the fish a creature that lives in water as we live in the grace of God. (The fish was also an ancient sign of Christ, and hence of Christians.) Often a shell is used to pour the water, and the shell is a symbol of John the Baptist.

Water is essential to life, to our very existence. It quenches our thirst. It cleanses and purifies us. All of these functions make water a primary and fundamental symbol of baptism. Water can also be lethal. The huge waves of a typhoon can wipe out whole villages; sudden cloudbursts can change life-sustaining streams to raging monsters. In baptism we die to sin and rise again in Christ. Three simple wavy blue lines may suggest water, but they do not indicate death and rising. A trickle of water does not express our identity with the crucified and risen Christ. A deluge does. Anyone who has had a near-drowning experience understands the concept of salvation and the awesome deadly power of water. On banners for baptism, the power of water is conveyed much more clearly by large splashing waves than by small, regular wavy lines. The effect is both more dynamic and more reflective of an understanding of baptism as a radical change of life.

Another part of the baptismal rites is the anointing with oil. Before the water bath, we anoint those to be baptized with plain olive oil that we call the "oil of catechumens." Since oil and water do not mix, this anointing symbolically ensures that those who go down into baptism's waters do not drown. Also, the oil of the catechumens is like the oil that athletes used to anoint their bodies. Just as it is hard to pin down a wrestler who is slippery with oil, the forces of evil can no longer pin down and defeat those anointed with this holy oil. The second, more important anointing happens after the water bath. This is the anointing with the royal oil of chrism: olive oil with a fragrant balsam added. Chrism is consecrated once a year in the cathedral by the bishop and then distributed to all the churches. It is a very old symbol of the grace of God, used liberally for anointing kings in the Hebrew scriptures.

The candle that the newly baptized Christian is given symbolizes the light of the world, the light of Christ. The new set of clothes—the fine linen garment—that the newly baptized puts on is a sign of becoming a new creation in Christ. Because the word of God is always read at any liturgical gathering, in paintings or other depictions of baptisms a large book is sometimes shown to indicate the word of God.

If the banner is being made for a specific person, the name of the person can also be a source of imagery. For example, the name "Daniel" is a rich source of visual imagery, including the lion and lamb as seen in Daniel's Baptism banner, made for Pam's third son. (See the photo on page 181, bottom.) The lion and lamb are good choices, because they point quite clearly to Christ as well. The lion calls forth the image of Christ as king and the lamb of Christ as sacrifice. The lion and lamb also appear in the famous passage in Isaiah,[6] pointing to the rule of Emmanuel. Note that Daniel's banner also includes a band of blue-green water and three silver fish, clearly identifying it as a baptismal banner.

It is better that a banner evoke these signs and symbols of baptism rather than depict them in a realistic fashion. For example, through texture, form, and color, water can be evoked without literal waves. The fabrics chosen can evoke the baptismal garment or the flame of the candle. Things like fish and shells can be stylized, or used as borders or in geometric patterns. To create a banner that depicts—as a photograph would—the font, the candle, and the robe is to run the risk of making a cliché.

Using Banners in the Baptismal Liturgy. Banners used in a baptismal liturgy help to set the mood of the celebration and identify the assembled individuals as people baptized in Christ. In addition, the use of one or more banners can help to highlight processional movement in the baptismal liturgy. Movement is an important element in liturgy and is itself symbolic. It is not just a means to get from one place to another, but symbolizes our "continuous walk toward the eternal pastures of the kingdom . . . Walking signifies life itself—searching, looking, deciding, departing toward that which gives meaning to existence."[7] Although procession is an element of every liturgy, this symbolic walking has particular relevance in the baptismal liturgy because baptism is the first step toward the fullness of life in Christ. The individual becomes a member of the church, a part of the Body of Christ, and both change as a result. God claims us as his own and gives us new life in Christ, while the church is enriched by our presence. Furthermore, God promises us that the grace of baptism will continue to flow for our lifetime, no matter how we respond or act. So this sacrament is very much connected with life's journey and our search for meaning.

Clearly, the opportunities for procession in the baptismal liturgy should be utilized to the fullest and highlighted with one or more banners. The number of banners depends on whether the parish chooses to use one banner for all being baptized, or to use one for each person. Multiple banners can be used quite effectively. Each person to be baptized could have a small banner, with the procession headed by either the processional cross or a larger banner. The individual banners would be of similar shape, color, and materials. If the banners are displayed after the baptism, the smaller banners could cluster around the larger baptismal banner to indicate the number of baptisms that week.

For the small individual banners, the simplest option would be ribbon banners, about 1' wide and 4' long, made mainly of white ribbons, possibly accented with silver, yellow, or gold. If your parish has a banner-making group, you might consider building a collection of small banners (12" x 18") with ribbons (4') from which each family could choose one to use in the liturgy. If the newly baptized or his or her family wanted a banner to keep, they could be given a kit or pattern to make their own. If these have a simple design and precut pieces, sponsors or parents could make their banner as a part of the parish baptismal preparation program. Ensuring that all the banners are finished would be the responsibility of the banner-making group committed to this idea, since it cannot be presumed that all parents have the time or skills needed to do so. This banner would become an heirloom and a cherished family possession, like an heirloom baptismal gown.

During the baptismal liturgy, let the banner travel with and stay with those to be baptized as much as possible. Being responsible for the banner can help an older sibling feel much more involved in an infant's baptismal liturgy. With adults, the sponsor, a spouse, or other family member could carry the banner.

In the Rite of Baptism of Children, the first part of the liturgy is the Reception of the Child(ren). It is intended that the child(ren), together with the parents and godparents, gather at the door of the church. The assembly normally stands inside. The rite of reception occurs at the door, and the entire assembly processes in together. If there is a suitable location close to the church, you can extend this procession. Because Daniel lived close to his church, friends and relatives gathered at his house and processed with the banner to the church, meeting the others at the door for the reception. In the Rite of Christian Initiation of Adults, this ritual reception is held long before the actual baptism. But it happens in much the same way. The beginning of the actual baptism—most likely celebrated at the Easter Vigil—is discussed in the previous chapter.

The liturgy of the word occurs next in any celebration of baptism. A good location for the main or single banner is next to the ambo. Smaller individual banners stay with those to be baptized. This calls for some kind of stand to hold them.

During or after the Litany of the Saints, child(ren), parents, and godparents process to the font for the baptism. The banner travels with the child to the font, where it remains for the celebration of the sacrament. After the conclusion of the rite, there is a procession to the altar, unless the font is located in the sanctuary. Again the banner travels with the child and stays with him or her until the conclusion of the liturgy. The final procession can include the newly baptized with their banners.

Confirmation

The second of the sacraments of initiation is confirmation. The church teaches that a Christian first receives the Spirit in baptism, beginning a journey toward union with Christ and fuller participation in the life of the community. Confirmation intensifies and strengthens (confirms) what has taken place in baptism, conferring the gifts of the Spirit in a fuller way, bringing us more fully into participation in the community.

This sacrament has two outward signs: the laying on of hands and the anointing with chrism. The laying on of hands calls forth the gift of the Spirit, with seven gifts being prayed for specifically: the spirit of wisdom, of understanding, of right judgment, of courage, of knowledge, of reverence, and the spirit of wonder and awe in God's presence.[8] Of course, these gifts have always been present. But the confirmandi are opened up to the power of these gifts, whose reception is ritualized in the sacrament. The anointing with chrism on the forehead, together with the words, indicates the effects of the sacrament; we receive the spiritual seal and the gift of the Holy Spirit.

Anointing with oil is a sign of abundance and joy; it cleanses (rubbed on the body after bathing), limbers (rubbed on the muscles of athletes), and heals. "It makes radiant with beauty, health, and strength."[9] With the anointing the bishop says the person's name and "Be sealed with the gift of the Holy Spirit." This seal "marks our total belonging to Christ, our enrollment in his service forever."[10] The title "Christ" means anointed one.

When the baptism and confirmation are separated by a number of years, sometimes those being confirmed take a new name. The name signifies becoming a new person. When serious thought is given to the choice, it can be an important part of the preparation for confirmation. What saint do I want to emulate? Who had qualities that I want to make my own?

Confirmation builds up the body of Christ, affecting not just the individual, but the whole community. Hence, programs of preparation for confirmation purposely stress a more active involvement and commitment to the life of the community. Ideally, the community helps with the preparation and celebration of the sacrament by sharing their gifts and stories with the confirmed, being prayer partners with them, or offering apprenticeships in ministry. The final prayer of the liturgy petitions the Spirit: "Make them ready to live [Christ's] Gospel and eager to do his will. May they never be ashamed to proclaim to all the world Christ crucified living and reigning for ever and ever."[11]

Colors and Symbols of Confirmation. The liturgical color for confirmation is red, like Pentecost. It is the red of the Spirit and should be an intense vibrant red shouting the presence of the Spirit!

Symbols for confirmation include the dove, fire, or anything associated with chrism, such as olives hanging on an olive branch. Seven tongues of fire represent the seven gifts of the Spirit: wisdom, understanding, right judgment, courage, knowledge, reverence, and the spirit of wonder and awe in God's presence. The intensity of fire and flame can be evoked quite naturally through simple ribbon banners. The use of seven banners has significance in number, symbolizing the seven gifts, and in reflecting the magnitude of the gift, the outpouring of the Spirit. The dominant color should be vibrant red, with burgundy, orange, and yellow-gold ribbons as accents. Resist the temptation to try to picture the seven gifts on these banners, as the ribbons alone carry the message.

If you choose to make a quilted panel depicting flames, these should be large and abundant, intertwined to reveal the interrelationship of the gifts, and full of life and movement. Likewise, a dove should be pictured as active and dynamic, a Spirit that changes our lives. A small white bird hovering in mid-air not only fails to evoke this powerful Spirit, but perhaps diminishes our notion of Spirit. An image more capable of bearing such an awesome weight might be a more generously sized dove in flight, surrounded by flowing, moving lines. Confirmation is a sacrament for life.

You might make smaller individual banners for confirmation, as for baptism, instead of or in addition to large banners for the group. These might be used to enhance the place of the assembly, and for the dismissal and final procession. For those being confirmed, the making of this banner could be a meaningful preparatory activity, and later become a reminder of their commitment to follow Christ. If the banners were constructed using fusible appliqué, the young people would be allowed a great variety in choice and interpretation of symbols, and would be able to make the banner top fairly independently. In addition to doves, flames, and crosses, these banners could have symbols particular to the saint whose name the confirmandi has chosen. Quilting, if desired, could be the project of a smaller group of students and adults who come together to finish the banners.

Using Banners in the Confirmation Liturgy. As a sacrament of initiation, confirmation can bear the use of an extravagant number of banners. While one fine banner will help set a vibrant tone, the reference in the rite to the seven gifts of the Holy Spirit suggests the use of seven banners. You might choose not to carry all your banners in the entrance procession, saving the greater impact of a larger number of moving banners for the recessional. Leading the newly confirmed out of church in this way illuminates the dismissal call to go forth, strengthened by the Spirit, and live as God-spirited people, witnessing the gospel. Consider using one or two to lead the entrance procession, placing them with the rest in stands during the liturgy.

Depending on the layout of your church, there are a few options for placement of the banners during the liturgy. One appropriate place might be near where the bishop will stand during the rite of confirmation, as long as neither altar, ambo, nor chair is obscured. (Banner bearers might even stand in a semi-circle behind the bishop while he is anointing the confirmandi.) Another choice would be to place them around the room where they are visible, but not blocking sight lines. A third choice would be to place them within the assembly, among the candidates for confirmation. The new confirmandi would carry the banners down the aisle during the recessional.

If you choose to make individual banners, these could be hung on the pew or be fastened aloft to the end of the pew where each candidate is sitting. If the small banners are processional banners, they would be carried out in the recessional.

EUCHARIST

Eucharist is the third and completing sacrament of initiation. Eucharist provides the spiritual food that nourishes the faithful in their baptismal commitment.

The celebration of the eucharist is the "source and summit" of our Christian life. It is an action of praise and thanksgiving to God by the whole assembly. Christ himself is the head of this assembly, present in the ordained ministers and in the baptized people. All present take an active part in this celebration. For all its similarity to theater, the Mass is not a show, with actors and an audience, but the prayer of a united participatory body.

The eucharist is a meal, uniting all who eat of the bread broken and blessed by Christ and forming one body in him. It is also a sacrifice, in that it makes present, or re-presents, the one sacrifice of our Savior. In the Mass the assembly enters "God's time," or eternity, in which past and future come into the present. It is a moment outside of time.

When a follower of Christ first joins in this banquet, it is a moment of life-changing significance. One cannot remain the same person after the intimacy of this encounter with the Risen One. Like baptism, participation in the eucharist changes us, sanctifies us, and unites us with Christ and one another. The Holy Spirit will plant in us the desire to eat of this food often, to strengthen our charity, to wipe away minor sins, to preserve us from major sins, to unite us in Christ, and to commit us to the poor. And once we begin to share in this spiritual food, we can never return to the simpler relationship of infancy. We are committed in a new way.

The greatness of this day is the reason we celebrate it so lavishly. Although customs vary from culture to culture, our clothing crowns this day, often helping us recall our baptism, for example, when the children wear white dresses or suits. We visibly express the connection of baptism and eucharist by wearing the color of baptism.

Colors and Symbols of First Communion. White is an appropriate color for first communion, recalling baptism. The family of yellow and gold, as well as silver, can support the white. Use any of the joyful colors of the rainbow in smaller amounts.

Symbols specific to first communion include the two fish and five loaves that fed the multitudes, grapes and wheat, and bread and wine. Consider using color to evoke the idea of bread and wine, rather than more literal images. (See, for example, the St. Francis Xavier Church First Communion banners, pictured on page 193.) The basic Christian symbol of the cross or chi-rho can be woven into the design.

Using Banners in the First Communion Liturgy. Any large group banners made would be used in the entrance procession. One or more banners can lead the procession. If the procession is long and continuous, intersperse large ribbon banners. Banners could be used during the procession with the gifts to the altar and to lead the final procession.

Banners made for first communion can be used on a variety of occasions in the future. The set of banners Pam made for a first communion celebration at St. Francis Xavier Church in St. Louis are now used every year on Holy Thursday, as well as during other celebrations of first communion. When the Dalai Lama visited St. Louis and led a prayer service of many faiths at St. Francis Xavier, these same banners graced the entrance procession.

You might decorate the places of the communion candidates with individual ribbon banners or single panels designed by the children. The children could carry these in the final procession out of the church. If the children will be designing their own banners to keep, simplify things by having precut pieces and a simple format, like a pieced block design (where they choose the colors and have some choice in design) or simple appliqué design. Small ribbon banners, made with narrow floral ribbons, would be simple enough for the children to make themselves with a parent.

Another way to use individual ribbon banners could be as a decoration for the altar or assembly. Gather them in stands or pots and hand them out to the children during the announcement period. The children would hold the banners during the blessing and carry them in the procession.

THE SACRAMENTS OF HEALING AND GROWTH

The church has two sacraments of healing and growth: reconciliation (or penance) and the anointing of the sick. The aim of both is spiritual healing and growth, and each sacrament can be received whenever necessary. The frequent reception of reconciliation is encouraged to aid in recognizing and owning our faults and failings in order to develop closer relationships with God and one another. The anointing of the sick is reserved for those with serious ailments, terminal or not, for which the recipient seeks grace to bear in order to grow closer to God.

RECONCILIATION

This sacrament is often known by a colloquial term popular before the Second Vatican Council (1962–1965) that emphasizes the action of the recipient: "confession," as in confession of sins. The new name of reconciliation changes the emphasis from the recipient's telling of sins to the opportunity for conversion and grace offered by God. It indicates a whole new attitude or frame of mind. Reconciliation signifies a "conversion of heart that brings about renewed union and more intimate union with God and with one another."[13] To reconcile means to bind together what was broken, to heal, to make whole again. The sacrament of reconciliation is meant to restore harmony and peace among people, to fix broken relationships, not only with people, but also with God and creation. Reconciliation is a mystery of the love and mercy of God "associated with the victory of Christ and the renewal within us of the gift of his Spirit, going beyond a mere psychological conception."[14]

The church has always associated this sacrament with the gospel story of Jesus' appearance to the disciples after the resurrection when he breathed on them and said, "Receive the Holy Spirit.

Whose sins you forgive are forgiven them, and whose sins you retain are retained."[15] John does not elaborate on the meaning of this action, but one can read in Jesus' words and actions forgiveness for the disciples' abandoning him days earlier. At the same time he gives them the power to forgive the sins of others. The gift of forgiveness from God provides power to forgive others.

When we celebrate the sacrament of reconciliation, we encounter Jesus who has risen from death. He forgives our sins, allowing us to rise from death, too. The Spirit he gives us "empowers us to die to our sinfulness and turn to God and one another in honesty and love."[16] Like baptism, reconciliation is an ongoing process. The whole church, as well as the individual sinner, is "at once holy and always in need of purification."[17] We continually need to turn to God whose merciful love has no limit.

Reconciliation is more than what happens during the rite. It is a constant mission or ministry, a way of life. As Paul writes, "So whoever is in Christ is a new creation: The old things have passed away; behold, new things have come. And all this is from God, who has reconciled us to himself through Christ and given us the ministry of reconciliation, namely, God was reconciling the world to himself in Christ, not counting their trespasses against them, and entrusting us with the message of reconciliation."[18] All members of the body of Christ are called to forgive and accept forgiveness, and to the extent that we do, we become this new creation.

The Roman church presently has three rites of penance: the rite of reconciliation of individual penitents, the rite of reconciliation of several penitents with individual confession and absolution, and the rite of reconciliation of several penitents with general confession and absolution. Both of the the communal forms include a liturgy of the word with hymns, scripture readings, a call to reconciliation (usually a homily), and prayers of praise and thanksgiving. Those assembled either confess their sins and receive absolution individually (the second form), or make a sign of contrition (such as kneeling) and receive absolution together (the third form).

Through the two communal rites in particular, we are beginning to realize the power of the sacrament of reconciliation to assist the church in developing a moral consciousness that is both social and global. The downtrodden have a rightful claim to our help and concern. The justice we serve goes beyond the established human laws. One who is moral must continuously struggle against all injustice. This extends to all creation. "We subvert God's justice when, instead of using the gifts of creation in common and respectfully, a privileged few use creation for personal possession, exploitation, fear or power."[19] As Eugene Walsh states, "The chief work of the church is reconciliation: to make peace; to bring justice, to lift up the broken, bringing them home and healing them; to search out the alienated, making them feel secure and wanted."[20]

Colors and Symbols of Reconciliation. The tone of this sacrament has changed with the new rite. The old individual rite was generally celebrated in a small, dark confessional box, in which the penitent and confessor were separated by a screen. The new rite takes place in a chapel, in which the penitent may kneel behind a screen for anonymity or sit facing the priest. Today we have a greater understanding that this is indeed an occasion of joy and reason for celebration. "The experience of the sacrament of reconciliation ought to be a joyful encounter with the risen Lord. It needs to be a celebration of the giving of the Spirit who frees us to live as brothers and sisters in Christ."[21]

The traditional color for this sacrament is purple. Although we may see purple as a somber, penitential color, it is also the color of royalty. We are a royal priesthood and a forgiven people who come to claim that forgiveness. White can be used as well, being symbolic of cleanliness or purity. Red is appropriate as an accent color, for as Isaiah says, "Though your sins be like scarlet, they may become white as snow; Though they be crimson red, they may become white as wool."[22]

Reconciliation does not claim the same sorts of specific symbolic imagery that we associate with other sacraments. One traditional symbol for the juridical or legal power of penance is the crossed keys of Peter, but this image may be lost on many today. A number of other images may work better to suggest the concept of reconciliation. The primary Christian symbol, the cross, most basically symbolizes redemption from sin. A cross with the body of Jesus is most appropriate.The dove carrying an olive branch is a universal symbol of peace. Other imagery that could be the topic for a reconciliation banner might include two people embracing, recalling the loving father and the prodigal son. The woman washing the feet of Jesus is a powerful image of gratitude for forgiveness. The image of King David, beloved and chosen by God, yet guilty of adultery and murder, is a powerful symbol for reconciliation, sometimes carved into the old confessionals in European churches. (Tradition has it that he composed the great penitential psalm, Psalm 51.) Obviously, there is room for imaginative interpretation of scripture and human experience in the making of a banner.

The Use of Banners for Reconciliation. Banners made for reconciliation can be used at a celebration of any of the three forms of the rite, but the ways they would be used differs. A banner can be displayed outside the reconciliation chapel as an indicator that a confessor is present, and as a reminder of the sacrament's communal dimension. (Some churches have more than one chapel.) In communal penance services, banners could be part of the entrance procession, and then move in coordination with the actions of the liturgy. Accordingly, during the reading of scriptures and homily, the banners would stand near the ambo. When it is time for individual confessions, the banners could be carried in procession to stand outside the door of the main reconciliation chapel. When there is more than one priest ministering, each could be led to his location for hearing individual confessions by banners that mark the location. If these banners were brought to the front or center of the church as each confessor finished, all assembled would be aware that it was time for the proclamation of praise and thanks. Using the banners in the recession would remind us of our obligation to share what we have received.

Anointing of the Sick

The sacrament of the anointing of the sick embodies Christ's compassion for all who suffer in body and soul. It is intended to strengthen those being tried by serious illness or infirmity. At one time, the sacrament was only given to people nearing death. However, like reconciliation, this sacrament has undergone significant change since the Second Vatican Council, including a change of name and focus. The new rite is part of a collection entitled *Pastoral Care of the Sick: Rites of Anointing and Viaticum.* Its focus has shifted from preparation for death to strengthening and preparation for the next phase of life's journey, be it physical healing or eternal life. Therefore, we no longer wait until death is imminent.

The suffering we experience during illness can cause us to become self-absorbed, angry, and depressed. This can lead to despair or to revolting against God. Paradoxically, the trials of illness and failure of the body can also have a refining effect, helping us to see more clearly what is essential in our lives. Bodily breakdown can be a milestone in our search, in our journey to God. The aim of the sacrament is to encourage and aid the recipient in every way possible on this journey to God. Its name, "pastoral care," indicates service and compassion.

Like reconciliation, the anointing of the sick is an action of the Christian community. Even when the sacrament is celebrated on the spur of the moment in a hospital room, the priest represents the Christian community's presence. The community reaches out to the sick, and the sick, in turn, minister to the community by revealing with their bodies the image of the Suffering Servant still with us. Through the experience of the illness and this sacrament, the sick both discover God and reveal God to the community. They remind us of our faith, looking in the face of death, hoping for new life, and rejoicing in the resurrection.[23]

When Jesus walked the earth, he healed many people of various diseases and afflictions. And he did so with great compassion for those who were suffering. It was a compassion that welled up from the depth of his being and expressed itself in unfathomable tenderness. Without hesitation, he touched the untouchables and changed their lives completely. Christ wanted this ministry to continue after his ascension. He told the apostles, "They (those who believe) will lay hands on the sick, and they will recover."[24]

The anointing of the sick may be celebrated with anyone who is seriously sick, even those who look healthy but have a potentially fatal condition, such as a bad heart, severe depression, or simply old age. In a sense, we all need the healing of the Divine Physician, but the anointing of the sick is intended for those whose physical health are seriously compromised. The rite contains a variety of texts to use in various situations: at home, in the hospital or nursing home, with the dying, and for a communal celebration for those who are well enough to be brought together with the rest of the parish.

Colors and Symbols for the Anointing of the Sick. There is no single strong symbol suggesting this sacrament. Since the oil of the sick is olive oil, the balm of many ancient Mediterranean customs, olives and the olive branch are associated with this sacrament. So, too, the crucifix, inasmuch as the suffering Christian is identified with the suffering Christ. Megan McKenna describes the ministry of this sacrament as "the church being a *Pietà*."[25] Like Mary holding the broken body of her dead son and Lord in her lap, we hold to our hearts the sick and the suffering, the dying, and the dead. The pervading feeling of this sacrament is compassion and sympathy, but at the same time there is a sense of hope and joy. The community gives spiritual support, standing with the sick in solidarity and hope. The color of vesture used in the celebration of this sacrament is violet. Purple and gray are colors of compassion. Green expresses life and hope. White, yellow, and other bright colors inspire joy.

The words of the rite are: "Through this holy anointing may the Lord in his love and mercy help you with the grace of the Holy Spirit. May the Lord who frees you from sin save you and raise you up."[26] The new catechism lists the effects brought by the Holy Spirit in this sacrament: strength, peace, courage, trust in God, and forgiveness of sins. All of these can lead to healing of soul and body. The sick person receives the strength to unite more closely to Christ's sufferings and contributes to the edification and sanctification of the church. An icon of Christ the Healer would be expressive of the compassion and caring we want to bring to this sacrament. There is a vast treasury of stories of Jesus' healing touch in the gospels to inspire such an icon.

The Use of Banners for the Sacrament of Anointing. On first thought, there does not seem to be an occasion to use banners at the bedside when this sacrament is celebrated at home or in the hospital with a single recipient. But Josephine remembers from childhood the "sick call set" containing a crucifix, candles, holy water, and cotton balls that her family kept tucked away in a bureau drawer. When the priest came to administer the sacrament to her grandmother, it was brought out. To grandmother, the items in this kit symbolized comfort, support, and continuity with the past. Could we not do the same by hanging a simple banner expressing hope and comfort near the bed during the rite? It could be left in the room to remind the recipient of God's grace and the tender support of the church community, and then passed on to those who follow, reminding them of the courageous people who went on before them.

For a communal service, processional banners would appropriately contribute to the mood. They could be made of a long gray panel with a few narrow purple ribbons hanging along the sides, perhaps with a depiction of Christ the Healer or a scriptural story of healing. They could be set up around a pedestal holding the oil of the sick. One banner would accompany the priest and ministers to each one being anointed, allowing all present to easily see to whom to direct their thoughts and prayers.

The Sacraments of Mission and Service

The sacraments of marriage and holy orders consecrate baptized believers, conferring on them particular missions. Thus each sacrament is directed toward the building up of the people of God.

Marriage

Christian marriage establishes between a woman and a man a lifelong covenant in which they come to know Christ's presence. Holy scripture affirms that male and female were created for each other, and Jesus raised the dignity of this covenant between baptized persons to that of a sacrament. There is an innate call, a fundamental vocation, in all of us to love. This is the way God made us. Since God is love, and we are made in the image and likeness of God, it cannot be any other way. A man and woman who choose to marry direct that call specifically to one another. Their mutual love becomes for all an image of the unconditional love of God.

For Christians, the call to love takes on an added dimension in the sacrament of matrimony, in that the covenantal love relationship of the wife and husband can be compared to the covenantal love relationship between Christ and his church. In order to keep this covenant, the married couple must love, honor, and treat each other as Christ does the church. They interact in the same way that the church is called to respond to Christ.[27] In fact, the two covenantal relationships are so closely related that one can be seen as a sign of the other.

Two people who love one another deeply visibly reveal invisible reality. The energy of their love comes from God and ultimately returns to God. Their intimate sexual sharing expresses the ultimate human risk, the risk of loving someone as God loved us in Christ and the risk of loving someone as Christ loved us—totally.[28]

To say that marriage is a sign of the union between Christ and the church is to reverence the reality of a loving human sexual relationship, to see it symbolizing in the strongest ways possible God's being-in-love with us, committed to us, calling us to constant growth in that love.[29]

Two people are committed to each other totally in marriage. They are partners and helpmates. This commitment enables them and frees them to grow and change, and to rejoice in this change. It also enables them to endure life's fears and disappointments and struggles.

The bonding of two people does not happen suddenly when the vows are exchanged, but begins when they first start caring for each other and grows slowly. They can then gradually become more Christ-like in the expression and depth of their love. They may grow to be sacraments to one another, fuller signs of Christ's love. Their love for each other nourishes a grateful way of living in which they feel compelled to share their joy and love with others. It is at this time that they will feel called to be strengthened and consecrated to share their love through the sacrament of marriage. The desire to reach out beyond themselves then becomes visible in many ways. They share the fruit of their love by bringing forth new life and by nurturing their children in all ways possible. They share through their interactions within their community and beyond.

This covenant of marriage is a life-long commitment. It requires fidelity. Just as God is *always* faithfully in love with us, two so bound must be faithful in their love. Love is always specific in its object, never general. As God loves each of us, so must we love one another.

In the Roman Catholic rite, the couple are ministers of the sacrament. Common courtesy requires that the couple greet their guests in the gathering area before they enter the church, or say a few words of welcome before the ceremony begins. Essentially, the nuptial ceremony consists of a declaration of consent to marry one another and an exchange of rings. It is in these actions in particular that they are the ministers of the sacrament. This is most effectively conveyed when the couple recites the words of the vows from memory, rather than repeating the words of the priest. During the vows and the exchange of rings, it is appropriate that the bride and groom face the assembly so that all can see.

When both parties are Catholic, the ceremony takes place within a Mass. Otherwise, the rite is celebrated in a liturgy of the word. In either case, processions are an important part of the rite.

Colors and Symbols of Marriage. The official liturgical color for weddings is white. The colors of the rainbow, which together create white light, help express joy even more exuberantly. These accent colors should be clear and light. If the banner is for the church, rather than for a specific couple, use accents that work well in the church.

A ring worn on the third finger of the left hand is a sign that a person is married. In a double ring ceremony, the bride and groom give each other this circular sign of their commitment to honor and love one another until death. The most frequently used symbol or sign for this sacrament is the two rings with the cross or the chi-rho, representing Christ. The two people become one through, in, and with Jesus Christ. Living out their marriage vows, the couple becomes a living sign of Christ's love. Two hearts blending into the heart of Jesus would also convey this mystery well. Any type of symbolism of two becoming one is appropriate. Light is another symbol for marriage, the light of Christ shining through the lives of the spouses and enlightening the lives of others. Think of images from scripture, like the story of the wedding at Cana, attended by Jesus and his disciples. Or the creation of Adam and Eve in the book of Genesis. Read and contemplate the Song of Songs for more wedding imagery.

Use of Banners during the Wedding Liturgy. The obvious time for using the processional banner at weddings, like all liturgical ceremonies, is in the entrance procession. If you read the Roman Catholic *Rite of Marriage*, you'll notice that the procession described there is not what we usually see: the men slinking in the side door while the women come up the main aisle, with the bride on the arm of her father, to be "given away" to the groom at the step before the altar. No, the rite envisions that the bride and groom walk in the entrance procession together, perhaps accompanied by their families, preceded by the ministers of the liturgy.

Perhaps three banners can be used in this procession, one evoking the sacrament, and two representing the individual families. The layout of the church determines how the procession can be structured and how the banners are used. If only the center aisle is wide enough for the procession, then all parties use that aisle. Alternatively, if the side aisles are wide enough, the bride and groom's parties could process in simultaneously using the side aisles. At the end of the aisles, the bride and groom would each leave their families and meet in the center. In both cases, a single wedding banner could be carried down the center aisle, followed by either the minister and altar servers or the entire wedding procession. If desired, a family banner could precede each of the wedding parties. At the conclusion of the ceremony, these two banners would be left at the altar, and the wedding banner could accompany the married couple down the aisle.

Julie and Greg centered their wedding procession around four ribbon banners made by Josephine. Julie and Greg wanted to symbolize in their procession that they were two persons becoming one in their vowed commitment to one another. The matron of honor carried a red ribbon banner, leading the bride from the sacristy down the side aisle to the main aisle. The best man carried a similar blue banner, leading the groom down the opposite side aisle to the main aisle. Here the banners were carried side by side, leading the flower girl and ring bearer, then the bride and groom walking side by side down the main aisle to the sanctuary. After the liturgy, two purple banners, each containing bits of blue and red woven to form a cross, led the newlyweds out of the church. Other couples might have chosen to use a single banner at this point, but they chose to use the banners to reflect the fact that they were still two distinct persons (two banners) now united (as shown in the colors of the banners) in their love and united in Christ. After the ceremony, Julie and Greg gave the banners to the church to be used during Advent and Pentecost in following years. (See the photos on page 182, left.)

Holy Orders

The sacrament of holy orders is the means by which the church provides leaders to continue God's work of salvation, mandating deacons, priests, and bishops to preach the gospel and administer the sacraments. Like marriage, holy orders is a sacrament of service.

The sacrament of holy orders has three degrees: diaconate (for deacons), presbyterate (for priests), and episcopate (for bishops).[30] The diaconate may be a transitional stage, followed by ordination to the presbyterate, or it may be permanent.

As Christians we are a priestly people. Baptism confers on us participation in the priesthood of Jesus Christ. Jesus was truly human; he was like us in every way but sin. He was the high priest, called from among us by God to offer his life as sacrifice to bring salvation to all. His priesthood is eternal, never changing. Through his death, he crossed over into resurrected life to be totally with God and yet remain with us. Because we follow him, we can, through him, ultimately die and rise again.[31] Through our share in Jesus' role as mediator between God and humankind, we give witness to Christ's presence and love by our actions. We are also peacemakers by confronting injustice, by loving our enemies, and by reaching out to all in compassion and forgiveness. We share in the priesthood of Christ in our worship, especially when we gather together as a community to celebrate the eucharist.

The ordained priest is a leader in a community of ministers. He is called from among us by the Holy Spirit and by the people themselves to speak on their behalf in Christ's name to them and to the wider community. He proclaims the gospel, celebrates the sacraments, and gives pastoral care. As the leader of the community, he calls forth many ministries from the people and puts them in order for the service of God's people. Since the Second Vatican Council, the sacrament of holy orders is seen as an ordering of ministries, "a ministry of ordering the holy."[32]

The priest is the symbol-bearer for the community, a reminder of the Word of God, the living sacrament of Christ reminding the community to be true to itself when it gathers.[33] Or as Megan McKenna writes, "The essence of priesthood is being the focus, the symbol of unity of a community. The priest is the gatherer, the animator, the shepherd, or, better yet, the sheep-gate, the open door into the community."[34] It is not a role of power, but one of service.

On the evening of the Last Supper, before he settled down and broke bread with the apostles, Jesus washed their feet and told them to do likewise. Priesthood also emcompasses the role of prophet or preacher, calling the people to repent and to embrace the gospel of love, truth, justice, and compassion.

The main purpose of the diaconate today, as in the early church, is service to the people of God. Deacons "are dedicated to the People of God . . . in the service of the liturgy, of the Gospel and of works of charity."[35] Their duties include administering baptism, dispensing the eucharist, blessing marriages, providing instruction for the sacraments, presiding at communion services, and officiating at funerals and burial services.

Bishops, in addition to their roles as priests, are ordained to govern the faithful in communion with the pope and the members of the college of bishops. Through "the imposition of hands and the words of the (episcopal) consecration, the grace of the Holy Spirit is so conferred, and the sacred character so impressed, that bishops in an eminent and visible way undertake Christ's own role as Teacher, Shepherd, and High Priest, and act in his person."[36]

Colors and Symbols of Holy Orders. White is the liturgical color for this sacrament. Other colors can be added to any banners to help express the joyfulness of the occasion. Consider especially gold and silver, yellows, reds, and oranges.

The laying on of hands, together with the words of consecration, are the outward signs of holy orders, so the image of human hands may be a starting point for your design. Images of biblical priests like Melchizedek or Aaron might be considered. For bishops especially, images of the apostles are appropriate. Saints Stephen and Lawrence are patrons of deacons—both were also martyrs in the early church. There is a tradition in which Jesus is portrayed as a priest, wearing priestly vestments, yet hanging on the cross. Images of Jesus the Teacher, common in Greek and Russian icons, are also appropriate.

Using Banners at an Ordination. A banner for each individual could be included in the entrance procession, as well as additional banners. Processions for ordinations are usually quite long; many deacons, priests, and bishops attend these liturgies, and all may be included in the entrance procession. Interspersing ribbon or other processional banners adds to the festivity. If time allows, consider also making banners for local dioceses, parishes, or patron saints; these may be used for other occasions as well. Banners made with symbols of the paschal mystery could, of course, be used for any liturgical service. Within the rite, carrying one or two banners serves to focus attention on the movement from one place to another. The banners could be used at the presentation of the candidates, as a backdrop for the bishop during the ordination rite itself, and in the presentation of the gifts. It is also appropriate for all the banners to lead the way out of church to the reception area.

Other Rites of the Church

Funerals, religious profession, and the dedication of a church building are not sacraments, although they most often occur in the context of the Mass. Nonetheless they are significant celebrations, and banners could appropriately be used at each.

Funerals

Using banners can add to the solemnity of the funeral liturgy, especially because processions form the basis of this rite. At the beginning of the funeral liturgy—whether it is a Mass or a liturgy of the word—the ministers meet the casket and the deceased's family in the rear of the church. A white cloth called a pall, reminiscent of the baptismal garment, is placed over the coffin. The casket is sprinkled with holy water, again reminding us of baptism. As baptism was a new birth into the life of Christ, physical death is a birth to a greater union with God in heaven. A processional banner held near the casket during this rite can function as a reminder of this mystery.

The processional banner could coordinate with the funeral pall, but care should be taken to respect their different functions. The pall should be white and relatively plain, since it is worn as the white garment of the baptized. The pall may have a cross in the center to help with placement on the casket, but should otherwise contain little additional decoration. It is not a large banner or message bearer. The whiteness of the pall is its message. Any other visual statements can be made through a processional banner. In fact, it can be highly desirable to use the processional banner as a medium of communication in this setting.

For example, Josephine's religious community experienced the loss of a greatly revered former provincial leader of the School Sisters of Notre Dame, Sister Bernadelle Zurmuehlen. When she died after a long illness, it seemed natural to use the Easter processional banner for her funeral liturgy. The white cross and the joyful colors surrounding it clearly expressed our belief that she who had died with Christ in baptism now would share in his resurrection. Although the Easter banner was not used for subsequent funerals (it could have been), using it helped the community realize that we needed a banner specifically for funerals. The funeral liturgy of each faithful follower of Christ is an appropriate occasion to celebrate her or his passover.

Colors and Symbols of Christian Funerals. The liturgical color for funerals is white in the dioceses of the United States, although purple or black may also be used. For banners made specifically for funerals, any joyful color could be appropriately added to the white, particularly yellows and oranges. Even deeper tones of purple and black can be used to support an image that as a whole conveys light. All the symbols of Easter or Resurrection are appropriate. These would include the triumphal cross, the sun and moon and stars, or the paschal lamb, for example. An image of the new and heavenly Jerusalem would also be fitting. (See the photo on page 182, right, for an example.)

The Latin hymn *In Paradisum* provides one inspiration—angels accompanying the soul to paradise. The emotion expressed in this hymn is deep compassion with hope and joy. That is what needs to be expressed in the banner as well.

Use of Banners at Funerals. The use of the banner in the church would begin with the draping of the casket during the opening ceremony. The banner would then be carried before the casket as it is moved toward the altar, and then placed in a stand near the casket. The placement of the stand should not block the assembly's view of the liturgical action. After the casket is incensed, the banner leads the procession out of the church.

Ideally, the banner would accompany the deceased to the cemetery and be held or placed in a stand by the burial plot for the final prayers. Since the final segment of the procession often involves driving, the pole may have to be made in segments for disassembly and transportation. Consider making the banner of nylon flag fabric for use in such situations.

Just as the funeral procession does not end at the church, it does not begin there either. It really begins at the funeral home, continues at the church, and ends at the cemetery. The use of a banner at all three locations helps reinforce their connection, while emphasizing resurrection and eternal life. Place the banner at the wake, carry it in the liturgy, and bring it to the cemetery. Ritually, one's journey on earth ends when the body lies in the grave.

Religious Profession

Since ancient times, men and women have responded to a call to focus on the search for union with God, living together in communities so dedicated. What distinguishes the search of the professed religious from others' is its exclusivity. "Religious pursue this quest to the exclusion of any other primary life commitment such as commitment to spouse or partner and family, profession or career, art, or economic or political projects. In this sense, all religious life is monastic (meaning single, only, sole, or unique), not because it involves the lifestyle elements of enclosed communities such as habit, cloister, common life, or choral recitation of the office, but because it is centered totally on what is identified as the one thing necessary."[37] Hence, responding to this call of religious life involves a radical choice of the gospel vows of poverty, chastity, and obedience.

For many years, entering religious life was perceived as fleeing from the world, the flesh, and the devil, all of which were considered evil! Today the attitude of professed members toward themselves and other people differs considerably. The whole cosmos is created by God and is good. Evil or sin is turning from the good that God created and promoting interests that lead us away from God. The covenant with God that members of religious communities make, promising obedience, celibacy, and poverty, is countercultural in a world that glorifies independence, self-indulgence, and possessions. They are prophetic, calling all God's people to conversion and new life.

The three vows of obedience, celibacy, and poverty do not emphasize self-denial as much as embracing life lived to its fullest. Religious say an unqualified "yes" to the gospel invitation to fullness of life. "I came that they might have life and have it to the full" (John 10:10). They do not hide from the world, but choose to be a sign to the world of what authentic human life, lived to its fullest, can be. In truth, every God-given vocation is a call to fullness of life. Today we recognize that perfection or holiness can be attained in any state of life. The three vows can be seen as related to the tendencies intrinsic in the continual cosmic process of life. Our instinct for life (survival) expresses itself in urges toward possessions, power, and sexual behavior. In all human beings, that instinct needs to be channeled toward the good of all with which we share this earth. When it is not, it appears as greed, domination, and lust, and becomes exploitative. Religious men and women vow poverty, celibacy, and obedience in order to direct their life energies toward the good of the whole species.[38]

Rites of Religious Profession. The rites of religious profession are usually celebrated in the church or chapel of the particular religious congregation to which the candidate is professing. The candidate goes through three rites: the rite of acceptance into the novitiate, temporary profession, and the final profession of vows. The rite for entering the period of the novitiate is very simple, performed in the presence of the religious community. It is not generally held within Mass. Upon completion of the novitiate, the temporary profession takes place. This rite is simple as well, without much solemnity. However, it is held within the context of a Mass, with the religious community and the broader community present. In this liturgy, the novice professes vows of poverty, celibate chastity, and obedience. He or she then receives the habit (if that is still the community's custom), any insignia (cross, ring, or pin) that identifies the community, and finally the rule or constitution of the community.

The final profession is celebrated with great solemnity. The entire community, including family, friends, and religious community, is encouraged to be present. It is at this rite that a processional banner would be appropriate, calling all to join in the celebration.

The sister or brother professes the three vows for life, according to the formula of the particular religious congregation.

Colors and Symbols of Religious Profession. The liturgical color of these celebrations is white. All other joyful colors can be used with the white in a processional banner, particularly any associated with the congregation. Symbols appropriate for vow ceremonies include the cross, as well as others referring to Christ or the Holy Spirit, such as the chi-rho or the dove. Symbols of virginity include lilies, a white rose, laurel, orange blossoms or the orange fruit, a lamp burning, and the unicorn. An image of the founder or a particular symbol of the community would remind the assembly of the charism of the community to which the candidate is professing. Because the vows are taken for the sake of the kingdom, symbols of the world or the universe could be the main focus of a banner, or provide a background for other symbols. Symbols of love are appropriate, since the vows are prompted from an undivided love for God, and expressed in a life dedicated to love for others. Images of light convey the liminal aspect of religious life, a beacon reflecting God's love to all people. Together, the color and the symbols should express joy and lavish generosity.

Because there are so many options available for designing a banner for a religious profession, you may feel compelled to try to put many symbols on one banner. Resist that temptation. Keep the symbolism in a single banner simple and uncluttered. Make more banners if needed. You might consider making one or more banners that a community would use for all professions, and one for each individual professing vows. A banner made for an individual would depict symbols relevant to him or her, and could then be presented to the newly professed at the end of the ceremony.

Dedication of a Church and Parish Anniversaries

The dedication of a new church or of a newly renovated church is a major event in the life of a parish community. The deeply moving prayers and actions of these liturgies clearly express the consecration of sacred place and its furnishings for worship through a rite that appeals to the human senses. In many ways, it is much like the rites of initiation.

The *Rite of Dedication* indicates that the assembly should gather outside or in another place and process to the door together. Candles are not used in this procession (for a specific reason—they are ritually lit later in the rite). The procession is joyous and exuberant, and banners are most fitting. This gathering of the people and procession of the entire assembly into the church itself provides a striking image of a pilgrim people. When they process behind a banner (or more than one), that banner helps enhance and embody this symbolism. It allows the assembly to take ownership of their worship place and symbolizes their commitment to continue that pilgrimage all their lives. On the following Sundays, the sight of the banner leading the entrance procession will remind them they are still part of the procession, and always will be, even though only the priest, servers, and a few other ministers are actually seen in the procession each Sunday.

Colors and Symbols for a Church Dedication. The liturgical color for dedications is white; gold is also appropriate. Any additional bright colors used in smaller quantities would help make a banner appropriately festive. Symbols for a processional banner for a church dedication could relate to the name of the church. Here the possibilities are vast: a design with a repeated rose motif could represent Saint Rose of Lima, the Little Flower, Our Lady of Guadalupe, or other titles of Mary. The symbol of the patron might be placed on a luminous sky background with a landscape of the area or the city skyline below it.

Motifs from the church's architecture might be used—arches or window shapes, for example. A parish might also choose to use a symbol to remind them that the church is the people, not the building, and that the building is significant because of the assembly that worships there.

A banner expressing this theology could contain the shape of the specific church building made of a collage of photos of the faces of all the parishioners. If the parish is too large, a random selection of faces could be used, making sure all generations are included. We describe the process of transferring photos in Chapter 8.

Another technique that would express this idea well is to write the names of all the parishioners in a drawing of the church. The names are the drawing. From a distance only the form of the church is distinguishable. Up close, the names are visible and the message is clear: We are the church. This drawing method is not nearly as difficult as it seems. See the directions in chapter 8.

Celebrations of parish anniversaries are also occasions for honoring the patron saint of the parish and remembering the history of the parish, the founding members, and the founding pastor. Photos of previous church buildings might be included in banners. Often renovations become controversial because parishioners do not want things changed in the building they have worshiped in for many years. Using photos of earlier buildings in the processional banner shows reverence for the past history of the parish and can help the grieving process associated with any future renovations proceed.

If you can't easily incorporate a photo of the church building in the design of the banner, put the photo on the back as part of the lining. You can transfer a black-and-white photograph as we describe in Chapter 8, or use a blue-printing process called cyanotype, also described in Chapter 8.

Notes

1. DeGidio, Sandra, *Sacraments Alive: Their History, Celebration, and Significance* (Mystic, Conn.: Twenty-Third Publications, 1991), p. 13.
2. Walsh, Eugene. *Celebration: Theology, Ministry, and Practice* (Portland, Ore.: OCP Publications, 1994), p. 11.
3. Matthew 3:13–17 (New American Bible).
4. Rowling, J. K., *Harry Potter and the Sorcerer's Stone* (New York: Scholastic Press, 1997), p. 299.
5. *Catechism of the Catholic Church*, #1272.
6. Isaiah 11:6.
7. Donghi, A., *Actions and Words: Symbolic Language and the Liturgy* (Collegeville, Minn.: Liturgical Press, 1997), p. 39.
8. Rite of Confirmation, #25.
9. *Catechism of the Catholic Church*, #1293.
10. *Catechism of the Catholic Church*, #1296.
11. Rite of Confirmation, #33.
12. *Catechism of the Catholic Church*, #1307, #1322.
13. Roberts, William P., *Encounters with Christ* (New York: Paulist Press, 1985), p. 161.
14. Sottocornola, F., *A New Look at the Rite of Penance*, trans. Thomas A. Krosnicki (Washington: United States Catholic Conference, 1975), p. 16.
15. John 20:22–23.

16. Roberts, p. 162.
17. "Dogmatic Constitution on the Church: *Lumen Gentium*," in *Vatican Council II: The Conciliar and Post Conciliar Documents,* ed. Austin Flannery, OP (Dublin: Dominican Publications, 1975), #8, p. 358.
18. 2 Corinthians 5:17–19.
19. DeGidio, p. 75.
20. Walsh, p. 75.
21. Roberts, p. 163.
22. Isaiah 1:18.
23. McKenna, Megan, *Rites of Justice* (Maryknoll, New York: Orbis, 1997), p. 155.
24. Mark 16:18.
25. McKenna, p. 155
26. *Catechism of the Catholic Church,* #1513.
27. Roberts, pp. 219–220.
28. DeGidio, p. 113.
29. Ibid, p. 120.
30. Roberts, pp. 196–197.
31. DeGidio, p. 137.
32. Ibid., p. 138.
33. McKenna, p. 188.
34. *Lumen Gentium,* #29.
35. Ibid., #21.
36. Schneiders, Sandra M., *Religious Life and Vows in Postmodern United States Culture* (Monroe, Mich.: Sisters Servants of the Immaculate Heart of Mary, 1998).
37. Prevallet, Elaine S. L., *A Wisdom for Life* (Nerinx, Ky., 1995), pp. 31–33.

Chapter 4

BASICS OF DESIGN AND HARDWARE

The success of a banner, both as a work of art and as an inspiration, depends on how well basic principles of design are utilized. Every banner contains lines, shapes, values, colors, and textures. How these basic elements are arranged constitute the design. Whether you create your own original design for a banner or interpret one of the designs illustrated in this book, you want it to be beautiful work that inspires viewers and helps them perceive a sense of mystery and awe.

> *Because the assembly gathers in the presence of God to celebrate his saving deeds, liturgy's climate is one of awe, mystery, wonder, reverence, thanksgiving and praise. So it cannot be satisfied with anything less than the* beautiful *in its environment and in all its artifacts, movements, and appeals to the senses. Admittedly difficult to define, the beautiful is related to the sense of the numinous, the holy. Where there is evidently no care for this, there is an environment basically unfriendly to mystery and awe, an environment too casual, if not careless, for the liturgical action. (*Environment and Art in Catholic Worship, *Washington: United States Catholic Conference, 1978, 34)*

Some in the assembly will recognize good design, others will not. But all have the innate ability to sense mystery and awe, to recognize the beautiful.

Artists share in the work of the Creator Spirit who fashioned our universe and delights in our attempts to reflect goodness, beauty, and truth. When designing banners, we must be committed to these ideals. Organizing and planning the design using basic principles does not curb creativity, but creates a framework for expression. Each artist expresses her or his individuality in the way she or he manipulates the elements of design. What stifles creativity is a lack of vision. Good design helps develop our vision.

The artist's prayer life also helps to cultivate artistic vision. Meditation and reflection on the stories of scripture, the texts of the liturgy, and the lives of the saints help bring symbols to life within us, so that we might convey them to others. When we approach these stories with a humble heart, ready to listen, our understanding of design acts upon what we have heard, producing designs that are gifts to the assembly and help open all to mystery and awe in the liturgical action.

Do not worry about your talent or lack of it. We all have some kind of talent, and all talent must be developed. The creative imagination can grow and be strengthened through exercise just as muscles can. The book that has become the classic for developing creativity is *Drawing on the Right Side of the Brain* by Betty Edwards (Los Angeles: J. P. Tarcher, Inc. 1979).

Elements of Design

The basic elements of design are line, shape, form, color, value, and texture. All visually perceptible objects can be described with these attributes. The manner in which these six elements are used creates two other elements, movement and pattern.

Line

There are many kinds of lines that can be used in a banner. Lines can be structural, like the lines of a quilt block or outline of an appliquéd symbol, or they can be purely decorative, in the pattern of the fabric. The quality and direction of these lines help create mood. Lines can be thick or thin—thick to express power or strength, thin to express delicacy and gentleness. Since banners are generally viewed from a distance, the perceptibility of thicker lines provides an advantage.

Lines can be curved or straight. Curved lines create a rhythmic movement and flow appropriate to banners. Straight lines tend to be more static, but using many in sequence also creates rhythm and movement, as we see in the design of many quilt blocks. The illusion of a curve can be created with straight lines.

Lines can be fast, busy, and jagged and or serene, slow, and slightly curved. A line's orientation also influences the feeling expressed. Horizontal lines are passive, restful. Vertical lines are alert or dignified. Diagonal lines are dynamic and moving. It is easy to remember these attributes by thinking of them as positions of the human body. The sleeping position is horizontal. Standing at attention is the military position for alertness, "standing tall" our expression for dignity. A person on a diagonal is either running, riding a bicycle, or falling. Because they convey alertness and action, vertical and diagonal lines are better for processional banners than horizontal lines.

Shape and Form

Lines also define shapes. Pieced quilt blocks utilize a small number of basic shapes to create a variety of geometric shapes. In banners that use symbols or figures, the symbol's shape is what communicates meaning to the viewer. Try positioning major shapes on the diagonal to give the most dramatic movement.

The background around a figure, or the negative space, should also be treated as part of the design. The interplay of negative and positive shapes provides appeal to many quilts. The positive shapes in one block can be negative shapes in the block next to it, depending on the fabrics used.

Form is related to shape; by adding depth to any shape, it becomes a three-dimensional form. With appliquéd symbols and figures, depth can be achieved with shadows or shading. In abstract or geometric designs, the appearance of depth is achieved by placing a dark color next to a light color, or a dull color next to a bright one.

Color

Color is a key element in banner making, particularly for liturgical banners. Probably more than any other design element, color helps to create mood. A banner's basic color is often determined by the liturgical season or feast being celebrated. A wide variety of shades, tones and tints of that hue can add drama. For example, red is the liturgical color for Passion Sunday, Good Friday, and Pentecost. Different reds can color the mood: a deep red for Good Friday and a fiery orange-red for Pentecost.

Many people are intimidated by color. We all know people who seem to be gifted with a sense of color, choosing colors that go well together without effort. If you struggle with colors, you can benefit greatly by developing your understanding of the color wheel and color harmonies. Buy a color wheel from an art supply store and use it to help you understand color harmonies. It will assist you in planning your projects.

Whole books have been written on color theory. For quilt makers, a good choice is *The Magical Effects of Color* by Joen Wolfrom (Lafayette, Cal.: C & T Publishing, 1992). She includes a chapter on how to achieve effects such as iridescence, luminosity, luster, opalescence, and transparency. Studying these effects will aid you in your quest to communicate mystery and awe.

Modern color theories are generally based on the six-point color wheel, which places the primary colors, that is, yellow, blue, and red,

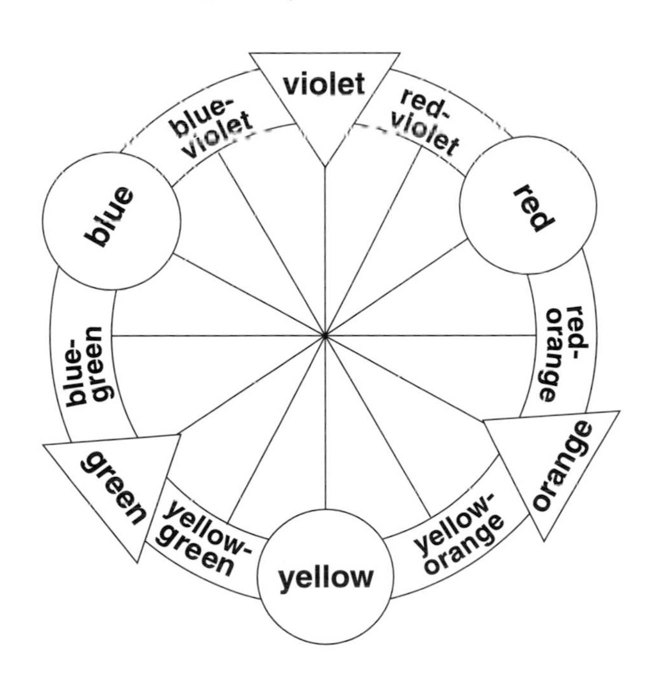

Color wheel.

at the points of an equilateral triangle. The secondary hues of green, violet, and orange form a second equilateral triangle, with green falling between yellow and blue, violet between blue and red, and orange between red and yellow. It is useful to make a further distinction in hue, that is, tertiary hues. These are half-way between each primary and its neighboring secondary color, that is, yellow-green, blue-green, blue-violet, red-violet, red-orange, and yellow-orange. White, black, and gray are not a part of the spectrum of hues, but add other dimensions to color: tints or pale colors, shades or deep colors, and tones or muted colors. Knowledge of the color wheel provides a basis for understanding how colors work together.

The principles for combining colors are called "harmonies." The most basic color harmony is monochromatic, meaning only one hue is utilized. Any tint, shade, or tone of that hue can be included in a monochromatic color scheme. The neutral colors of white, black, and gray can be used as well. While the principle sounds simple enough, it can be difficult to match commercially available fabrics to stay within a monochromatic scheme.

Analogous hues lie next to each other on the color wheel. An analogous color harmony usually uses three adjacent hues, the central of which is primary or secondary. Using an analogous color scheme centered on blue is very effective in banners depicting water. Blue comes alive with the addition of smaller amounts of blue-green, blue-violet, and white. Likewise, the orange of fire radiates when complemented with red-orange and yellow-orange. Because the hues vary in an analogous color scheme, quilters find it much easier to find appropriate fabrics.

A complementary harmony contrasts two colors opposite each other on the color wheel, highlighting each other. We use these complements naturally, in the decorative colors for Christmas and Easter, that is, red and green, yellow and purple. Even a small amount of a complementary hue sparks a color. The tiniest amount of red or burgundy in a green Ordinary Time banner will make your ribbons dance. Even complementary tertiary colors are striking. If your church interior clashes with emerald green, consider using blue-green or teal as your dominant hue and add red-orange highlights.

Split-complementary color harmonies are similar to complementary harmonies except that they involve three hues instead of two. Rather than using the directly opposite hue, split the difference and use the two hues adjacent to the opposite. It's like using an analogous color scheme for your opposite, except that you drop out the central hue. This approach would turn the red-orange highlights in our blue-green banner to bits of red and orange. As with complementary colors, the contrast is great, so the colors can be seen well from a distance. The effect is striking, even more interesting than a straight complementary color harmony.

Triad color harmonies use three colors that form an equilateral triangle on the color wheel. We already know that the primary colors form an equilateral triangle, so they also form a triad color harmony. The secondary colors form another. Two more triads are formed from the tertiaries: red-violet, yellow-orange, and blue-green, and red-orange, yellow-green, and blue-violet. The neutrals of white, black, and gray can be used with any of these color harmonies.

Besides hue, color has two additional properties: value and tone. In order to use color effectively, we need to understand these properties as well. Value refers to a color's lightness or darkness. Every hue on the color wheel has a full range of pastel colors called tints, which a painter would obtain by mixing various amounts of white with the pure hue to lighten it. It also has a full range of shades, obtained by mixing black with the pure hue to darken it. Contrast in value is critical for the perception of form, particularly from a distance. Medium red and medium green may contrast in hue, but they do not contrast in value. If you want your form to be readable from a distance, choose values of those hues that do contrast, such as light red and dark green. Value contributes to the mood of a color as well. Generally speaking, high-key or light colors are cheerful; low-key or dark colors more somber.

Tone refers to the saturation or intensity of hue. Pure hues have maximum intensity. The addition of gray, that is, both white and black, lessens a color's intensity. Colors of high intensity express exuberance and joy, while toned-down colors convey a shadowy calm. Contrast in tone can provide depth to your piece. If you look carefully at paintings of the old masters, you will see that even small bits of pure hues among toned-down hues look glowing and full of color.

Texture

Because we work with fabric, the surface texture and pattern, or visual texture, of the fabric must be considered as design components. Fabrics can be shiny or matte, smooth or rough, textured or flat. Pattern can be dense or open, defined or random, undulating or linear. In most of our work we use 100% cotton fabrics because they handle easily, don't slip, and are available in a wide range of colors and patterns. We avoid cotton/polyester blends, since they do not keep their shape as well. They tend to sag in a completed piece. Raw silk has a richness and depth of color unsurpassed by any other fiber. Its rough nubby texture makes it relatively easy to handle. If you wish to use more slippery shiny silks, back them with iron-on interfacing before cutting. Metallic fabrics create highlights that catch the eye of the viewer. Buy either bonded metallics or bond them yourself with iron-on interfacing.

Working with pattern provides one of the great joys of quilt making. Any quilt or fabric shop will provide a great variety of patterns printed on 100% cotton. If you want a simple, bold design, choose solid color fabrics, as seen in Amish designs. Solids stand out when you mix them with prints, so control that effect carefully. Prints tend to mix better with each other. Subtle prints, sometimes called printed solids, are now a quilting basic, complementing prints of more contrast. Prints come in a variety of scales and patterns, from little flowers to large-scale botanicals, to stripes, plaids, batiks, and ethnic designs. Vary the scale and type of patterns within a piece. Using only small-scale calicoes can be dull and boring, while too many large-scale prints can be confusing. Combine small and large, sharply defined patterns and flowing hand-dyes. We generally avoid stripes and polka dots with a lot of contrast, because they tend to draw attention to themselves. Use that effect carefully. Constants in our use of fabrics include hand-dyes, batiks from Bali, leaf prints, and hand-painted fabrics.

Basic Principles

The basic elements of design must all work together to form a pleasing composition. A good design utilizes the basic principles of unity, balance, contrast, emphasis, and rhythm. There are also principles of harmony, coherence, repetition, gradation, and dominance. These overlap the basic principles or are other names for them.

Unity

All lines, shapes, colors, and textures contribute to a banner's design. Therefore, they should look as if they belong together. In other words, they should provide an impression of unity. If any single element clashes with the others, the banner will lack unity. One color might clash with the others. If used in too large a proportion, it disturbs rather than complements the design, causing the banner to lack unity. Likewise, a line or shape might stand out from the rest of the composition, making it look as though it does not belong in the design. Periodically throughout the design process, ask yourself if the design appears unified.

Balance

Balance in design means that colors, shapes, lines, and textures give the appearance of being equally distributed on both sides of the work of art. A symmetrical, or mirror image, design is one example of balance, but symmetry is not necessary. There is asymmetrical balance as well.

To understand asymmetrical balance, consider a see-saw. Obviously a see-saw works if two people of equal weight sit at the end of each arm. This is symmetrical balance. However, two people of unequal weight can see-saw if the smaller person sits at the end of one arm and the larger person sits closer to the center on the other arm. This is asymmetrical balance. Balance requires that the two sides of a design have equal visual impact, even if they are not identical. In a banner design, a larger shape close to the center on one side can balance a smaller shape on the edge of the other. A brighter color near the center can balance a toned-down color further from the center. All the elements should be distributed through the design to create balance.

Contrast

Contrast creates interest. Sameness quickly becomes boring. Contrasting light versus dark, bright versus dull, rough versus smooth, large versus small, creates a tension that attracts attention. Banners that display a good use of contrast have an energy that draws people into the action of the liturgy. Contrast also increases the visibility of the banner from a distance.

Emphasis

Good design has a center of interest, or a point of emphasis. This center of interest is usually, but not always, near the center of the design. One way to achieve emphasis is through contrast. A shape can also be emphasized by arranging other shapes and lines in the composition in such a way that they lead to it. One shape should dominate the rest, as several shapes of equal importance create confusion in their bids for attention.

Rhythm

Rhythm is that quality in a work of art that gives it a feeling of gracefulness. It is the repetition of lines and colors that encourage the viewer's eye to move from one part of the design to another. When making a banner with quilt blocks, the repetition of the same lines and shapes creates a strong rhythm. In the Pentecost banner of red and yellow flames, the repetition of the curved vertical lines creates another kind of rhythm. Just as with music, the rhythm can be slow or fast, staccato or smooth. The kinds of lines and colors used produce different qualities.

Gradation is a type of rhythm, one that Pam uses extensively. It can be quite effective. Gradually changing a color from light to dark, or a shape from large to small, not only creates an obvious rhythm, it also implies depth. Gradation in hue can also be used. Josephine used a hue gradation when designing an angel for a banner. She recalled that in the traveling *Angels of the Vatican* exhibit of a few years ago, few of the angel wings were white. They were many different colors. Because the person commissioning the banner requested lots of color, she decided to use all the hues of the rainbow except greens in the wings. The range of hues helps leads the eye around the banner. (See the photo on page 183, top.)

As you work with these principles and design your next banner, bear in mind simplicity is best. A processional banner provides a fairly small surface for design, when compared with a bed-sized quilt, and is nearly always viewed from a distance. For greatest impact, make the design simple and limit your color palette. Experiment with detail and sparks of complementary colors within broadly defined areas. Indiscriminate use of texture, pattern, color, and line causes elements to compete for the viewer's attention, rather than highlight and support each other. Be selective.

HARDWARE

The support system for a processional banner can be constructed of wood, or metal pipes, or even PVC tubing. The method we describe is a combination of these materials. There are three basic sections: the top to which the banner is attached, the pole by which it is held high, and the stand to support it when it is not carried in procession.

The shape of the top section is determined by the shape of the banner. We will describe the three that we use most often. The first is the simplest and would be used for most ribbon banners; it is for banners with a straight horizontal line at the top.

HORIZONTAL BAR

To make a horizontal top section, you will need a length of 1/2" PVC plumbing pipe as long as your banner is wide plus 1', one 1/2" tee joint, and the adhesive manufactured specifically for PVC tubing. This adhesive is toxic, so be sure to use it only outdoors or in a

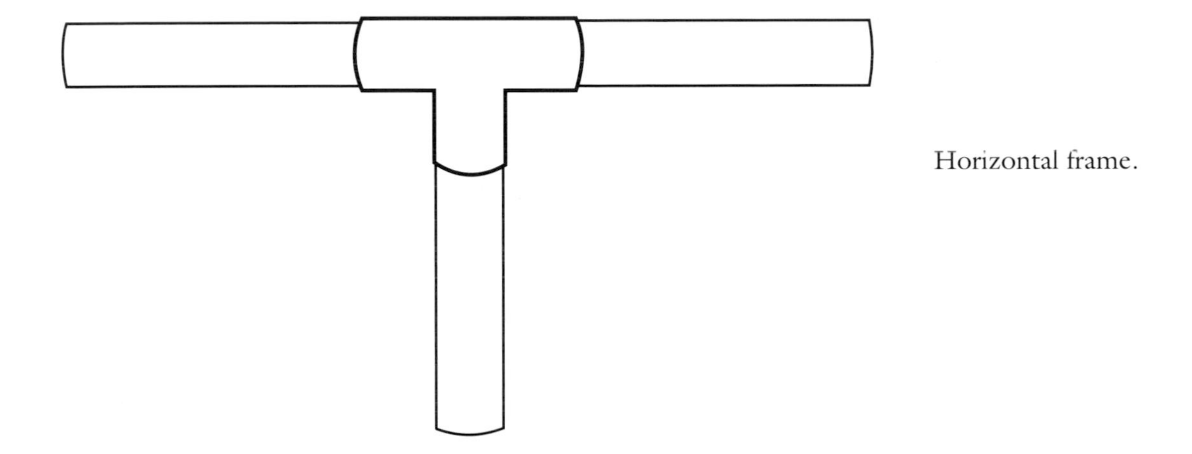

Horizontal frame.

room with an exhaust fan. Place layers of newspapers on the table or counter where you assemble the top.

Following the instructions on the can, apply the adhesive to one end of the pipe and to the inside of one side of the tee joint. Once these are securely attached, measure from the center of the tee and mark half your banner width. Cut the pipe with a hacksaw or electric jigsaw. Glue the cut pipe to the other side of the tee. Measure, mark and cut as before. Attach the remainder of the pipe into the bottom of the tee joint.

Inverted V

The second type of top section is for diamond-shaped banners, or those with an inverted V shape at the top. For a banner with 24" sides, purchase PVC adhesive and the following PVC pieces: one 90° elbow, three tee joints, two 45° elbows, and a 60" long piece of 1/2" pipe. Cut the pipe into sections, one 9" length and two each of the following lengths: 18 1/4", 3 3/8", 1 1/4", and 1". Following the directions on the can, glue these together according to this diagram. Be sure the two slanted sections form a perfect right angle centered over the 9" segment. The 18 1/4" segments can be lengthened or shortened according to the size of the banner.

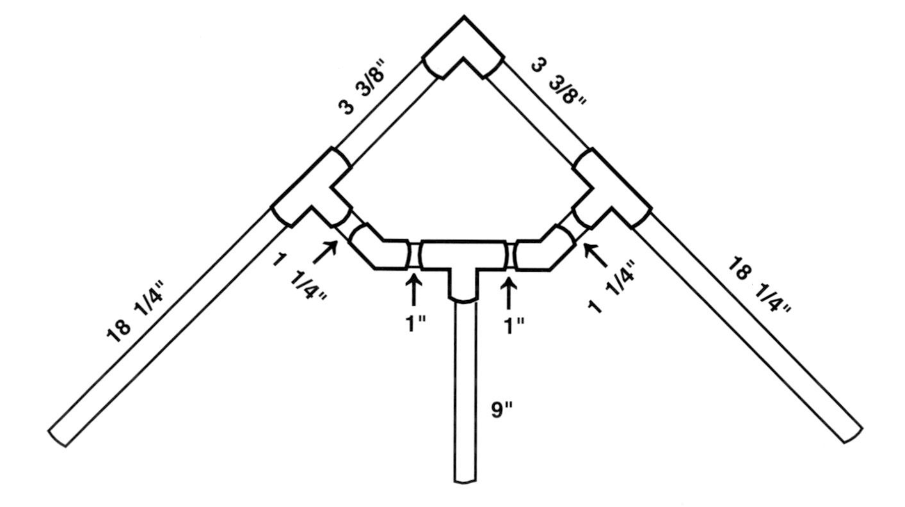

Inverted V frame.

Octagonal Frame

An octagonal frame is used for the woven ribbon banners described in the next chapter. Construct the framework according to this diagram. Use the 1/2" PVC tubing and joints. You will need 8 45° elbows, 1 tee joint, one 8' pipe, and PVC glue.

Cut the following pieces: five 13" pieces, three 4 3/4" pieces, and two 2" pieces. Use the PVC adhesive outside or in a room with an exhaust fan. Spread layers of newspaper on a table and arrange the pieces on it according to the diagram. Following the directions on the can, glue the pieces together using a carpenter's square or the edge of the table to ensure that the sides are straight.

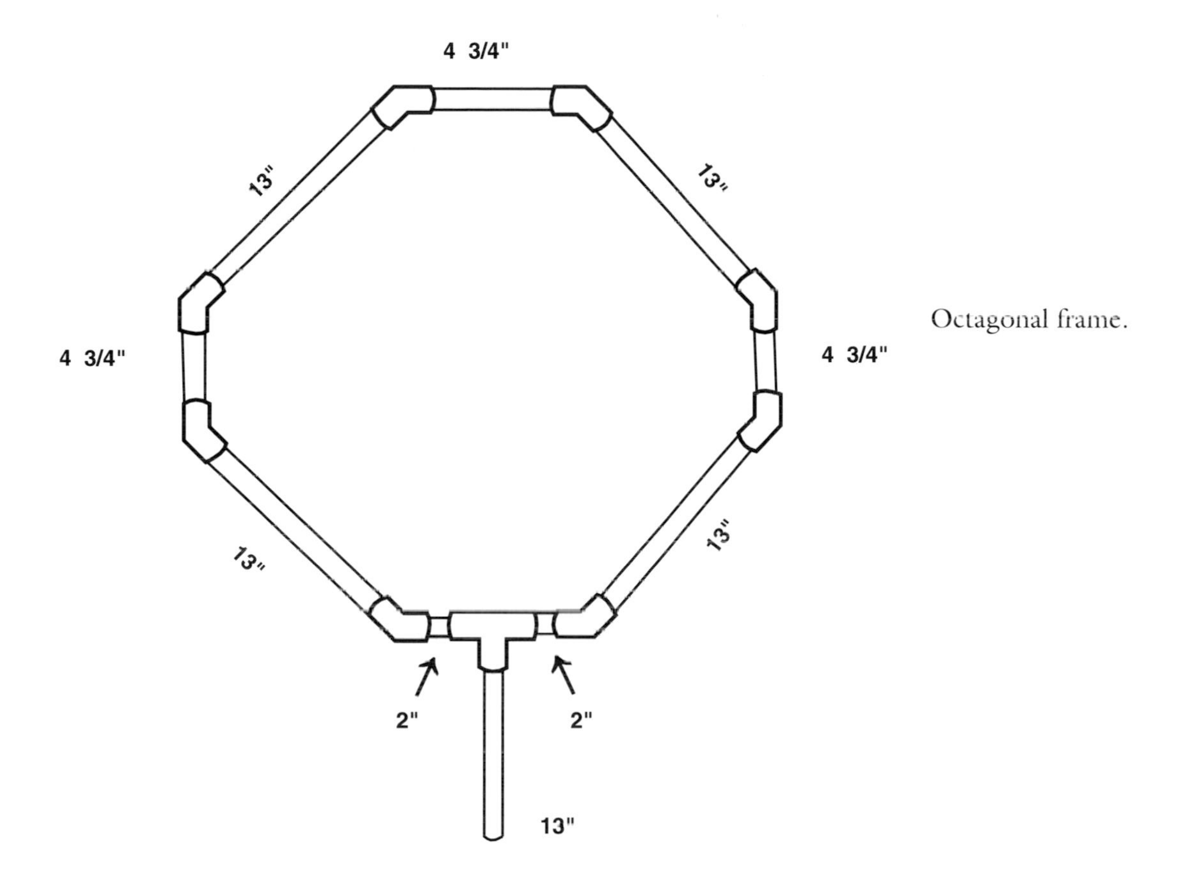

Octagonal frame.

POLE

The pole can be any hollow metal pole that is light enough to carry gracefully in the procession: 1" aluminum conduit works well and can be found in the electrical supply section of your building supply store. The inside diameter of your pole should about 3/4" or slightly more, so that the vertical segment of the top section can slide into it.

The length of the pole is affected by the size of your space and the size of the person who will carry the banner. We find that 8' to 10' poles work well in many parishes, using a longer pole where there is a higher ceiling. If the banner will be carried by a child, the pole should be short enough for smaller people to handle comfortably, that is, 6' to 7'.

Because aluminum is lightweight, it works the best. If you cannot find long aluminum poles, clothesline props work well. Simply saw the hook off the top. To make a pole longer, cut the extra length needed from a second piece of the same material. Attach a segment of PVC tubing inside the first pole where the segments will join so that it sticks up half its length. Drill holes through the pole and PVC and secure with a bolt and nut. Slip the added pole over the PVC that sticks up, and secure in the same way.

The vertical segment of the top section needs to fit snugly inside the pole so that the banner does not swivel. Wind masking tape or electrical tape around the vertical segment to make it fit snugly.

Stand

If the banner will be displayed during the liturgy, a stand is needed to hold it upright and stable. There are many ways to construct a stand. One simple, attractive method is shown below. The main requirements are that it have a wide base for stability and a tall and narrow opening to hold the banner upright. Wood is attractive, and can be painted or stained to match the interior of the church.

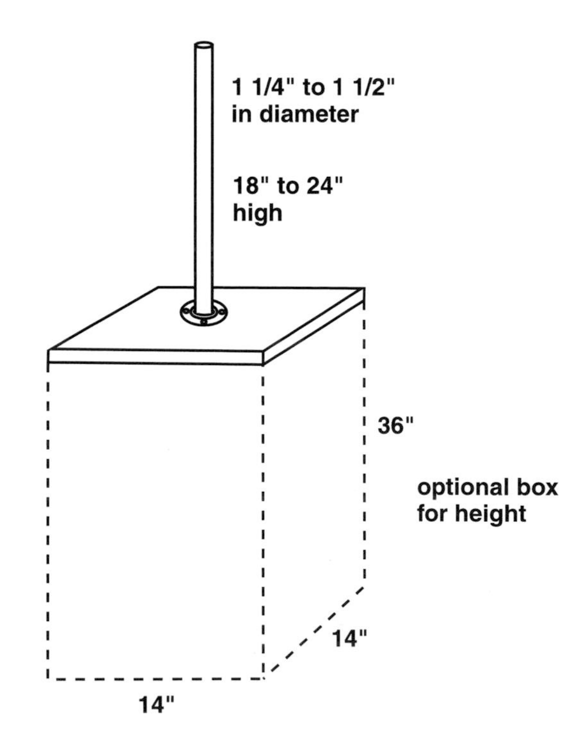

Stand for banners.

An unobtrusive stand for holding the banner for display can be made of a standard plumbing pipe and plywood. Purchase a 12"–24" length of pipe threaded at one end, of a diameter large enough to accommodate your banner pole: 1 1/4" or 1 1/2" pipe should be sufficient. Screw on a flat flange of the same size. Spray-paint the pipe and flange with metallic gold or silver paint. Screw the flange to the center of a 14" square of plywood that has been stained and varnished.

If your church has very high ceilings, you should raise the banner higher off the floor. To raise the stand, construct a vertical box (14" square x 28"–36" high). Place a sandbag inside the box to give it stability. Nail the stand to the top of this box, and stain and varnish the box to match.

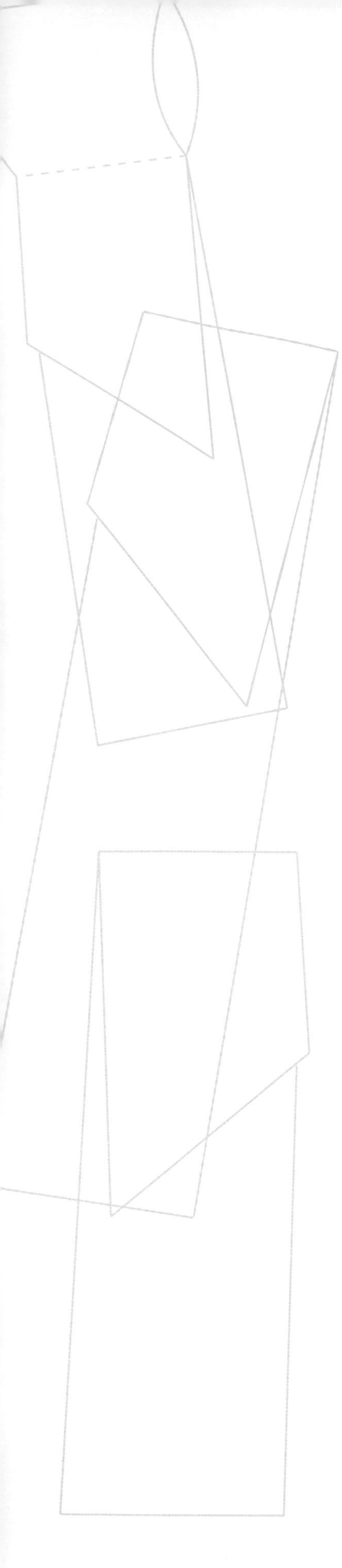

Chapter 5:

RIBBON BANNERS

Banners carried in liturgical processions are usually tall and narrow, and carried high on a pole. Their height allows the banners to be seen above the heads of the assembly, and narrowness ensures that the banners do not obstruct the view of those carrying them in the procession. These attributes also function well when the banners are placed in a stationary position for the duration of the liturgy. A tall banner may be made up of streamers or ribbons alone, or streamers and ribbons may be added to a fabric panel. As the banner moves, the ribbons float gracefully behind the bearer, emphasizing the movement of the procession and adding to its festivity.

Ribbons alone are sufficient to indicate the liturgical season, but further elaboration of a season's symbolism or a specific design requires the use of a fabric panel, or what is usually thought of as a banner. The design of such panels is taken up in detail in Chapter 6. As a preliminary step, make sure that a panel is of an appropriate size for the space in which it will be used. The interior volume of some churches can have a diminishing effect. To avoid surprises, make a plain paper pattern the size of your banner and attach it to a pole. Carry the paper dummy in the church and decide whether the size needs to be adjusted. Test the paper dummy in a stand if the banner will be displayed during the liturgy.

Ribbons and Streamers

Ribbons or streamers can be used either on their own or in combination with a fabric panel. Depending on the intended uses and life of the banner, different kinds of materials may be used. Ribbons commonly used for sewing, such as satin and grosgrain, silk, metallics, and other similar ribbons work well for the streamers. They come in an astounding array of colors, move nicely, can be ironed and cleaned, and are relatively forgiving. While less expensive, floral or craft ribbons are usually stiffer and do not move as well. Some have unfinished edges which will eventually fray. A crumpled craft ribbon's appearance can be improved by ironing, but creases caused by handling or storing will never entirely disappear. Clearly, these ribbons should be used only for banners with a limited life span. Craft ribbons are good for projects done with children, because their lower price allows more lavish use of the material.

The length of the ribbons depends on the height of the pole. A pole to be carried by a child should not be more than six or seven feet tall, while an adult can carry a ten-foot pole. Proportionally, the length of the ribbons should be at least twice the width of the banner; three times the width is even better. The longest ribbons should end no lower than a foot from the floor when the banner is placed in the stand. Cut each ribbon at an angle to prevent raveling. While you may cut them all off at the same length, consider cutting the ends at random lengths or graduating them to form a V shape. When preparing to cut ribbons for a banner, suspend a bar from the ceiling at the height of the banner's top. Hang the ribbons from it, taping them in place. Arrange the ribbons as desired. Then cut the ribbons to the desired length.

To attach the ribbons to the cross bar, sew a loop in each ribbon, making the loop slightly larger than the circumference of the bar. Allow the shorter cut end to extend about an inch below the loop. (See diagram, next page.) Maintaining the order of your design, slide each ribbon loop onto the bar after you sew it to keep everything straight and tangle-free. Tie a narrow ribbon to each end of the cross bar to keep the ribbon loops from slipping off. If all your ribbons are narrow ($^{1}/_{2}$" or less), they can simply be tied to the crossbar.

Sewn ribbon loop.

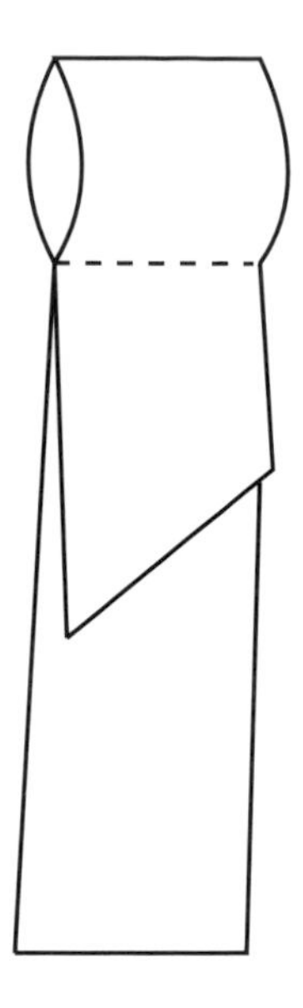

If the banner has a fabric panel, the ribbons can be attached another way. Sew the ribbons to a sleeve which will be attached to the fabric panel, through which the crossbar will be threaded. To make such a sleeve, cut two pieces of fabric, each 1" longer than half the length of the cross bar and 1" wider than the circumference of the cross bar. Finish the short ends with a 1/4" rolled seam, and iron a 1/4" fold on each of the long edges. Lay the casings wrong side up and end to end. Pin the ribbons (with ends cut straight across) to the bottom edges, making sure to arrange them in the order of your design. Continue across the center gap between the halves of the casing where the vertical pole will be. The ribbons may touch each other, but, since you are sewing them in place, you may elect to leave gaps between them; 1/8" to 1/4" spaces between ribbons can be effective. Gaps of up to 2" to 3" create groupings that can be interesting; however, don't overdo it, or the ribbons will look sparse. Once the ribbons are pinned, sew them down with slightly less than a 1/2" seam. Fold the casing in half lengthwise and zigzag the edges together. If the center ribbons are narrow, they can be used to tie the two halves together across the vertical pole. Otherwise, tack two short, narrow ribbons to the sleeves to serve this purpose. Tack the sleeves to the back of the fabric panel.

A simple ribbon banner can be effective for any of the liturgical seasons. Buy ribbons in a variety of colors and widths. The widest or most dominant ribbon used should also be the brightest shade of the liturgical color. Narrower ribbons can be in lighter or darker shades, or in related hues. The very narrowest ribbons can be in a contrasting color for sparkle, if desired. Metallic ribbons can be used with any liturgical color. Gold ribbons work well in a white or red banner, while silver can highlight a green banner.

Painted Ribbon Banners

Most ribbons available commercially come in solid colors. However, ribbon banners can be enlivened by painting some of the ribbons. Because most fabric paint is transparent, only white or light-colored ribbons can be painted. Satin ribbons tend to be extremely absorbent, making them more desirable for a soft-edged design. Waterproof floral ribbon is non-absorbent and more suitable for harder-edged designs. You can use specially made fabric paint, but ordinary acrylic paint thinned with water works just as well. Permanent markers are possibly the easiest to use. Unless the markers or paints are non-toxic, work outside. Whatever medium you choose, experiment with small pieces of ribbon until you are confident you can achieve the desired effect.

Spread layers of newspaper on the countertop or table. Pin the ribbons to the paper, arranging them as they will be in the banner. Now paint to your heart's content! Let the paint dry before moving the ribbons.

Rubber Stamped Ribbons

Rubber stamps can also be used to create beautiful designs on the ribbons. Many tourist and gift shops sell remarkable collections of rubber stamps. Large bold designs would be the most effective. You can also create your own designs by drawing on a large rubber eraser and cutting away the negative spaces with a single-edge razor or an X-acto knife. You can use one rubber stamp over and over in your banner, or many different rubber stamps. One way to make a single rubber stamp design interesting is to use varieties of colors in the stamp pad inks. Wide ribbons probably work best, at least 1" wider than your stamp design. Because even the largest rubber stamps are relatively small, single images will be unreadable from a distance. Strive for a design where repetition of the image creates a lovely pattern.

Woven Ribbons

Stunning processional banners can be made by weaving satin ribbons on a frame made of PVC tubing. Josephine made one showing the glorious cross for the Easter season at Holy Family Church in St. Louis. With many long ribbons trailing from the cross as it is carried in procession, there can be no doubt about the exuberance of the celebration. This method is also used for the wedding banners discussed in Chapter 3. Directions for making this banner, shown on page 183, bottom, follow.

Easter Cross Woven Ribbon Banner

Construct an octagonal frame for the woven design at the top of the banner by following the directions on page 85.

To make the banner illustrated you will need the following colors, lengths, and widths of satin ribbon:

— white (4 yds. $1\frac{1}{2}$" wide, 17 yds. $\frac{7}{8}$" wide, 6 yds. $2\frac{1}{4}$" wide)
— yellow ($8\frac{1}{2}$ yds. $\frac{7}{8}$" wide, $8\frac{1}{2}$ yds. $1\frac{1}{2}$" wide)
— metallic gold (15 yds. $\frac{5}{8}$" wide)
— orange ($6\frac{1}{2}$ yds. $\frac{7}{8}$" wide)
— maroon ($12\frac{1}{2}$ yds. $\frac{7}{8}$" wide)
— red (10 yds. $\frac{1}{4}$" wide).

Or you may select your own colors. You might choose white and gold for festive occasions. Accent colors could be other than orange and maroon; turquoise or teal might be better choices for your worship space.

If you have difficulty finding these sizes of ribbons, buy narrower ones and use more, or leave spaces. Very narrow ribbon ($\frac{1}{6}$") is often on sale by the spool. These can be used between the other ribbons, arranged in a symmetrical design.

To weave these ribbons on the frame, you will attach the center horizontal ribbons to the vertical sections of the frame, and then attach and weave the center vertical ribbons through the horizontal ribbons. Finish by filling in the remaining horizontal and vertical areas. To keep the cross in the center white, you will not weave any of the colored ribbons through them, but let the colored ribbons lie behind the three center white ribbons in both directions. The ribbons that fall below the frame will vary in length.

1. Begin by attaching the center horizontal ribbons to the frame in this manner. Center 32" of $1\frac{1}{2}$" wide white ribbon horizontally on the frame (with the ends cut diagonally in opposite directions) and wrap each end around the frame. Pin it to itself on the back, making it as taut as you can. Place one 32" length of $\frac{7}{8}$" wide white on either side of the center ribbon and secure likewise. Next pin 32" of the metallic gold ribbon above the central ribbons and 8' of the metallic gold ribbon below the central ribbons. Taking the narrow red ribbon, pin a 5' length above and a 10' length below the central ribbons. So, to clarify, these ribbons extend horizontally across the frame, in order from top to bottom: $\frac{1}{4}$" red, $\frac{5}{8}$" metallic gold, $\frac{7}{8}$" white, $1\frac{1}{2}$" white, $\frac{7}{8}$" white, $\frac{5}{8}$" metallic gold, $\frac{1}{4}$" red.

2. Sew these to the frame by machine with invisible thread. Remove the pressure foot and needle to get the frame under the sewing machine. Using the zipper foot, sew as close to the frame as you can. You may find it easier to secure the ribbon ends by hand.

3. Next weave the center vertical ribbons through those already in place. Begin with 8' of $1\frac{1}{2}$" wide white ribbon. Since this ribbon will hang in the center, cut the ends in a V shape. Starting in the center of the frame, center the ribbon over the widest white horizontal ribbon, and weave under the ribbon above it, over the next, and under the top red ribbon. Pull the ribbon over the top of the frame and pin it to itself on the back allowing an inch to overlap beyond the pin. Finish weaving down from the center and let the end hang free.

4. Pin over the top of the frame on either side of the central vertical ribbon lengths of $\frac{7}{8}$" white ribbon 2" shorter than 8'. Make sure the diagonal ends go in opposite directions. Weave through the center horizontal ribbons, pull around the bottom of the frame, and pin them to themselves on the back. Next pin to each side 8' long metallic ribbons, allowing 6" to hang freely in back. Weave and wrap them around the bottom of the frame and pin them to the back. Cut two 7½' lengths of the narrow red ribbon and pin to either side at the top, allowing 8" to hang free. Weave, wrap, and pin.

5. Sew the ribbons at the top and the bottom as closely as you can to the frame, either by hand or machine. Note that the center ribbon has not been pinned at the bottom; hold it taut and sew through it. It cannot be wrapped around the frame because the extension that will fit into the pole is in the way.

6. Now you are ready to fill in the remaining sections of the frame. Center 4' of maroon ribbon across the top of the horizontal ribbons, wrap the left side around the frame and pin it to the white ribbons on the back. This ribbon will wind around the frame at a slant. Because it covers both the narrow pipe and the wider connecting joint, it will have a gap in it. This can be tucked and whipped into place after all the ribbons are firmly attached. Weave the maroon ribbon, wrap it around the frame on the opposite side in a similar manner, and pin it to the back.

7. Cut a second maroon ribbon 3' long and center it below the horizontal ribbons. Wrap the left end around the frame upward to the back and pin it to the white ribbons. Weave and pin it to the white ribbons on the back.

8. Now work in the vertical direction. Cut a length of maroon ribbon 15' long. Center and pin to the back of the center vertical white ribbon just below the stitching. Pull the ends around the front (shiny side up), next to the red ribbons, and weave them in and out of the horizontal ribbons, starting on top of the first maroon ribbon. Wrap them around the bottom of the frame and pin them to the white ribbons.

9. Working horizontally again, cut 50" of the orange ribbon and weave it above the horizontal ribbons; do not weave it over the center white ribbons so that the cross design will show up effectively. Wrap both ends around the back and pin them to the white ribbons. Cut 6' of orange ribbon and weave it below the horizontal ribbons, again skipping the center white ribbons. Wrap the ends around the back and pin them to the white ribbons.

10. The vertical orange ribbon is 9' long. Pin the center of it to the center back at the top where the stitching is. Bring both ends around the front next to the maroon ribbon and weave them, again skipping the center white ribbons. Wrap these around the back and pin to the white ribbons.

11. Next comes a horizontal 7/8" yellow ribbon cut 28" long. Place this under the horizontal ribbons and weave it, skipping the white ribbons in the center. Wrap the ends around the frame and pin them upward to the ribbons in the back. Place a 6' length of the yellow ribbon above the horizontal ribbons and weave, skipping the white ribbons in the center. Wrap and pin to the back.

12. The vertical yellow ribbon is 17', centered on the back below the orange ribbon and pinned. Bring the ends around the front next to the orange ribbon and weave, skipping the center white ribbons. Bring around to the back and pin to the orange and maroon ribbons.

13. Working with the 1½" wide yellow ribbon, cut 26" and place below the horizontal ribbons. Weave, skipping the center white ribbons. Wrap and pin to the back. Center a 7' length above the horizontal ribbons. Weave, skipping the center ribbons. Wrap and pin to the back. Center a 16' length to the back below the narrow yellow ribbon. Bring the ends around to the front and weave, skipping the center white ribbons. Wrap and pin to the orange ribbons.

14. From the metallic gold ribbon, center a 26" length below the horizontal ribbons. Weave, skipping the center white ribbons; wrap and pin the ends to the back. The horizontal ribbon that goes above the center horizontal ribbons will take a vertical turn at each end. Cut 16' of metallic gold and center it above the horizontal ribbons. Weave, skipping the center white ribbons, and wrap the ends under and around the diagonal of the frame. Continue weaving downward through the horizontal ribbons, skipping the center white ribbons. Wrap the ends around the frame and pin them to the back.

15. Using the 7/8" white ribbon, center a 4' length above the top horizontal metallic gold ribbon. Weave through all the ribbons, including the center white ribbons. Wrap the ends around the frame and pin them to the back. Center a 7' length under the horizontal ribbons and weave. Wrap the ends around the bottom of the frame and pin to the back. Center a third length 12' long on the back below the top horizontal gold ribbon and pin. Bring each end around the front and weave them through the horizontal ribbons. Wrap the ends and pin.

16. Finish filling in, first with the 2¼" white ribbon. Cut two pieces 2' long; center horizontally at the top and bottom and weave. Wrap around the frame and pin to the back. Cut two more 2' lengths. On either side, pin them to the back below the narrow white ribbon. Wrap around the frame and weave vertically. Allow the bottoms to hang free between the yellow ribbons. Switch to the ⅞" wide white ribbon and cut four 18" lengths. Weave in the remaining space on all four sides; wrap around the frame to the back and pin.

17. By hand or machine, sew all the ribbons as close as possible to the frame. Stabilize the ribbons, especially those in the center, by tacking adjacent ribbons with invisible thread.

Chapter 6:

GENERAL TECHNIQUES FOR QUILTED FABRIC PANELS

Adding a fabric panel to a banner greatly extends the range of possibilities for the banner maker. While ribbons alone are sufficient to suggest the liturgical season and enliven the atmosphere, a fabric panel creates a focus for the processional banner. It can also carry symbolic imagery beyond the symbolism of the flowing ribbons and their colors. In fact, when most people hear the word "banner," fabric panels, rather than ribbons, usually come to mind. The unfortunate heritage of banner making in the church in the recent past has also firmly attached the picture of burlap, felt, glue, and all-too-literal words to a concept of banners, and we are ready to leave that behind. A few more skills, a bit more time, and quality materials can make a banner that is a treasured work of art.

Most of our fabric panels are pieced or appliquéd, and then quilted. While the number of books available with designs for appliqué banners attests to its popularity, these designs are usually sewn on a foundation fabric and left unlined. We go a step further and treat our fabric panels as quilts, which allows greater design flexibility. We use a very thin quilt batting and line the panel with a coordinating fabric. The lining makes the panel look finished from the back. In addition, quilting the banner, or stitching through all three layers, holds the layers together and creates an additional opportunity for surface design.

The quilting process also opens up other avenues and techniques for banner design, such as patchwork. While the base fabric can hide the raw edges of appliqué pieces, the nature of patchwork precludes the possibility of producing a finished back in a similar manner. Lining the panel eliminates the need to finish the reverse side, and opens up possibilities for using various styles of patchwork.

The popularity of quilting in our time constitutes a distinct advantage for amateurs over other banner making techniques, like silk-screening, which require specialized skills and equipment. Many church communities today include members interested in quilting and willing to share their skills for the benefit of the church. Organize these people, coordinate with the people responsible for worship in your community, and you are on your way to more color-filled celebrations. In this chapter, we present basic considerations for designing the panel, general instructions for quilting, and inspirations and instructions for a number of quilted panels.

Basic Considerations

When making a fabric panel for a banner, consider several things in addition to the color and design of the panel. Determine a basic shape for your panel, the size and proportions of the panel, and how it will be attached to the carrying frame and pole.

Shape

The rectangle is the basis for most of the banner shapes you will see. The straight upper edge makes it relatively easy to devise a frame for carrying and hanging these banners. The proportions of the rectangle may vary considerably, from a square to a long narrow pennant. An examination of your space may help you decide what kind of shape will work for you. Taller spaces will naturally suggest longer banners.

As long as the top is straight, the bottom and sides of the rectangle can be shaped as desired. You might choose to end your panel with a point. The architecture of a church can be a good source of inspiration for such cutaway shapes. Gothic architecture in a church suggests the use of an inverted arch shape; a plain, spare, rectangular worship space suggests the use of similar shapes.

Another source of inspiration for the shape is the design on the panel. You could choose to shape the sides and bottom to flow with the design, cutting away from the basic rectangle, not adding. If your banner depicts a single large figure, like an angel, you could sculpt the bottom edge of the panel to match the bottom of the figure, so that, for instance, the hem of the angel's robe forms the end of the banner.

The shape of the top of the panel is somewhat less flexible, in that its entire edge must be supported. Therefore, the shape of the framework limits you. Obviously, there are choices beyond the straight horizontal bar, as illustrated with our description of the construction of an inverted V frame and an octagonal frame. The inverted V will allow you to use a square on point, that is, a diamond, or any shape with an inverted V at the top. The octagon frame provides similar options. You may find it possible to make a semi circular frame by bending PVC or some other material, and attaching the curve to two 90° elbows pointing upward on either end of a straight horizontal bar frame. Three-dimensional frames are also conceivable. The only limits are your imagination and the type of supporting framework you can devise.

Size and Proportions

Once you have decided on a basic banner shape, the size and proportions of the banner need to be considered in conjunction with the size and proportions of your space. For most churches, a fabric panel two to three feet wide works well and is comfortable to carry. In smaller churches, especially when multiple banners are being used in close proximity, 18" may work better. Before you make your fabric panel, it is a good idea to bring some paper or plain fabric to the space in order to experiment. Tape the paper to a pole of the proper size, carry it down the aisle, and put it in a stand where it might be placed in an actual liturgy. Look at it and assess it from all angles. Make sure the size and proportions of your shape feel right in the interior of the building.

The importance of sizing things with paper shapes became clear when Pope John Paul II visited St. Louis. The eucharistic liturgy was to be held in a football stadium. Such mega-spaces dwarf anything brought into them, including people. The environment committee for the event was concerned that members of the assembly seated in the highest seats would be so far away that they would hardly be aware of the entrance procession as it moved along the length of the floor. Because there were thousands of people in the procession, it was decided that ten banners would be used. Each banner consisted of a 5' x 6' nylon panel carried on a 12' vertical pole. Thirty-foot streamers were attached and draped over two additional poles. The undulating of the blue streamers as the procession advanced effectively conveyed both the waters of baptism and the waters of the nearby confluence of the Mississippi and Missouri Rivers. (See the photo on page 184, top.)

Experimenting with materials like bed sheets, rolls of paper, or lengths of muslin fabric would be an effective way to determine the size for such a project. While most of us will never be challenged with planning for a Mass with the pope in a giant football stadium, using paper mock-ups to determine a basic size and form can be extremely helpful, particularly if you are working with a large space.

Attaching the Banner

Before you begin construction of your fabric panel, it is wise to consider how you will attach it to the supporting hardware, and how to attach any ribbons you might use. We present two of the many techniques we've experimented with for attaching the panel to the framework. Both allow you to remove the banner from the framework for safe handling. Both are placed before finishing any edges of the banner.

Method 1 is to sew strips of hemmed fabric to the top of the panel that will cover the top framework without covering much of the pole or the quilted back of the panel. This method can be used with either a straight-edged top or an inverted V. For a straight-edged banner, start with two 2¼" wide strips of backing fabric that are each half as long as the banner is wide. For each one, hem one long edge and the two short edges. Cut two pieces of Velcro the length of your strips. Sew the pile Velcro to the hemmed edge of the strip, edge-stitching around the outside edges of the Velcro.

Before finishing the edges of your banner, pin the two strips to the top edge of the banner so that there is a small space between them in the middle. Then bind or sew a self-edge as usual. Sew the hook Velcro to a strip of backing fabric $1/2$" larger than the Velcro. Turn the edges under and sew this by hand to the back of the banner, so the hook Velcro is beneath the pile Velcro of the flap.

The casing for an inverted V banner is sewn similarly, but requires three pieces: a large right triangle and two 3" wide strips. Begin by cutting from the backing fabric two 3" strips the length of one arm of the inverted V less 8". On the first strip, hem one long edge and turn the corner to hem the next short edge. Do the reverse for the second strip, so they are mirror images. Cut two pieces of Velcro the length of these strips. Sew the pile Velcro to the strip at its hemmed edge, edge-stitching around the Velcro's outside edge.

Before finishing the banner's edges, pin these strips on either side of the banner top, so that the finished short edge on either side is $1/2$" in from the edge of the banner. Sew the hook Velcro to a piece of backing fabric $1/2$" larger all around. Turn the edges under and sew it by hand to the back, placing it so the two pieces of Velcro meet.

Now cut a right triangle with the shorter sides 12" long (the diagonal half of a 12" square). On either side of the (right angle) corner of the triangle, fold a $1/2$" tuck about 1" from the corner and baste. Hem the long edge of the triangle. Cut two 1" pieces of Velcro. Center the two pile pieces on the hemmed edge, leaving a 1" gap in the middle. Sew around the edges of the Velcro.

Pin the triangle in place on the back of the banner at the top center and baste in place. Tack the triangle to each side strip where it overlaps. Sew the 1" pieces of hook Velcro to pieces of background fabric $1/2$" larger all around. Turn in the edges and sew them to the backing beneath the 1" pieces of pile Velcro.

Method 2 involves sewing an extra lining to the back of the panel that will cover the crossbar and the top of the pole. This can be an easier solution for an inverted V and can be adapted for use with any banner that has an unusual top edge. Cut or piece a lining $1/2$" larger all around than the unfinished banner. Make a small roll hem on the two bottom edges. Pin two $1/4$" tucks in the raw edges, each 1" away from the top corner and baste.

Now cut two lengths of Velcro the measurement of the edge less 2". Sew each strip of pile Velcro to the wrong side of the lining, $1\frac{1}{2}$" from one of the top raw edges and 1" in from the finished edge. Lay the lining right side up over the quilted, but not bound, banner so that its raw edges line up with the top edges of the banner, and pin in place.

Sew each piece of hook Velcro to a piece of fabric 1/2" larger all around. Turn under the edges and sew to the banner's back, so that the hook Velcro is beneath the pile Velcro. It may help to remove the pins from the lining as you sew the Velcro. Re-pin the lining and bind the banner.

Make the ribbons detachable for purposes of cleaning and storing the banner and ribbons. Do this by sewing the ribbons to a strip of fabric that matches the backing of the quilted panel.

Cut a strip of the backing fabric 2 1/2" wide and as long as the banner is wide. Fold the strip in half lengthwise with the wrong side out, and sew 1/4" seams on both ends. Turn it right side out and pin the top edge of the ribbons to the raw edge of the fabric. Sew a 1/4" seam along the raw edge. Pull the ribbons away from the fabric, allowing the seam to turn in. Press flat with a cool iron.

Cut a length of Velcro as long as the fabric strip. Sew the pile Velcro to the fabric strip on the side where the ribbons are right side up. You will need to sew a strip of hook Velcro (first machine-sewn to a strip of the backing fabric) to the back of the banner to attach the ribbons. For an inverted V banner, sew the hook Velcro across the center of the back. If you have a straight-edge banner, you can attach the Velcro to the bottom or top.

To attach the ribbons to the bottom, just sew the hook Velcro (on its fabric foundation) on the bottom of the banner back. Placing the ribbons at the bottom allows viewers to see the quilting from the back. To camouflage the back, sew a piece of hook Velcro to the other side of the ribbon strip (it will have hook Velcro on one side and pile Velcro on the other), so the ribbon strip can be sandwiched between the banner and the attached flap.

For the saddle-style banner that hangs down on both sides of the pole, discussed in the colorwash section, it is better to attach the ribbons to the pole. Construct a fabric sleeve that fits around the horizontal bar by cutting two pieces of fabric 2 1/2" wide and half the width of the banner. Sew small pieces of pile Velcro one inch from each end of these strips centered widthwise.

Lay the ribbons next to each other on one long edge of each sleeve, right sides together with the fabric sleeve. Pin and sew them in place with a 1/4" seam. Fold the sleeves in half lengthwise right sides together and sew a 1/4" seam at one short end of each sleeve. Sew a tiny hem in the other end, including a 12" piece of narrow ribbon in the hem. Reinforce the attachment of the ribbon by pulling it away from the fabric and stitching several times over the hem where they are joined.

Turn the sleeves right side out. Pull the long ribbons flat and allow the raw edges of the seam to turn in. Iron with a cool iron. Turn the remaining long edge of the sleeve in 1/2" and topstitch over the ribbons.

Slip the two sleeves over either end of the rod and secure them together by tying the two 12" ribbons together. Hang the finished saddle-style banner over the rod and place pins in the back where the Velcro squares touch it. Sew the hook Velcro to the banner in these four places. As a finishing touch, hand-tack a wide ribbon over the center of the bar to cover the pole.

General Instructions for Pieced and Quilted Fabric Panels

A quilted panel is composed of three layers sandwiched together: the surface or design layer, quilt batting, and a backing. The layers are held together with hand or machine stitching that goes through all three layers. This stitching, or quilting, adds an additional element of surface design. In quilt making, the quality of your materials and the precision of your technique influence greatly the success of the finished piece. We begin our general instructions with a discussion on material choices, provide some general information on technique, and finish with instructions on layering and quilting the piece.

Material Choices

The array of fabrics available in any fabric store today is astounding. How is one to choose what is most suitable? In our quilts, our bias is toward using natural fabrics whenever possible, for their beauty, ease in handling, and honesty. We primarily use 100% cotton fabrics available for quilt making in fabric stores. However, we often supplement with many other kinds of fabrics to enrich our pieces.

These include raw silk, which has particularly brilliant colors, is not overly difficult to work with, and may be used alone or in combination with other fabrics. Other materials we have found useful include bonded metallic fabrics, which catch light and sparkle, hand-woven fabrics from Guatemala and India, batiks from Bali, and drapery fabrics. You can also find many wonderful prints, batiks, and mudcloths from Africa. Netting can be a useful material to add to the top of the quilt for variation in the surface texture. As artists, we search out and purchase a variety of fabrics without necessarily having a specific intention for their use, in order to have on hand the kinds of things we know we will need. Many of our designs use a wide variety of fabrics. If you don't already have a stash and need to purchase all the fabrics for a project, you will probably find that in most shops the minimum cut of fabric is a quarter-yard. Some shop owners will cut eighths.

Fabrics to avoid include polyesters or polyester blends and most rayons. These fabrics slip easily and can be hard to quilt through. Fabrics that are too loosely woven may ravel in a quilted piece. If you need to use one for your design, attach iron-on interfacing to the back of it before you cut out your piece. Then zigzag the edges of the piece before sewing it. In general, look for the best quality and most beautiful and interesting fabrics you can find. Your time in constructing it and the length of time the piece will be enjoyed far outweigh the cost of quality materials.

The backing should be made of a single large piece of cotton fabric that coordinates with the front and with the ribbons. It should be of a muted design, since it will be seen when the banner is carried in procession; soft prints work best for this purpose. Look at the fabric from a distance; squint at it for an even greater distance effect. For most banners, 45" wide fabric commonly available will suffice to make a lining without seams. Some cottons are available in a 60" width. The backing should be at least an inch or two larger all around than completed top.

For the inner layer, or batting, use one of the modern cotton battings available. These battings have an inner synthetic layer through which the cotton is punched, making them extremely stable. Unlike some polyester batts, they will not pill or allow the layers to shift while you are quilting. Warm and Natural™ (The

Warm Company, 954 East Union St., Seattle WA 98122, 1-800-234-9276) and Quilter's Dream™ (Kelsul, Inc., 3205 Foxgrove Lane, Chesapeake VA 23321, 1-888-268-8664) are high quality products available at quilt shops. Warm and Natural comes in one weight in 90", 124", and 34" rolls. The Deluxe weight in Quilter's Dream is the equivalent. However, the slightly lighter Select is probably most suitable. All weights come in 92" and 46" wide rolls, and in natural or white. A 121" x 121" white batt is also available.

General Techniques

There are a variety of ways of marking the fabric pieces before you cut them out. If your style is different, make sure you understand how it is different from what we describe so that you can adapt our instructions appropriately. Whatever your technique, you will have the greatest success in getting your banner to lie flat if all the pieces are cut with the grain and the stretch of the grain goes widthwise in your finished piece, rather than lengthwise. For marking fabric, we generally use a plain #2 pencil. If the fabric is dark and the pencil does not show up, use a pencil with white or yellow lead.

Start by drawing a diagram of your panel. Mark each piece on your diagram with arrows pointing upward. Make your pattern pieces and transfer the arrows to them. If you will be sewing by machine, add a 1/4" seam allowance to each pattern piece (the pattern pieces in the back of this book have these seam allowances included). Place each pattern piece on the wrong side of the fabric with the arrow aligned with the selvedge (or parallel to the direction that has less stretch).

If you will be sewing by hand, allow for a 1/4" seam allowance, and pin the pattern pieces to the fabric. Draw around the pattern piece for a sewing line, and measuring by eye, cut 1/4" away from that line all the way around.

For your own designs, you can either add 1/4" to the pattern piece as we did and draw the cutting line with a pencil, or add the seam allowance when cutting with a rotary cutter and ruler. When using the rotary cutter, use flat-headed flower pins to pin the pattern piece to the fabric. Then lay your ruler on the pattern piece so that it extends 1/4" out over the edge you wish to cut. Cut with your rotary cutter, and continue likewise to cut the other sides.

No matter which method you have chosen, once you have finished cutting, carefully lay the pieces out with the grain arrows pointing up.

Now you will pin the pieces together to sew them. If you sew by hand, make sure you put the pins exactly through the pencil sewing lines on both sides of the seam. Sew in a small running stitch along the seam. End at the pencil line. If you sew by machine, you will have precise 1/4" seam allowances. Pin the edges of the fabric together. Determine where on your machine you need to place your fabric to get a 1/4" seam allowance. Put a piece of tape on your machine to help you keep the fabric lined up at that point. Sew from one end of the seam to the other, without back-tacking. You do not have to cut the thread after sewing two pieces together; just continue sewing the next two pieces and form a chain.

After sewing a chain of pieces, we press the seams to one side. We try to press to the darker side when possible. We are not strict about this, however, and prefer to have seams pressed in opposite directions when they will meet. So, for example, if you were sewing four squares together into a four-patch, you would first sew the top two together and the bottom two together. Press the seam on the top section to the right, and the one on the bottom to the left. When you put the two sections together to sew them, feel the area where the seams come together between your finger and thumb. The seams should just come together, with no overlap and no gap. When you sew the seam joining the two halves, you should be able to open it and find the top and bottom seams line up.

Many of the fabric panels based on quilt blocks that we have designed have a border surrounding the quilt block. This gives a finishing touch to the design, as a frame does for a picture. These look more professional if the corners are mitered. However, if you are a beginning quilter, you might wish to simply sew straight rectangular borders on your piece; sew the two sides on first, and then sew on the top and bottom. The length of the two sides will match the length of the piece, while the top and bottom will be the width of the piece, plus the width of the two side rectangular borders.

Layering and Quilting the Piece

Once the top is completed, you are ready to assemble the layers, and quilt the piece. There are two ways of proceeding at this point, depending on whether you want the edges to be finished with a binding, as most quilts are, or whether you want a self-edging, which is often preferable for a banner. The procedure is less complex when you use a binding. In order not to overwhelm the smaller size of a banner (as opposed to a bed-size quilt), use a binding that matches the border of the banner when possible. Otherwise, the banner may look overly busy. We'll start with a bound-edge quilt.

1. Bound-edge Quilts. Iron the backing and lay it flat with the wrong side up. Laying it on a carpeted surface often works well, as long as the carpet is looped and has a low pile. Spread the batting smoothly on top of the backing. If necessary, trim the batting so none of its edges overlap those of the backing. Carefully iron the top from both the wrong side and the right side. Spread it smoothly right side up over the batting.

Now the three layers must be basted together. If you are going to quilt by hand, use thread to baste the quilt. Starting in the center, stitch in very large stitches (two inches or so) to the top, bottom, and center of each side of the quilt. Then fill in the corners with lines of stitching that radiate from the center. If you quilt by machine, use safety pins manufactured for quilters to pin the layers together. Start at the center and pin every three to four inches to the top, bottom, and center sides. Fill in the corners with pins spaced three to four inches in each direction. When you have finished, cut the batting and backing layers 1/4" larger than the top.

For the quilting, mark the top where you would like the stitches using a chalk wheel or a light pencil mark. Avoid soap or pens with disappearing ink. Use quilting thread in a coordinating color and a quilting needle. Knot the thread near the end and take one stitch through the top layer and batting only. Pull the knot through the fabric and lodge it in the batting so that it's hidden. Quilt through all three layers with a small running stitch where you have marked your design. Finish with a knot pulled to the inside.

For machine quilting, we prefer to use invisible thread in the needle and cotton thread to match the backing in the bobbin. Invisible thread comes in clear, which is good for light fabrics, and smoky, which blends better with darker fabrics. Use a walking foot if your machine has one. Start each line of quilting with a series of very tiny stitches (.5mm) and increase to a larger stitch (3mm) for the line itself. End similarly and cut the threads with sharp scissors. Trim the edges, cutting off the extra batting and lining.

When you have finished the quilting, the final step is to finish the edges. The most common way to do this is to bind them with bias binding. Cut a $2^{1}/_{2}$" wide strip of your chosen fabric on the bias (45° angle). Leave the ends of the strip at a 45° angle and piece strips until you have a piece long enough to go around the quilt. If you do not have enough fabric to cut it on the true bias (45° angle), cut it with the straight of the grain.

Fold the strip in half, wrong sides together, and iron it. Starting in the center of one side of the banner, pin the raw edge of the binding, matching it to the raw edge of the quilted layers. Leaving the first few inches free, sew this with a $^{1}/_{4}$" seam. Place a pin in the first corner you come to, exactly $^{1}/_{4}$" from each edge. Sew the seam up to this pin, and leave the needle in the fabric. Pivot the quilt 45 degrees and sew straight to the raw edge of corner. Fold the binding back over the tiny diagonal seam and fold it again toward yourself so that this fold lines up with the edge you have just finished.

Now sew the second, third, and fourth sides, repeating the procedure just described at each corner. When you return to the first side, stop sewing four or five inches before the place you started. Carefully measure where the binding strips meet and mark each with a pin. Add a $^{1}/_{4}$" seam allowance to each end and cut. Open the binding and sew the ends right sides together. Thumb-press the seam apart and refold the binding. Sew this remaining section. To finish, fold the binding over to the lining side so that it covers the line of stitching. Pin and whipstitch in place by hand.

2. Self-edge Quilts. Quilts with a self-edging end up with their layers in the same order, but they are not ordered the same way initially. Start by laying down your batting and smoothing it. Iron the quilt top carefully, first from the wrong side and then the right side, and lay it right side up on the batting. Pin these two layers together every four to six inches with safety pins. Trim the batting all around so that it is even with the top. Iron the back and lay it down by itself right side up. Then take your pinned top and batting and lay them face down on the back. Smooth any wrinkles. Pin around the edges and sew 1/4" away from the edge of the batting all around the edges. Make sure you leave a 6" gap for turning. Trim the backing so it is just slightly bigger than the batting. Turn the piece right sides out.

Before you can begin quilting, the edges must be flat. Working your way around the quilt, pull the seam you just sewed flat so that you can see the edges of the stitching. Smooth out the front and back and pin the three layers every couple of inches with pins perpendicular to the edge. Whipstitch the opening shut and pin that as well. Once the piece is flat, lay it down front side up and smooth any wrinkles on the top and bottom. Re-pin the safety pins through all three layers and add some pins in between those you already have so that it is pinned every three to four inches.

From this point, you can elect to quilt it by hand or machine. If you hand quilt it, you will need to replace the pins with basting thread. Make sure your quilting lines extend to the edge. Alternatively, quilt around the panel at a distance of 1/4" from the edge.

Inspirations for Pieced and Quilted Fabric Panels

The designs for the fabric panels illustrated in this book range from simple to complex. We provide instructions for the banners pictured in this book, but the coloring, fabric choices, and the designs themselves are meant to be springboards for your own creative ideas. Look back to the chapters on the liturgical year and the sacraments to find further inspiration for your banner. The history and depth of our tradition provide a range of possibilities that will feed a banner maker for a very long time. For each of the banners pictured, we provide some background, telling for whom it was made and for what purpose. And we try to give some explanation of why the design has meaning for us. Read, enjoy, and create.

Chapter 7

BANNER DESIGN PART 1: BLOCK DESIGNS

Thousands of quilt block patterns have been developed over the centuries of time that people have done patchwork and appliqué to construct and embellish bedding and other household articles. Many quilt blocks are relatively easy to sew, making sewing in blocks an ideal format for the beginning banner maker. Yet the variations possible in value and color and in combining blocks yield enough possibilities to hold the interest of even expert quilters for quite some time.

There are many books and computer programs that contain treasuries of blocks (we list some in the Resource section). Look through these compilations with an eye to what might work well for a banner. Try different shadings of the pieces and different placements of colors.

SINGLE QUILT BLOCKS ILLUSTRATING BASIC TECHNIQUES

In this section, three single block banners are illustrated with detailed instructions. Pattern pieces are located in the appendix, beginning on page 171. Even if you are not making one of these banners, reading the instructions will provide you with some useful tips for construction. We also present several line drawings for blocks that you might find useful as you begin designing banners.

Amish Cross for Ordinary Time

The Amish Cross block is an original block, and one of the first processional banners Josephine designed. As in many Amish quilts, the colors are solid fabrics of deeper hues, and there are large areas of black. Because it was made for Ordinary Time, the color green predominates, in a teal shade. With its subdued colors, this would make an ideal banner for the winter weeks of Ordinary Time. Though the overall panel is dark, the cross is joyful and victorious. The teal green frame reminds us that in each liturgy we celebrate the life, death, and resurrection of Jesus Christ. See the photo on page 184, bottom.

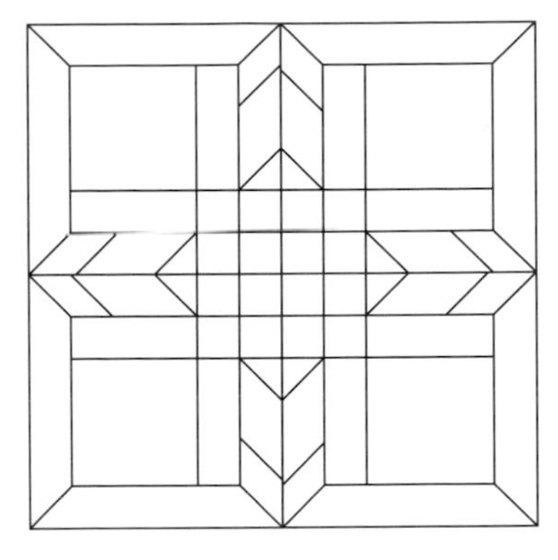

Amish Cross.

The Amish Cross banner is 24" square and backed in solid black fabric. The finished size of the small squares (piece C) in the middle is 2". You could easily change the dimensions of the block to make the banner 36" square by making piece C 3" square, and changing the sizes of the other pattern pieces accordingly. Likewise, an 18" banner would be based on a 1½" square. For the 24" size, you will need ⅔ yard of solid black fabric, and fat quarters or scraps of the following solids: medium blue, teal blue, violet, red, and teal green.

Cut the following quantities of each pattern piece (found in the appendix, page 172) in the specified colors:

Piece	Quantity	Color
A	4	Black
B	8	Violet
C	4	Blue
C	4	Black
C	4	Teal Blue
C	2	Violet
C	2	Red
D	8	Red
E	4	Blue
F	4	Teal Green
G	4	Teal Blue
H	4	Red
I	8	Teal Green

The panel is made from four nearly identical blocks that are rotated and joined together in a four-patch. The directions are for sewing one 12" block. Follow the construction diagram as you read through the instructions. Sew four of the following block units:

1. Sew B to A.

2. Sew a black C to a second B.

3. Press both seams to the black side. Sew #1 and #2 together as in the diagram. Press to the large square.

4. Sew the 8" side of I to #3 on one side of the large black square. Begin and end the seam on the sewing line, 1/4" in. Do not sew to the end of the fabric. Backtack at each end. Press to the outside.

5. Repeat Step 4 with a second I along the other edge of the large black square.

6. Sew F to E. Press to the blue.

7. Sew D to E of #6. Press to the red.

8. Sew a teal blue C to #7. Press to the teal blue.

9. Sew #8 to the top of #5. Begin the seam with a backtack 1/4" in on the triangular end. Press to the outside.

10. Repeat steps 6, 7, and 8 using G, H, D, and a blue C. Note that the parallelogram points in the opposite direction, so that the shapes of #8 and #10 are mirror images.

11. Sew a red (two of the blocks have a red square here, two violet) C to the blue square in #10. Press to the blue.

12. Sew #11 onto #9. Sew to the end of the fabric at the square end, and 1/4" in on the parallelogram end. Press to the outside.

13. There are now three diagonal corners to sew. Unfold the seams. Use pins to line up the ends of the seams. Sew from the edge of the fabric on the outside of the corner to the point where the seams meet (1/4" in) on the inside. Backtack on the inside. Press to one side.

14. Arrange the four completed and pressed blocks in a four-patch, so that the teal green strips form a border and the red and violet blocks form a checkerboard in the center. Sew the top two together, and press toward the side with the red square. Repeat with the bottom two.

15. Sew the top and bottom together, matching all seams.

Assemble the panel according to the general directions. If you machine-quilt it, you could stitch all the seams in the ditch and use a fleur-de-lis quilting pattern, or a similar design of your own, in the center of the 6" blocks. The ribbons for this banner matched the colors in the quilt panel as closely as possible.

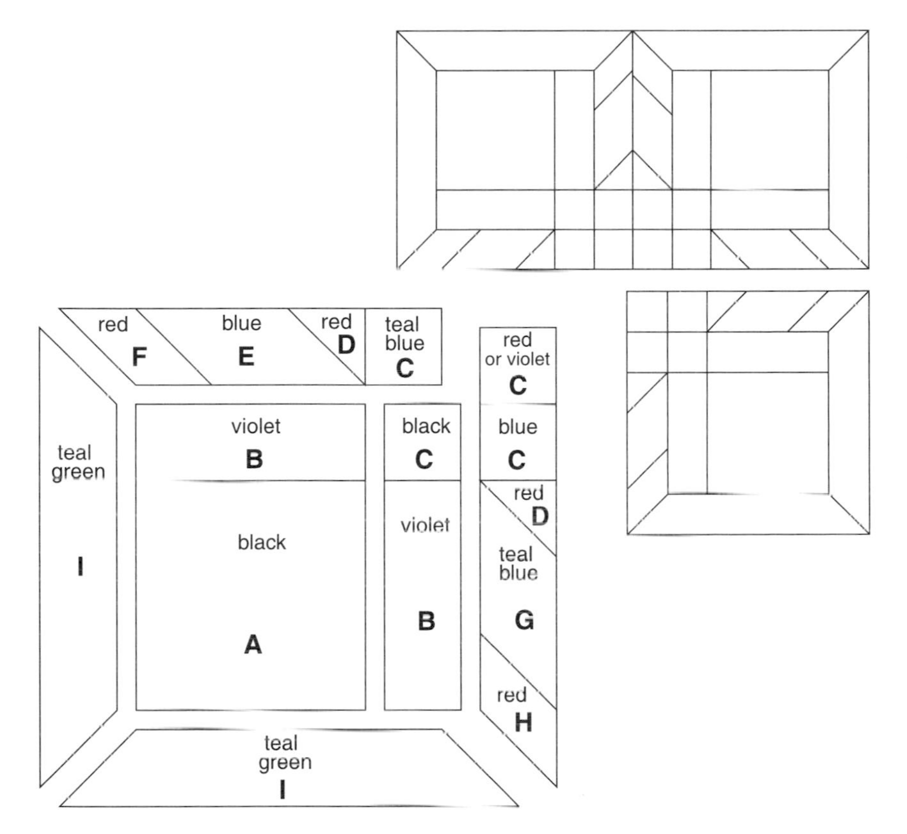

Amish Cross construction diagram.

Advent and Christmas Star

Star imagery abounds during the Advent and Christmas seasons. We are all familiar with the story of the three wise men following the star. We too are pilgrims seeking God in our lives, following the light of Christ. The use of a star banner during these seasons reminds us the light that illuminates our journeys.

This star pattern is an adaptation of a nine-patch star pattern. It was made for Our Lady of Loretto Church in St. Louis, Missouri, where it harmonizes with the colors of the stained glass windows

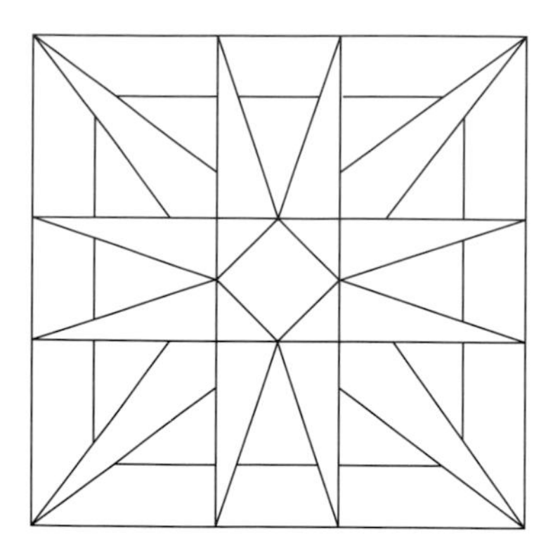

Advent and Christmas Star.

and the vestments. You might consider making the same banner in two versions, one with a background of blues and purples for Advent and the other with hunter green and burgundy for Christmas. Thus each season would have its own distinct banner, but the common theme and shape of the star would unite them. See the photo on page 185, top left.

The original panel used a mixture of printed and solid fabrics. The prints used were solid-looking, with textures of sky and clouds, and a star print. The prints add interest when the banner is viewed at close range. If you choose to use a metallic fabric, either use one that comes bonded or back the fabric with iron-on interfacing. Metallics can melt at temperatures for cotton, so use lower temperatures and a translucent press cloth.

The size of this block is 22". Since the square is set on point, the actual width of the banner is 31". To make the star, you will need one yard of black for the binding and lining, plus fat quarters or scraps of the following colors: white (a brocade with metallic gold was used), bright red, gold metallic, teal blue, royal blue, purple, medium blue. The pieces are lettered on the diagram. Actual size pattern pieces can be found in the appendix. Cut:

Piece	Quantity	Color
A	1	white
B	4	red
C	4	teal blue
D	4	black
E	4	white
F	4	white
G	4	royal blue
H	4	black
I	4	purple
J	4	black
K	4	metallic gold
L	4	medium blue

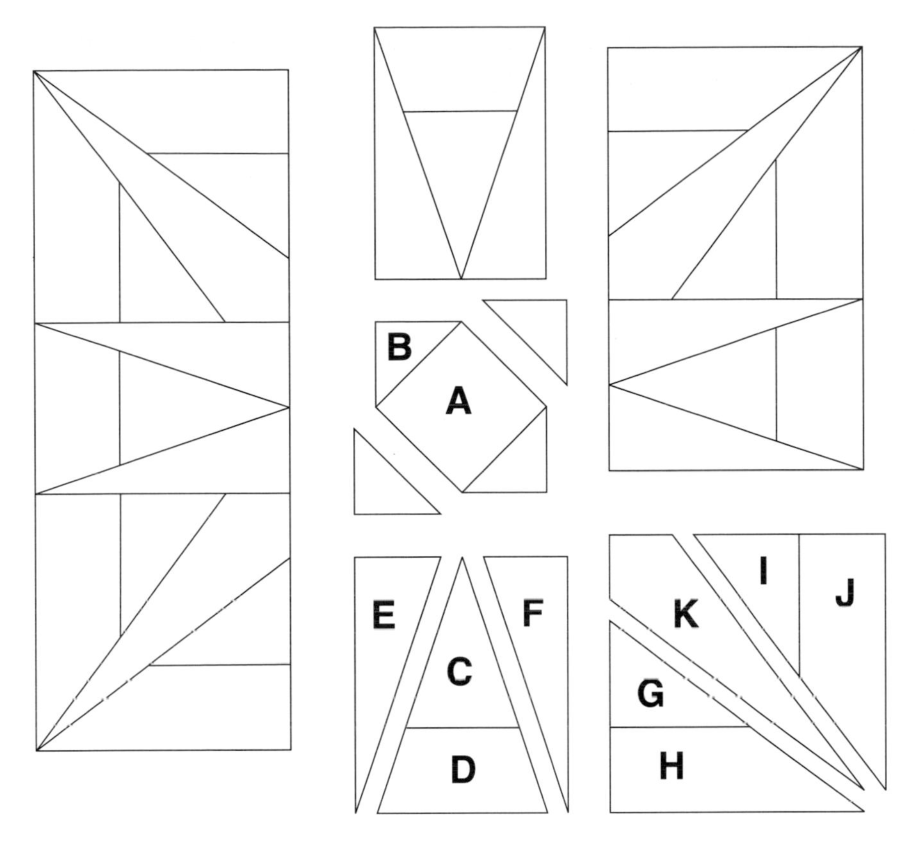

Advent and Christmas Star construction diagram.

1. Sew two B's onto opposite sides of the central square A. Press the seam out. Sew two B's to the remaining two sides and press out.

2. Sew triangle C to parallelogram D to form a larger triangle. Repeat 3 times. Press to D.

3. Sew triangle E to the left side of #2. Repeat 3 times. Press to E.

4. Repeat step 3 with triangle F on the right side of #3.

5. Sew one #4 to #1 and another to the opposite side, with triangle C pointing toward square A. Press out toward #4.

6. Sew triangle G to trapezoid H to form a larger triangle. Repeat 3 times. Press to H.

7. Sew triangle I to trapezoid J to form a larger triangle. Repeat 3 times. Press to J.

8. Sew #6 to elongated kite K, as indicated in the diagram. Repeat 3 times. Press to #6.

9. Sew #7 to #8 to obtain a 6" square. Repeat three times. Press to #7.

10. Sew one #9 to either side of rectangle #4 as in the diagram. Repeat once. Press to #6.

11. Sew one of strip #10 to either side of strip #9. Press.

12. Sew a medium blue border (not pictured in diagram, L in pattern pieces) to each edge of the block. The shorter edge of the parallelogram will line up with the block. Start and end the seam 1/4" in and backtack. Repeat 3 times.

13. Use a pin to help you line up the diagonal corners. Starting at the corner, sew from the edge and stop 1/4" from the end, where the stitches converge and backtack.

Festive Cross: Drunkard's Path Pattern

The Festive Cross banner was made by Josephine for the celebration of the fiftieth anniversary of ordination of the pastor at Little Flower Parish in St. Louis. Since this special celebration, the parish has used the banner during the Easter season. The circles in the design, and the brightness of its white, yellow, and gold colors, highlighted by the contrast with the darker blue and purple background, make it an appropriate and joyful symbol of the season. While the use of the traditional pattern "drunkard's path" might seem irreverent in this context, or at least paradoxical, it is actually quite appropriate. In sacred scripture Jesus says he came to heal the sick, not the healthy. He came to save sinners, not the self-righteous. Thus, even a drunkard's path can end up leading to salvation and glory. The coloration of this banner makes it appropriate for any festive occasion. See the photo on page 185, top right.

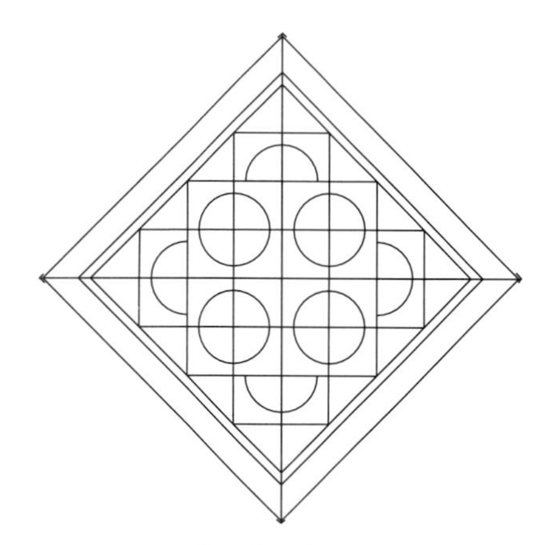

Festive Cross.

This quilt block is about 21" square or 30" on point, as designed. The measurement of the individual square block for which we provide the pattern (in the appendix) is 3". The individual square block is composed of two pieces (A and B) forming a quarter-circle in a square. To ensure smooth curved seams, draw in the seam allowance of pieces A and B the hatch marks provided on the pattern pieces. When you pin an A and a B together, you begin by matching the central hatch marks. Insert the pin perpendicularly through the matching points on either side, line up the fabrics carefully; holding the fabrics together near the pin with one hand, turn the pin and stick the end through both fabrics with the other hand. Follow the same procedure at each end of the arc, and then work out from the center for the remainder of the pins.

One yard of fabric is required for the lining and binding. Quarter-yards or scraps of the following solids or small prints are used: white, gold and white brocade or print, medium light neutral, medium dark neutral, light orange, yellow-orange, red-orange, deep red, blue-green, medium blue, dark blue, purple, and gold lamé (use bonded lamé fabric or fuse with iron-on interfacing). Cut:

Piece	Quantity	Color
A	8	gold lamé
A	4	yellow-orange
A	4	light orange
A	4	red-orange
A	4	deep red
A	2	white
B	2	gold and white brocade or print
B	4	medium light neutral
B	4	another medium light neutral
B	4	medium dark neutral
B	4	yellow
B	4	blue-green
B	4	purple
C	8	purple
C	4	dark blue
C	4	medium blue

Lay out the pieces carefully according to the diagram. Use a piece of white flannel or batting as a base to lay the pieces on. This will keep them in place. Each quarter is laid out exactly the same, except that in two quarters the central V (labeled white or brocade) piece is white and in the other two it is the gold and white brocade. Sew

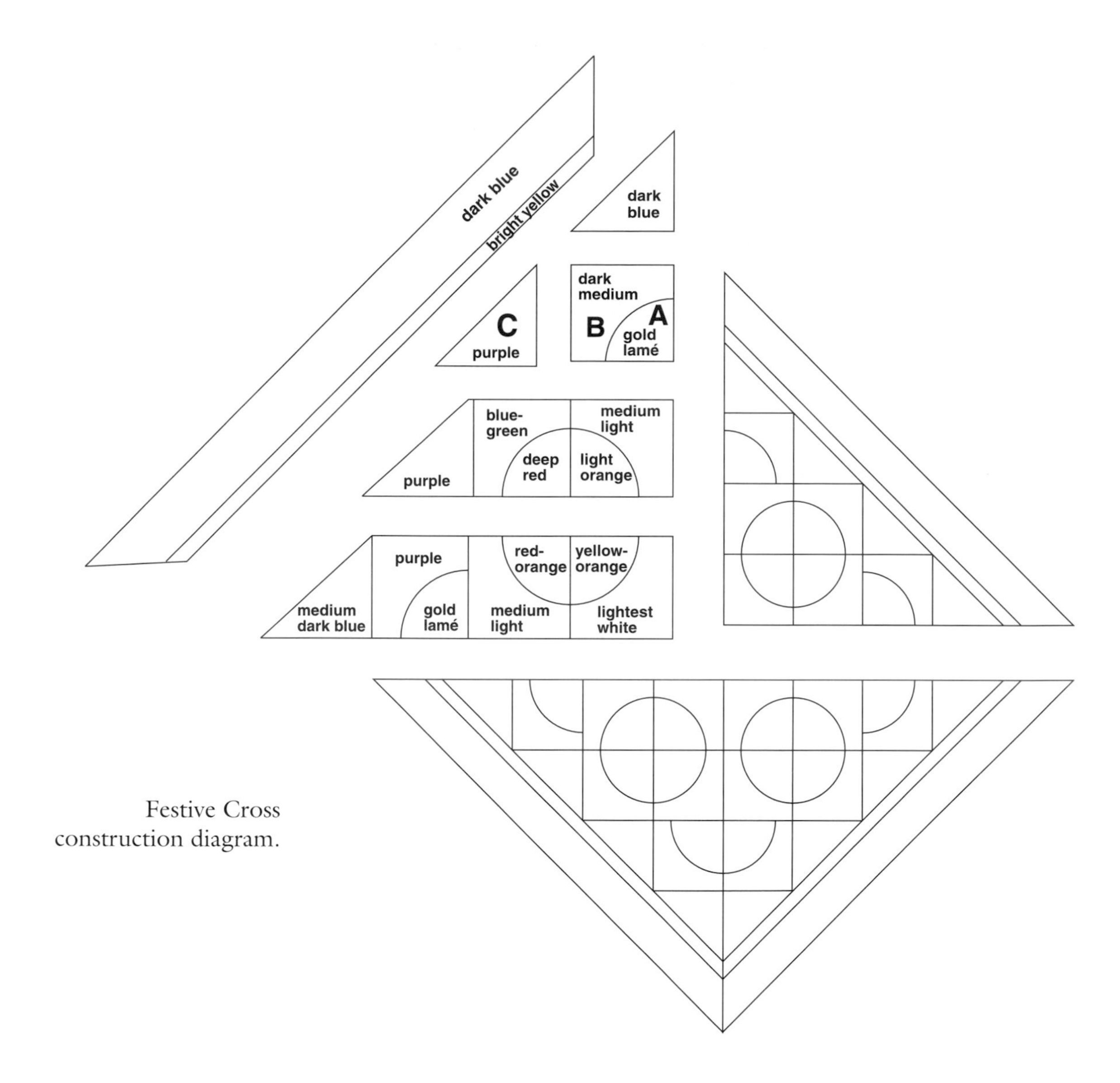

Festive Cross
construction diagram.

the curved arc in the drunkard's path blocks first, and then follow the assembly diagram.

Once you have sewn one row of blocks, press all the seams in one direction. After sewing the next row, press the seams in the opposite direction. The third row is again opposite, or like the first. When you sew these rows together, you should find that the seam allowances at the junctions are pressed in opposite directions, minimizing the bulk. Use these sets of opposing seams to help you line up the intersection; when you feel the seam, there should be no overlap and no gap. Pin and sew the rows together.

Finish each quarter by adding the two borders. First sew on a 1" wide strip of yellow, allowing a 2" overhang of yellow at each end. Then sew on a 2½" wide strip of dark blue, again allowing a 2" overhang at each end. Iron both border strips to the outside edge. Using a ruler, draw a line extending the edge of the triangle into the border and cut off the excess. Assemble the four quarters into a square.

Cut the lining and batting a little larger than the finished top. After securing the top, batting, and lining with safety pins, quilt the banner ¼" from all the seams, or be creative and design your own pattern, perhaps with curved lines radiating from the center.

Most of the ribbons on this banner are a combination of white and the bright colors in the banner. A few narrow strips of the dark colors are added for contrast. To attach these ribbons and finish the banner, follow the directions given in the general instructions.

To make the simple cross lining design, cut one 4½" deep red square, four light rectangles 4½" x 14½", and two 12½" medium squares. Cut the large squares diagonally. Sew one of the 4 ½" rectangles to the central red square, and another to the opposite side of the square. Sew one triangle to each side of the two remaining strips, forming two large, flat-topped triangles. Trim the extra fabric to form a right triangle. Sew the large triangles to opposite sides of the center strip. Roll-hem two adjacent sides of the lining. Lay the lining over the quilted banner so that the raw edges of both pieces line up. Pin and baste these edges together. Bind the edges with fabric that matches the outer border on the front. Sew pieces of pile Velcro near the two side corners so the banner can be attached to the PVC tube structure, to which you will glue hook Velcro in the corresponding positions.

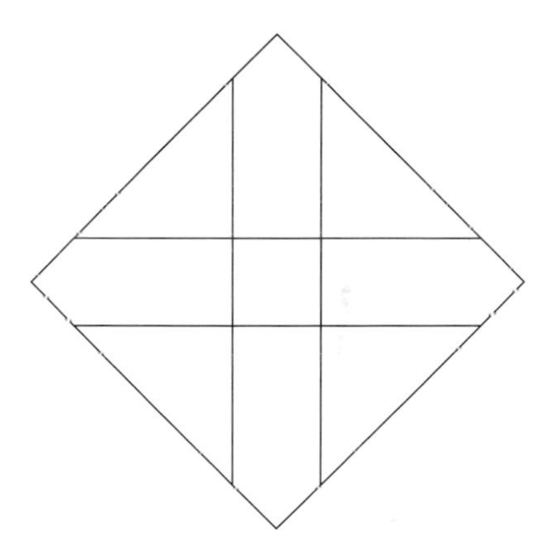

Simple cross for lining.

To attach ribbons to a banner with a lining, sew the ribbons horizontally to a strip of fabric and attach them to the quilted panel with Velcro. This fabric strip goes across the center back of the quilted panel; the lining will cover the straight line of this attachment.

Lenten Cross: Ocean Waves Pattern

Lent is a season of penance, a time of renewal, and a time to rededicate ourselves to the Christian practices of prayer, fasting, and

Lenten Cross.

almsgiving. Is the use of processional banners appropriate during Lent? While the spirit of Lent is different from the flames of Pentecost or the abounding joy of Easter, it is important to remember that we celebrate the resurrection of Our Lord at each and every liturgy. So, it is for each parish to decide whether the use of a processional banner would enhance the mood of their lenten services. A lenten banner could be used specifically for the special rites of the RCIA during Lent. If a parish has candidates and catechumens in the RCIA, a banner might accompany them in the three rites of scrutiny during Lent and lead them out of the assembly afterward. They are nearing the end of their long journey, and we celebrate their willingness to look deeply into their hearts and lives. See the photos on page 185, bottom.

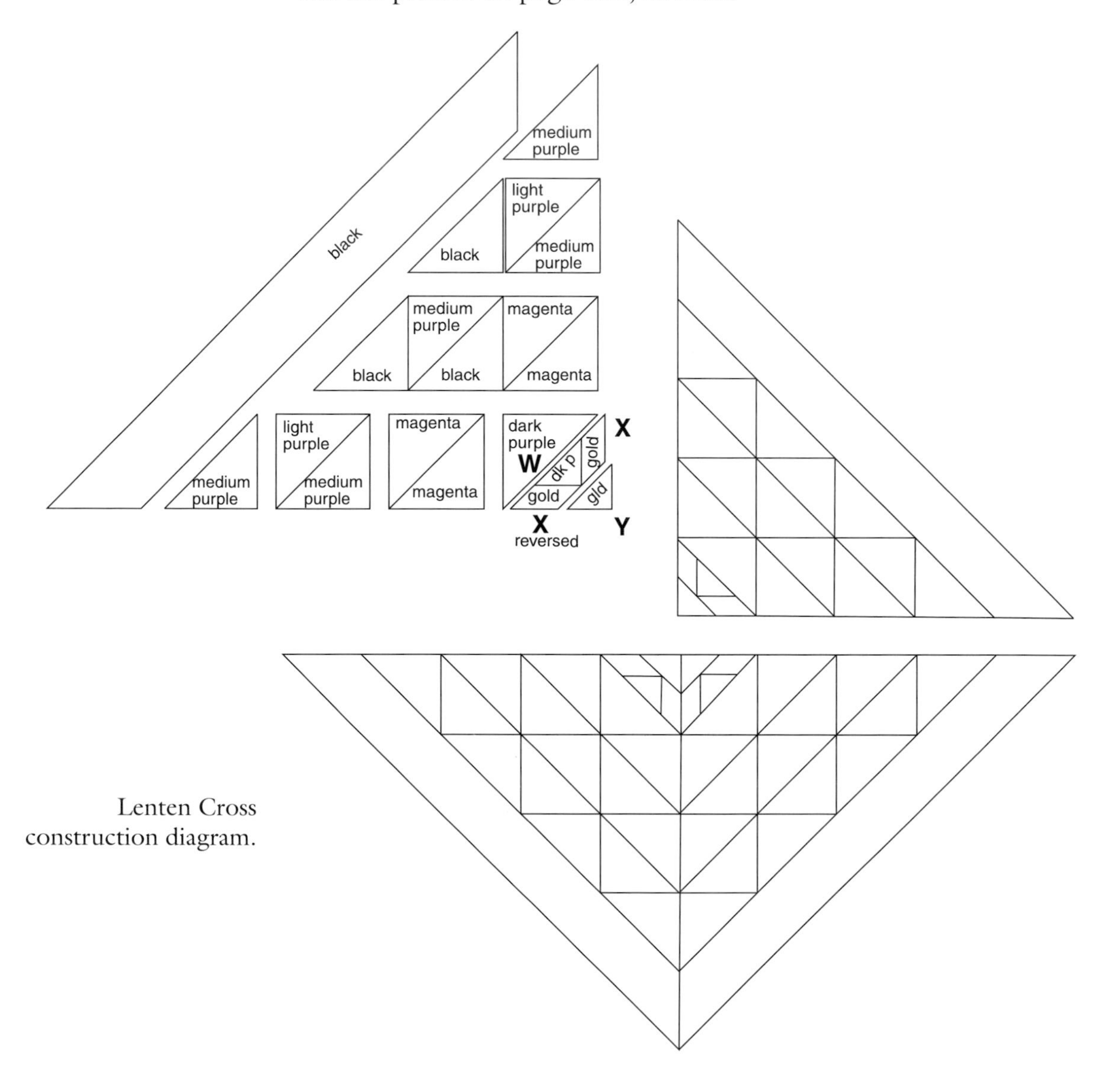

Lenten Cross construction diagram.

Josephine designed the Lenten Cross banner for St. Joseph Church in Martinsburg, West Virginia. The cross is made entirely out of triangles, a variation on the Ocean Waves pattern. Use W, X, and Y in the appendix. The colors used are written on each piece in the construction diagram, opposite. Follow the diagram for order of construction. Add borders as in the directions for the Festive Cross. Before you actually begin piecing the banner, lay out all the triangles on flannel or batting to make sure you are satisfied with the arrangement. Substitute pieces as needed.

Consider using this pattern with other colorings for other seasons. To maintain the cross image in the banner, you must place the lightest lights and the darkest darks in the same positions as those in the Lenten Cross. If you choose, you can vary the design by changing the placement of the light and dark colors. Because the design is created by the contrast of darks and lights, you can make any symbol that can be created solely with horizontal, vertical, and diagonal lines.

A Library of Blocks

The tradition of quilting in America evolved in a society of few books, where the only book a family may have owned was a Bible. Hence, many traditional pieced blocks have some obvious religious significance, such as Jacob's Ladder and King David's Crown. While the design of a block like the Carolina Lily might have been inspired by a plant, Christ's reference to the lilies of the field makes it appropriate for use as a banner design. Similarly, banner designs can be based on blocks like the Ohio Star or other star blocks (for Advent and Christmas), the palm leaf (Passion Sunday), basket blocks (containing fishes and loaves), the tree of life, and various flower blocks. Look for blocks whose traditional titles relate to Christ or to the saints, for example, Crown of Thorns.

We have selected a number of blocks that would lend themselves to banner designs for churches. For some blocks, alternative arrangements for using the block are given. We discuss a few of the blocks here in detail. As you study these blocks, note that the configuration (arrangement and coloring) of many of these blocks is what creates the design. The cross shape is probably the easiest to work with, and we use it over and over in this book.

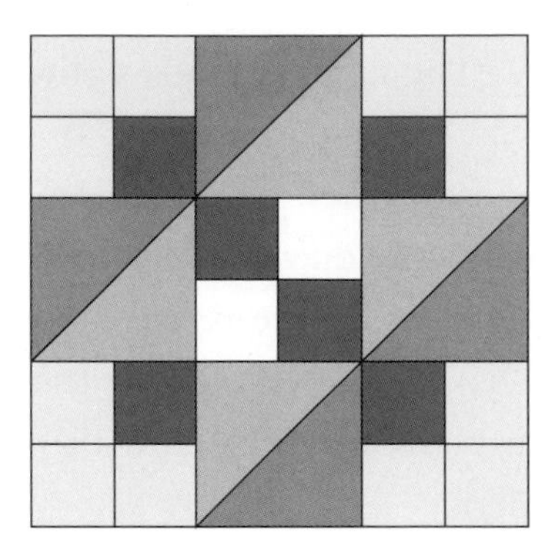
Jacob's Ladder.

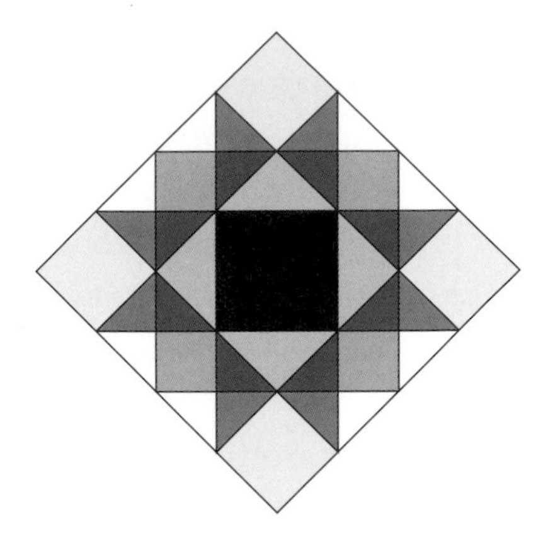
Square and Stars, set on point.

Memory.

Miller's Daughter.

Tree of Life.

Sawtooth Basket.

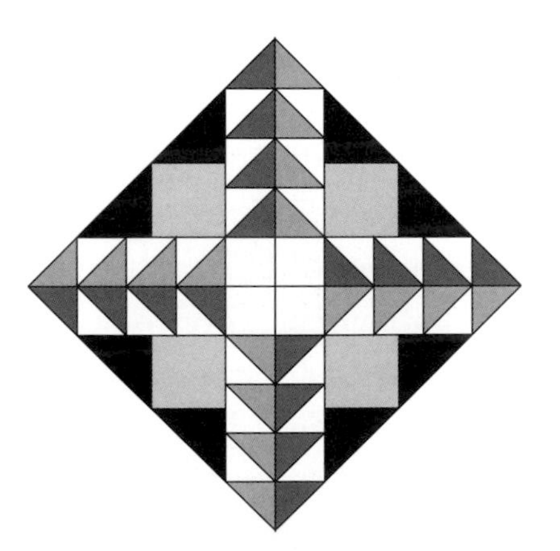
Sawtooth Cross.

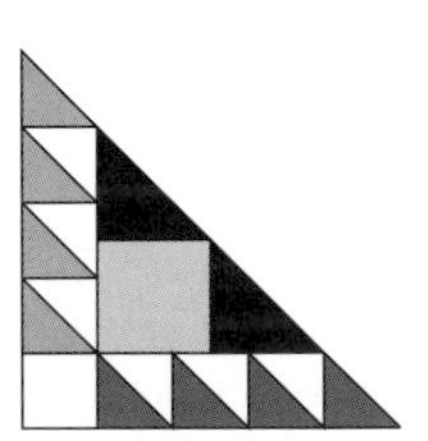
Sawtooth block.

Palm Leaf block.

Palm Leaf, four-square variation.

Palm Leaf, another four-square variation.

Carolina Lily block.

Carolina Lily, four-square variation.

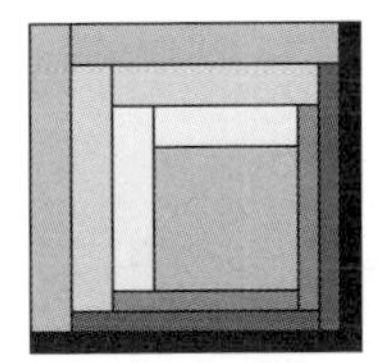

Log Cabin Cross block.

Log Cabin Cross.

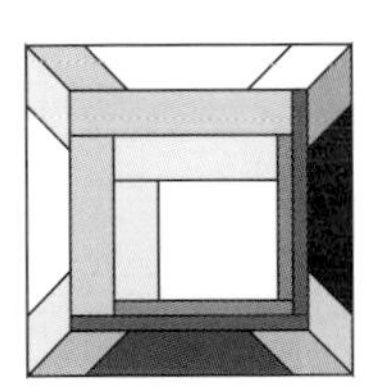

Log Cabin Star block.

Log Cabin Star.

Lilies.

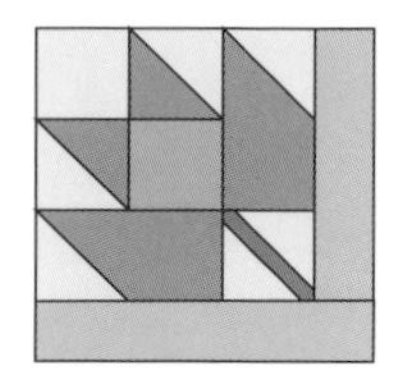

Maple Leaf block.

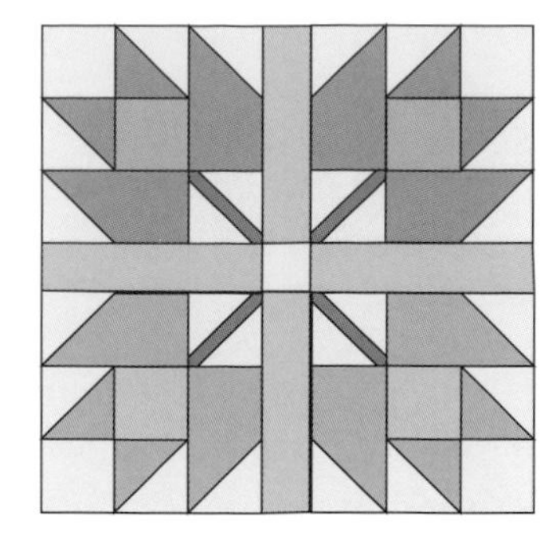

Maple Leaf.

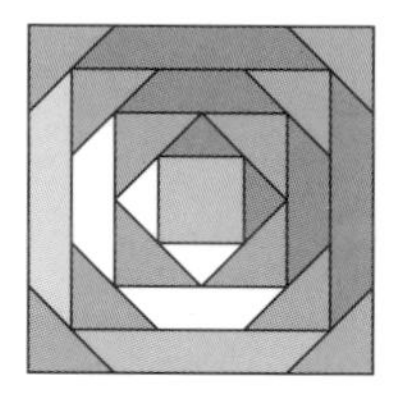

Pineapple block.

Pineapple Cross.

Feathered Friend.

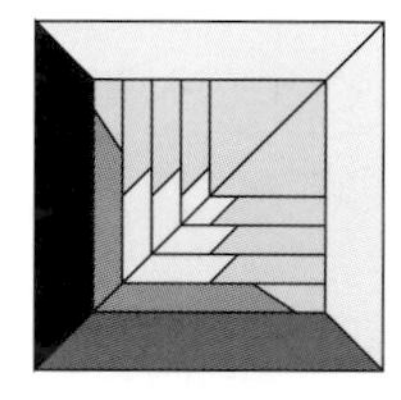

Rose of Sharon block.

Rose of Sharon cross.

The first block illustrated is Jacob's Ladder. One large block, with or without borders, can be used as the design for the banner. Jacob's Ladder would work well for a lenten banner using purple fabrics in the center sections to create a cross. Consider using a long panel of a loosely woven purple or gray fabric, such as dyed cheesecloth, rather than ribbons for a more penitential mood. The reference to the covenant in Jacob's dream is appropriate for any liturgical season.

Square and Stars is a variation of the Rising Star block placed on point. It would make a wonderful Christmas banner with the star in the center of the cross. At Christmas we are not merely celebrating Christ's birth; we commemorate his birth because it was the first step to the redemption he achieved through his death on the cross.

Note that Memory is also a cross and star design. It can be used as is or on point. The Tree of Life is a symbol found in many ancient traditions. It reminds Christians of the tree of life on which Adam and Eve were forbidden to eat the fruit, and its connection to the tree of the cross on which Christ won our salvation. Thus the tree of life is a rich symbol, and would be appropriate for a banner to be used in any sacramental liturgy.

Some blocks that make a fine banner design on their own, such as the Palm Leaf, yield complex and interesting designs when four or more blocks are used. In one Palm Leaf variation, the basic block is simply repeated four times to form a larger square. In another variation, the block is rotated around a central point. Likewise, the Carolina Lily also works well as a single block design or repeated four times and rotated around a central point.

Other blocks form satisfying designs only when four or more blocks are used. The Log Cabin block is generally used in multiples to form a design. Judy Martin has adapted this traditional block by adding diagonal lines in the outer strips to create a star. We've further adapted her design by narrowing the two dark inner strips to create the Log Cabin Star. The Log Cabin Star would make a fine Christmas banner in white, gold, red, and green. The Star of the Sea, named after one of Mary's titles, provides inspiration for an alternative coloring: tints and shades of blue (shading into blue-green) and white, with a gold star in the center.

Combining four blocks may yield promising designs with other types of quilt block patterns. Adding sashing in between the blocks results in a cross shape design, as in the Lilies and the Maple Leaf. Experiment with the width of the sashing and with different color squares in the center.

There are so many possibilities when designing a banner with quilt blocks. You need not even limit yourself to multiples of a single block, but can combine more than one block in the same banner. Later, we will provide you with instructions for a banner that uses three different blocks.

The skills you need to sew any design based on square blocks are possible to develop with some practice. The only real limitation in creating banners with quilt blocks is your own imagination and creativity. You can easily find more quilt block patterns by visiting your local library and perusing books of quilt blocks. If you like working with a computer, there are now multiple quilt design programs you can choose from, including EQ4 (available from the American Quilter's Society, 5801 Kentucky Dam Road, P.O. Box 3290, Paducah KY 42002-3290, 1-800-626-5420).

Miniature Quilts

Miniature quilts have gained tremendous popularity in recent years. Miniatures duplicate a large quilt pattern in a small format, usually on a scale of about 1:12. You can reduce any quilt block design and use multiple blocks for a memorable processional banner. Color some blocks light and some dark. Alternatively, choose a block that has a strong diagonal line, and make the contrast in values on the two sides strong.

Reduce the size of your block to 6" or less. For a 24" square banner, a 6" block will allow you to make a design 4 blocks by 4 blocks, while a 3" block allows more possibilities for design at 8 x 8 blocks. The Gemstones banner is an example of a banner done in this technique. See the photo on page 186, top left.

The block is an original design created for a queen-size quilt with 12" blocks. The banner uses 3" blocks in two colorings, one light and one dark. The design of the banner results from the arrangement of the light and dark blocks. Note that with this same

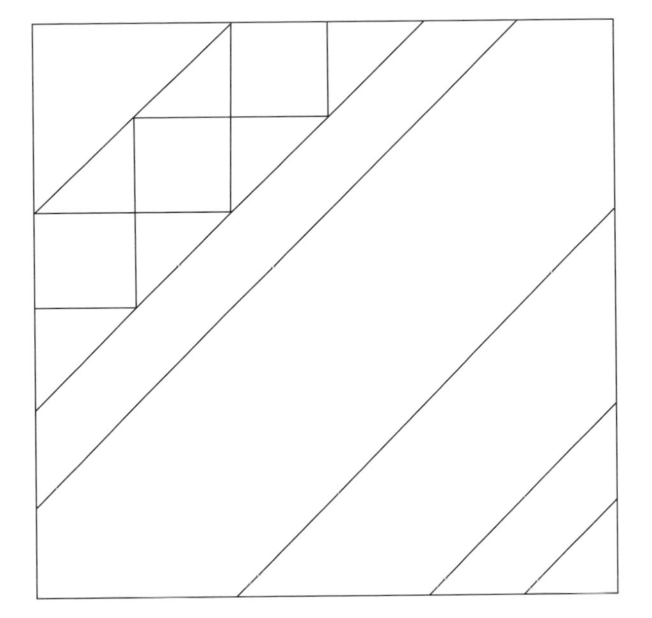

Gemstones, actual size.

block, one could contrast the diagonal halves of the block in value for a different set of design possibilities.

It is called Gemstones because the three squares in the original quilt were many bright colors surrounded by black, giving them the appearance of jewels. Three is always a reminder of the Trinity, so this block is very appropriate. Jesus died on the cross for our salvation, but the Father gave us his only-begotten Son for this purpose, and the Holy Spirit is the spirit of love emanating from the Father and Son through this ultimate act of love.

Combining One or More Block Patterns

All of the pieced banner designs that we have discussed thus far have utilized one block design, whether singly or in multiples. The possibilities for designs using blocks broaden when blocks are used in combination. We show one banner design using multiple blocks here; consult books on combining blocks or experiment on your own for more possibilities.

The construction of some block designs is made much simpler and more accurate by using the technique of foundation, or paper, piecing. Certainly, this is true for any block based on the Log Cabin, Fans, and many other types of blocks. You can opt for either paper piecing or regular piecing with this project. If you use regular piecing, remember to add 1/4" seam allowances around each pattern piece. Sew the pieces in the same order.

Resurrection Rose.

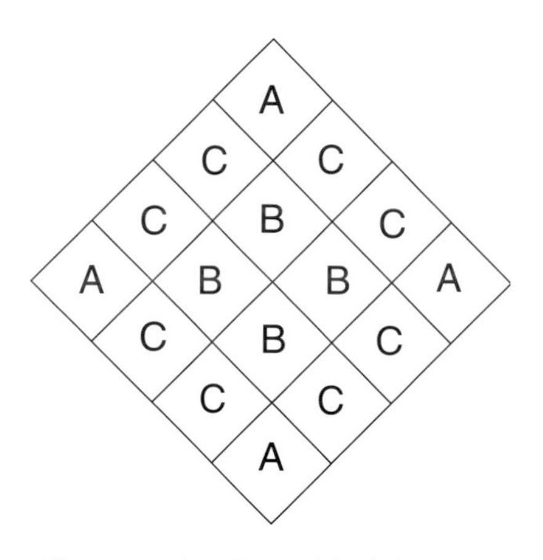

Resurrection Rose block layout.

Resurrection Rose

This is an example of a design that utilizes three different blocks. Blocks A and B are flower blocks that are variations of the basic Log Cabin block. Block C is simply a square composed of two right triangles with 5" sides, forming a 5" square; an optional curve can be used to make your banner look like the photograph. Used together, they form a blooming cross, appropriate for Easter and springtime. See the photo on page 186, bottom left.

Begin by making copies of the block patterns (in the appendix). Use a medium-weight uncoated paper for foundation piecing, such as copy paper. Avoid newsprint, tissue paper, or any other lightweight paper. Trace by hand or copy on a very accurate copier. These sheets of paper become the foundation of your blocks. For this banner, make four copies of Block A, four of Block B, and eight of Block C.

Select three shades of rose and two shades of green. Block A uses a sky-blue print background fabric and Block B has a white-on-white background. Begin each block with a piece of the lightest rose fabric somewhat larger than the center square (piece 1) of your

A
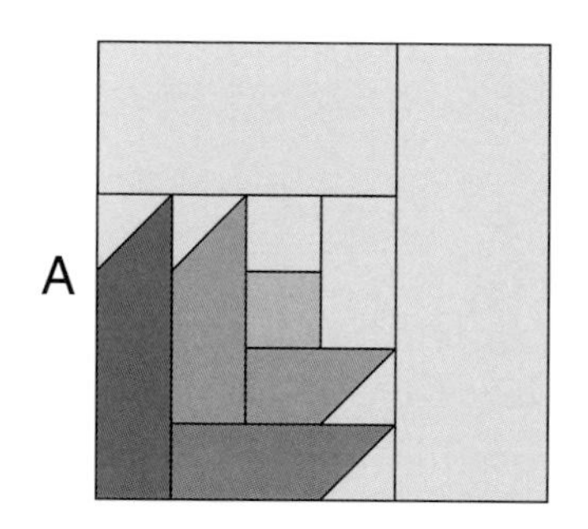

B
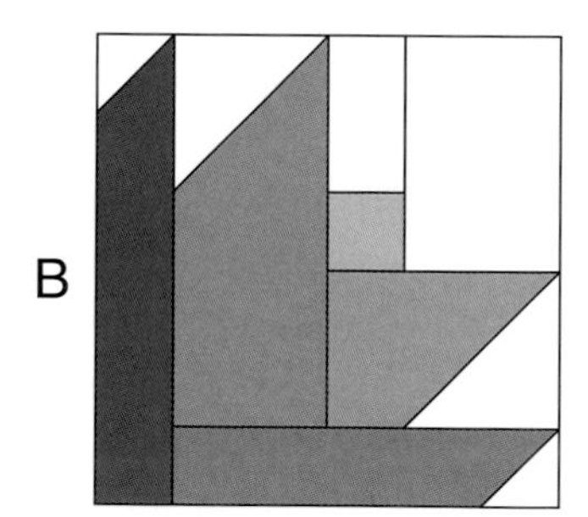

C
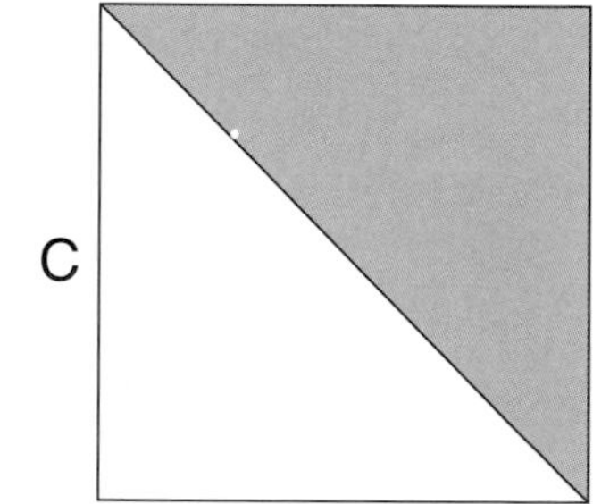

foundation. Pin the rose square to the back side of the paper so that you can see it centered over the square when you hold it up to the light. The wrong side of the fabric should be against the paper, so the right side is facing up.

Next, cut a piece of the background fabric 1" bigger than piece 2. Place it right sides together over the central square you just pinned to the foundation. Turn the paper over and sew on the line between 1 and 2 with a very small stitch. Trim the seam to about 1/4", fold piece 2 so it is right side up, and press the seam from the right side. The third piece will also be of the background fabric. Cut it 1" larger than rectangle 3 on the pattern, and place it over pieces 1 and 2. Turn the paper over and sew the seam between piece 3 and the unit formed of 1 and 2. Trim and press open. Continue, following all the numbers until the block is finished.

Sew the blocks together according to the diagram. After all the blocks are sewn together, tear the paper away from the back by folding along each stitching line and tearing the paper. Carefully extract any remaining bits of the paper. (For further information and patterns for paper piecing, see books by Carol Doak, including *Easy Machine Paper Piecing*.) Block C has a large white triangle and a large sky-blue triangle. If you choose to add the rounded earth image, divide the blue triangle into a pie shaped green earth piece and a sky-blue background. Arrange blocks A, B, and C as in the photograph.

Colorwash Banners

Colorwash, or watercolor, quilting has been popular in quilting in the past decade or so. It is particularly suited to liturgical banners, especially as backgrounds for overlaid designs. The flowing use of color and subtlety of tone echo the feeling of much Impressionist art. A quilt done using this technique can give the impression of light filtering through mist or fog, as in a painting by Monet.

Colorwash quilts are pieced from units of the same size and shape, usually 2" squares. The simplicity of the shape allows the artist to focus on color and value. Subtle gradation of these attributes is the primary means of attaining the colorwash effect. The right kinds of prints can be arranged so that they blend gradually from light to dark, like washes of a watercolor painting. Medium to large scale flower prints can be used, as well as prints that do not have a small regular pattern. Avoid polka dots and stripes, and any fabric that contains a strong contrast of value. You want a dappled kind of effect.

Select a number of fabrics and cut several 2" squares from each. Arrange them in a rectangular grid, preferably on a flannel board or wall where you can leave the work undisturbed for a period of time. If you want a shape or an edge to stand out in the grid, then make a sharp contrast of value. Otherwise, keep the squares flowing in color and value from one to the next. You may have to rearrange the squares many times until you have a pleasing blend. Do not get discouraged if it takes a while, as this is the nature of the technique.

Once you are satisfied with your grid arrangement, sew the squares together in rows. Many quilters save time and thread by chain-piecing the squares. If you chain-piece in a particular way, the pieces will stay in order as the rows are sewn. To do this, work from the left and turn over the second block in the top row on top of the first, right sides together. Do the same thing for the remaining rows and stack these pairs of squares in order from top to bottom, carefully maintaining their orientation.

Sew a 1/4" seam on the right-hand side of the first pair of squares. Without cutting the thread, sew a 1/4" seam on the right-hand side of the next pair of squares. Repeat for the remaining pairs of squares. When you have sewn the last pair of squares, detach your string of squares from the machine, but cut no other threads.

Stack the third squares in each row, maintaining their order from top to bottom. Sew the top square, which will be the third square in the first row, to the right-hand square in the first pair of squares in your chain, that is, the second square in row 1. Without cutting the thread, sew the next square in the pile to the right-hand square of the next row, and so on. When you have finished adding the last square, you can detach the construction from the machine, but cut no other threads. Continue likewise until you have completed sewing together each of the rows. The rows will all be linked to each other by pieces of thread at each seam. Do not cut these threads, so that you maintain the ordering of the rows.

Iron all the seams in the first row in one direction. Then lay the construction on the ironing board so that all but the first and second row hangs off the edge. Press all the seams in the second row in the other direction. Continue in a likewise manner to press the seams in alternate directions. Finish the top by sewing the horizontal rows together, matching up the seams. Press the horizontal seams in one direction.

There are quite a few quilt books written on this technique that will give you more details in selecting fabrics and many more possibilities for designs than we give here. One source is *Colourwash Quilts—A Personal Approach to Design and Technique* (That Patchwork Place, 1994), by Deirdre Amsden, who originated the style. As you view quilts done in the watercolor style, remember that banners used in liturgy should be easily seen from a distance, and watercolor quilts do not necessarily fit that requirement. If you choose to form a symbol within the watercolor arrangement, rather than using watercolor blocks as a background for an appliqué, the symbol must contrast sharply with the background. Step back from your design wall occasionally and squint to get an impression of what the design looks like from a distance. It is easy to get caught up in the process of blending colors and tones while working with the two-inch squares and forget the power and impact needed for distance viewing. See the photos on pages 186, right, and 187.

EASTER CROSS: SADDLE BANNERS

Josephine designed the Easter Cross banner for use by her community, the School Sisters of Notre Dame, in St. Louis. It is a saddle-style banner, that is, it drapes over the pole so the back is the same size and shape as the front. Both sides have a design, so that the banner is appealing from the back as well as the front. The image of the cross is a part of the watercolor design itself. The solid white fabric used for the cross makes it stand out, both because there is a contrast of solid versus print, in addition to the necessary contrast in value. See the photo on page 186, right.

To make this watercolor Easter banner, you will need 16 2" blocks across and 28 down. A few solids of yellow, orange and red will brighten the piece. If solids contrast too much, you can tone down the effect by choosing one-color prints in the same colors. Note that the cross is ten squares of white fabric. If you choose to cut out larger rectangles instead of squares, note that each square measures 1½" without seam allowances.

After piecing the squares, the top will measure 32½" x 56½". Note that the piece folds in the middle; if the orientation of the back design matters, lay it out upside down. Then when the banner is folded in half, both the front and back will be oriented properly.

All 4 corners are cut to make the rounded bottom. To mark the curve, use a yardstick compass set with a radius of 16¼" and center it 16¼" from the end. Draw a half-circle from side to side and cut along the line. Repeat at the other end.

Ordinary Time Banner: Inserting a Large Square

This Ordinary Time banner is also in the collection of the School Sisters of Notre Dame. It is a saddle banner, much like the Easter banner. A gold anchor was first appliquéd to an 8½" square of white fabric. Because this larger square spans more than one row, you must accommodate it in the construction. First assemble the three short rows on either side of the large square. Sew each set of three rows together, and then inset the large white square. See page 187, top.

Grapes and Vine Banner: Overlaid Appliqué

Josephine designed this Ordinary Time banner for the Archdiocese of Chicago's Office of the Laity. She took her inspiration from the section in John 15 in which Jesus identifies himself as the vine and his disciples as the branches: "He who lives in me and I in him, will produce abundantly." "My Father has been glorified in your bearing much fruit and becoming my disciples."

The design for this banner illustrates how colorwash can be used as a background for appliqué, which substantially increases that technique's usefulness. The Grapes and Vine banner is also a saddle banner, with the same basic shape as the Easter banner. In the area where the grapes and vine were to be appliquéd, Josephine used a concentration of lights and whites, which allows the appliqué to stand out. Notice how the colors of the ribbons match the patches of the quilted standard. See page 187, bottom and right.

Ideas for a Wedding Banner Using Colorwash

The technique of appliqué over colorwash has many possibilities for use in processional banners. It would make an appealing and appropriate wedding banner. Use light floral prints around the edges, perhaps in colors harmonizing with the clothing of the wedding party, and blend into off-whites and whites in the center. Appliqué a symbol of marriage over this background, in a darker print or perhaps silver or gold lamé. The symbol most often used is the interlocked rings with the Chi-Rho or the cross. Alternatively, you could piece two darker interlocking rings from the Double Wedding Ring quilt block pattern and appliqué them over the colorwash grid. For the ribbons, let white and off-white predominate, accented by gold, silver, and pale colors harmonizing with the wedding party's colors.

Chapter 8

BANNER DESIGN PART 2: WORKING FROM A FREE-FORM DRAWING

Although the tradition of working in blocks has dominated quilt design for many years, quilters have always used other techniques, some of which offer greater flexibility to the banner maker. These methods include whole-cloth quilting, hand and machine appliqué, and pieced pictures. What these methods have in common is that the quilter generally works from a full-sized drawing.

In whole-cloth quilting, a single piece of cloth is used as the foundation for a design composed entirely of quilting stitches. The dimensionality of the stitching, sometimes highlighted by a form of stitchery called *trapunto,* produces the design. Whole-cloth quilting is often used for bed quilts. Creative use of the technique can produce fascinating designs. Although not traditional, gold or silver metallic lamé fabric will fit better with most church interiors than plain white muslin, and can be worked fairly easily.

The versatility of appliqué is readily apparent to any viewer of modern quilts. Any shape can be appliquéd, or layered and sewn, onto a background fabric. Even complex shapes that would be difficult to sew in any other way can be used. Appliqué can be sewn either by hand or machine, although we prefer machine appliqué for speed and durability. With machine appliqué, the thread used to stitch down the appliqué generally shows, offering an additional design feature that you can use to highlight a symbol.

Pieced pictures is a technique of piecing that allows nearly the same flexibility as appliqué, but leaves smooth flat pieced edges.

There is no thread line left on top, which can be an advantage. Pam prefers piecing, both as a technique and for the resultant smooth edges, and uses it as her primary technique.

In order to use any of these three techniques, you need to know how to enlarge a drawing. You have our permission to enlarge any of the drawings in this book for personal use or use in your own church. You may not sell any item made using our drawings. The use of drawings from other published sources requires permission from the publisher, unless that publisher clearly states that the drawing is free of copyright.

We begin by explaining three methods of enlarging, followed by the techniques themselves.

Enlarging a Drawing

Enlarging a drawing is generally prerequisite to the techniques described in this section. While you can work directly, drawing in full size, it is usually easier to enlarge a small drawing to the appropriate size. There are a number of ways to do this; the easiest involve extra equipment, such as a blueprint copier, a regular copy machine, an overhead projector, or an opaque projector. If none of these are available, use the grid method explained beginning on page 136.

If your local copy center has a blueprint copier, you may be able to enlarge your drawing to fit on a single sheet of paper. The process is relatively expensive, but simple, saves time, and produces an exact image with no distortion. Bring your drawing to the copy center and specify how large an image you will need.

A regular copy machine can also be used to enlarge images, but you will probably have to piece the final image from multiple sheets of paper. To get the percentage enlargement for the copy machine, divide the width of the finished banner image by the width of the drawing and multiply by 100. For example, if you would like a banner to be 30 inches wide and your starting drawing is 6 inches, divide 30 by 6 to get 5. Then multiply by 100 for a 500% enlargement. You may have to go through more than one generation of enlargement if the copier will not enlarge that much at one time. Note that each enlargement distorts the image slightly, so minimize the number of enlargements to be made by using the highest percentage enlargement possible each time. Since your banner will probably be larger than a piece of copier paper, draw a grid on the drawing, label the sections, cut it up and enlarge each section by the same percentage. Join the enlarged sections by carefully taping them together, so that the taped paper is flat.

Using an overhead projector or opaque projector eliminates the cumbersome process of taping paper, as you can buy paper in large rolls. Use a good quality medium weight white paper. With either projector, begin by taping a sheet of paper slightly larger than your banner size to the wall. Use painter's masking tape, and be sure to remove the tape within 48 hours to avoid damaging the wall. Place the projector high enough to project the image straight on, without distortion. Move the projector forward or backward until the image is the right size for your banner and is in focus. When the projected image is clear and measures the right size, trace its lines onto the paper using a pencil. If you don't have enough space to back up far enough to project the image at the size you want, try enlarging the source image with a copy machine.

Overhead projectors are used with transparent source images. Sheets of acetate, 8½" x 11", are made to use with overhead projectors. You may draw your design directly onto a sheet of acetate using a permanent pen, or you may photocopy it onto a sheet of acetate. Specially coated acetate sheets may be used in your computer's laser printer. Overhead projectors are often available at libraries, schools, and churches. If you find one that seems not to be working, try replacing the bulb.

An opaque projector is used in the same way, except that the source image is on opaque paper, not transparent acetate. The paper can range from 8½" x 11" down to 4" x 5".

Using either projector is easiest if the whole source image fits on the projector surface. It is not easy to line up an image and keep it square if you have to project it in pieces. Pam likes overhead projectors because they can take an 8½ x 11" image, the image is sharp, the projectors are a reasonable size, and they are commonly available.

The grid method can be used to enlarge an image without any extra equipment. Begin by drawing a square grid on your image. To determine the size of the squares you will need for your enlarged grid, multiply the size of the squares in your small grid by the width of the enlarged image and divide by the width of the original image. So, for example, to enlarge a 6" image drawn on 1/4" graph paper to a size of 36", multiply 1/4 by 36 and divide by 6 and make an enlarged grid of 1 1/2" squares. Draw this grid on a sheet of paper appropriate for the size of the enlargement. Then transfer your image square by square, making sure the lines of your image cross the grid lines in the same places on the large drawing that they do on the small drawing. It's harder to get the same quality of results with this technique, so it's worth the extra effort to get a projector if you can. Regardless of your enlarging method, correct your finished drawing to make sure the straight lines are straight and the curves are smooth.

Whole Cloth Quilting

In a whole cloth quilt, the quilting alone forms the design. Traditionally, plain white fabric was used for whole cloth quilting. The color white is not necessary, but the stitching does show up best on a solid fabric. Tissue lamé produces striking results that fit well with most church settings. The appropriateness of gold and silver is obvious, but many other colors are available. Raw silk comes in many rich colors and is easy to work with. Cotton sateen also comes in rich colors with a nice sheen, yet is not slippery. You might try searching for a two-tone fabric woven with different-colored threads in the horizontal and vertical directions, which would catch the light differently depending on point of view. Whole cloth quilting calls for a fabric that is not slippery and whose color complements your purpose.

The design for a whole cloth banner should have areas of dense quilting that contrast with open areas. The quilted areas recede and the open areas come forward, so plan carefully to accent the right elements. Celtic quilting designs can show you how contrasting areas of quilting complement each other and provide design inspiration. The Japanese have a long history of whole cloth quilting, which may prove valuable for inspiration as well.

Because marking fabrics like tissue lamé and raw silk can be difficult, mark your pattern on the backing fabric and sew from the back. Even if you use an easily marked fabric, consider working from the back to avoid the difficulties of completely removing marks from the front. The backing fabric should be an easily marked cotton, but need not be solid or even light-colored. To mark the design, use a #2 pencil, a silver or yellow colored pencil, or a fine-line chalk marker, whichever shows up best.

If you are machine quilting, the thread that will show on the front should be loaded onto the bobbin, since you will be sewing from the back. It might be cotton thread that matches or contrasts with the front fabric, or metallic thread. The thread used in the needle should be a cotton thread that matches the backing fabric. Experiment with threads and designs on 6" square quilt sandwiches to find pleasing combinations.

Wedding banner.

Whole cloth quilting is a particularly good technique for wedding or anniversary banners, since names can be incorporated into the quilting design. We don't ordinarily design banners with words, but for these events we would break that rule. Use a bold typeface from a computer or seek out a book of typefaces. Enlarge the letters to the appropriate size and trace onto your design. Outline the letters with quilting and fill in the spaces between the letters with close quilting. Leave the letters themselves open.

The Wedding banner that Pam designed is a good example of a whole cloth design that could include a family name. Put the name across the bottom of the banner and fill in with rays. When your design includes letters and you plan to quilt from the back of the banner, make sure to draw the letters in reverse so that the name can be read correctly from the front. This banner could be used for a wedding or silver anniversary, and could be hung in the couple's home and used again for a renewal of vows. The top is silver tissue lamé, quilted with gold metallic thread. See the photo on page 188, top left.

Machine Appliqué

If you are looking for a technique that offers flexibility in design, look no further than machine appliqué. Whether you want to work from a drawing or work directly with fabric shapes, you can do it with appliqué. Basically, you cut out a shape, lay it on a background fabric, and sew around the edges. Any shape you can dream up can be sewn down.

The two concerns in appliqué are that the shape lies flat and that the edges are secured neatly by the stitching. The first concern is easily taken care of by using a bonding agent or fusible webbing (such as Wonder Under or Heat 'n Bond Lite). We recommend a fusible with paper backing, useful for transferring shapes from your enlarged drawing. It is necessary to reverse the shape for tracing on the fusible so that the resultant piece will look like your drawing. To reverse the shape, lay your enlarged drawing wrong side up on a light table, or hang it in a window or door so that you can see through it to trace. When you cut out the fusible shape, leave a margin of 1/4" or so around the pencil line. Iron the fusible to the back of your selected fabric, following the directions provided with the fusible. Cut out the shape along the line, and peel off the paper. Then place the shape on the foundation fabric and iron it into place, again following the directions provided.

Once that the shape has been fused flat to the foundation, the edges should be secured with stitching to produce a durable banner. A medium width zigzag satin stitch in a matching color is normally used to both secure and cover the edge. However, the thread could be chosen to contrast with the shape if you want it to stand out. Invisible nylon thread sewn with a more open zigzag downplays the edges, but does not cover them.

There is an alternate method for machine appliqué that produces neater edges and on which the stitching barely shows. However, it involves an extra step of lining the shape. This is especially suitable for cotton fabrics and designs in which one piece of fabric is used as the background or foundation of the design.

Each shape to be appliquéd is cut with a 1/4" (or less) seam allowance and a duplicate is cut from very thin fabric, such as light non-woven interfacing. Pin the fabric, right side down, to the interfacing and sew on the seam line around the entire circumference of the piece. Cut a slit in the interfacing and turn the piece right side out. Use a pointed object to turn the corners completely. Iron the unit flat and pin it in place on the foundation fabric (trace the entire design on the fabric to facilitate placement). Blind-stitch or hem-stitch it in place on your machine with invisible thread. This stitching will be almost invisible.

We now describe, step by step, an actual project made with the basic method of machine appliqué.

Pentecost Fire.

PENTECOST FIRE: STEPS OF APPLIQUÉ

The Spirit of God is manifested in many ways. In scripture, the Spirit is depicted as, among other things, a dove, tongues of fire, a gently whispering wind, and a mighty wind. Those who experience the Spirit change; they are moved to do amazing things. For this reason symbols of the Spirit must be forceful and dynamic. In Pentecost Fire, the flames of the Spirit are bold, filled with color and life. Not bound or contained by a tight border, the curved lines of this design move beyond the inner border to the outer frame. See the photo on page 188, top right.

These curved lines led to the choice of appliqué for the construction technique. The simple background of an inner square surrounded by an outer border was pieced first. The flames were machine-appliquéd with cotton thread that matched each flame as closely as possible in color. The panel is a 24" square set on point, so that the panel is about 30" across.

The background requires generous half-yards of black and blue-green. Cut the 18½" inner square from the black fabric. For the blue-green border, cut four long rectangles, 3½" x 24¾". To miter the corners, trim each end of these border pieces at a 45° angle to form trapezoids whose shorter edge (minus seam allowances) measures 18". If you want to draft a paper pattern for these border pieces to ensure a proper fit, begin with a 24" line. Center an 18" parallel line 3" below. Connect the two lines at each end with 45° angle lines. Add ¼" seam allowances all around. Piece the borders to the square.

The flames require quarter-yards of dark red, red-orange, orange, yellow-orange, and bright yellow solids or prints. You also need one yard of bright red, which will be used for the back as well.

Enlarge the Pentecost Fire diagram so that the edge of the square measures 24". Draw upward-pointing grain-line arrows on each piece. To make the banner look like the drawing, turn the drawing over before tracing the shapes onto fusible webbing. Use a lightbox or tape the drawing and webbing to a window to see through it. Trace each shape to be appliquéd onto the paper side of the webbing, leaving a little bit of room between shapes. Transfer the grain-line arrows onto the fusible webbing. You may find it helpful to code each shape on the drawing and on the webbing, to help you remember how the pieces correspond. Cut out the shapes drawn on the fusible webbing, leaving about 1/4" around each shape.

For the flames, you can follow the colors in the photograph, or lay out your fabrics on the drawing to determine your own arrangement. Once you've selected the fabric, lay the fusible webbing shape on the wrong side of the fabric. The paper side of the webbing should be up and the arrow lined up with the grain line of the fabric. Iron the fusible webbing shape to your fabric, following the directions that come with the fusible webbing. Cut out the fabric/webbing sandwich carefully, following the pencil line of the pattern piece.

Once the pieces are cut out, pull the paper backing off each one and arrange them on the background. When you are satisfied with the arrangement, press with a hot iron (again following the directions that come with the fusible webbing). Using a medium width satin stitch, zigzag around each piece. You may use thread that closely matches the fabric, black thread to emphasize the lines, or metallic thread to add sparkle. Sparkle can also be added by quilting in bits of prismatic foil scattered like confetti, as in this banner. Finish the banner with red, yellow, and orange ribbons, a red lining, and a teal binding.

Mighty Waters Banners: Working with Nylon Fabric

For the pope's 1999 visit to St. Louis, Josephine made ten large-scale (5' x 6') nylon banners with a water theme. Reflecting the theme of the papal visit, "Salvation for All," the banners of waves splashing high conveyed a sense of place as well; the Missouri and the Mississippi rivers converge at St. Louis. Because these rivers had flooded in recent years, this assembly would be appreciative of the power and force of water, of death and rebirth. Josephine tried to capture a sense of water as a defining force in our lives. See the photo on page 188, bottom.

Mighty Waters.

Lightweight nylon was used to construct these huge banners so that they could be carried in procession. The waves were appliquéd to a solid navy background in a technique similar to that described in Pentecost Fire. When fusing nylon to a background, use a fusible web that works at a low heat setting (such as Therm o Web's Heat 'n Bond Lite. 505 Spray & Fix should also work and requires no heat. It's available from Clotilde, B3000, Louisiana, MO 63353-3000, 800-772-2891).

Banners for outdoor use need to withstand the weather, rain or shine. Nylon flag fabric is lightweight and water-resistant. Look in the appendix for sources. If the banners will remain outdoors for a long time, they need to be fade-resistant. Use Solarmax fabric.

Flag makers usually cut away the background fabric so that light can shine through, giving a brighter look. While cutaway appliqué was not appropriate for such a large and complex project, consider using it if your project is smaller and simpler. Fix the appliqué to the background with a fixative such as 505 Spray & Fix, zigzag the edge with a matching or invisible thread, and cut away the background, leaving an edge of 1/4" or less. Note that you can place a new piece of fabric over what you've already sewn and cut away behind that. You may find it helpful to sew on a tear-away foundation fabric (also available from Clotilde).

Unless specially treated by the manufacturer, nylon fabric frays easily. The best way to cut it is to use a hot knife, which cuts the fabric by melting it, sealing the edges at the same time. Contact Para-Gear Equipment at 708-679-5905 for information. Work on a piece of glass to protect your surface, and keep a ceramic plate or other heat-resistant surface nearby on which to rest the hot knife so that you don't burn holes where you don't want them. A metal ruler or narrow strip of plate glass can be used as an aid in cutting straight lines. Make sure you have adequate ventilation or work outside, as the fumes from melting nylon are toxic.

Harvest.

AUTUMN ORDINARY TIME BANNERS: APPLIQUÉ ON A PIECED BACKGROUND

The choice of construction technique is not an either/or situation. Sometimes a banner design benefits from a combination of piecing and appliqué. In fact, many of the designs made by the School Sisters of Notre Dame's organization, Liturgical Fabric Arts, do combine techniques. Use the technique needed to get the effect you want most easily.

The period of Ordinary Time that begins after Pentecost stretches through high summer into the bare branches of November. Since Ordinary Time has no overarching theme by definition and spans three of nature's seasons, there is no reason to treat it as a unified whole. The environment committee at Holy Infant Parish commissioned Josephine to design banners for Christ the King and Thanksgiving. See the photos on page 189.

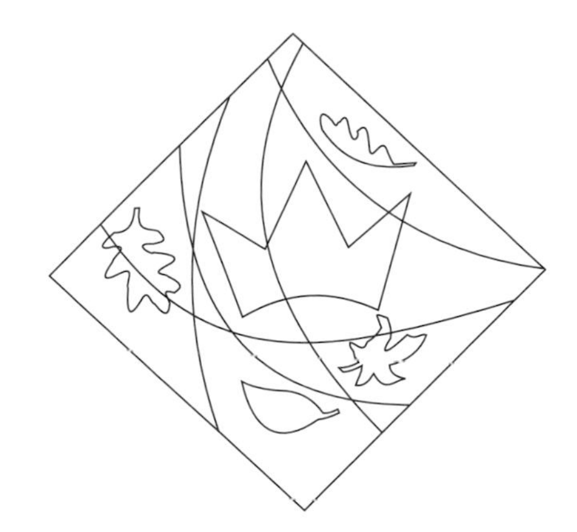

Christ the King.

Foliage prints of brown, forest, and olive green form a pieced background for the glowing oranges and yellows of autumn. Bright solids and a metallic gold help the appliqués to really stand out. The symbols were appliquéd first on black to heighten the contrast with the background. Cut the black so about 1/4" remains around each piece and appliqué the whole unit to the background with black thread. General directions for constructing a free-form image can be found in the section on pieced pictures.

Sacred Heart and Eucharist Banners: Working in Sections

The Sacred Heart and Eucharist banners were worked in sections. They combine symbols appliquéd on a solid fabric with stripes pieced on a fabric foundation. Piecing on a foundation combines the steps of piecing and quilting, for an easier and faster result. When the church building for St. Margaret Mary Alacoque Church in south St. Louis County was dedicated, these Sacred Heart and Eucharist banners were carried in procession. They are now used occasionally throughout the year, but since they generally remain stationary, free-flowing ribbons were not used. See the photos on page 190.

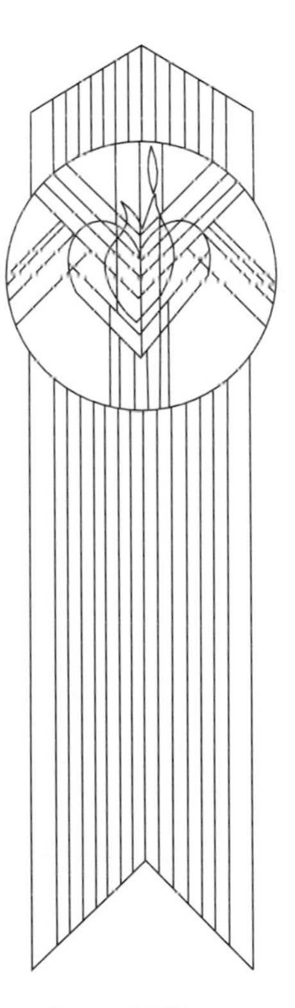

Sacred Heart.

Usually it is best to avoid dominant circles when designing banners, as they tend to draw too much attention. But since the structure of this church building cascades from a circular tower, the architecture itself suggested the form. An M shape, inspired by the stained glass windows in the style of Frank Lloyd Wright, divides the circle and reminds viewers of Margaret Mary, the parish's patron saint. The heart and its emergent flame present a contemporary turn on the traditional Sacred Heart image.

Many of us tend to dismiss traditional images like the Sacred Heart as uninteresting or irrelevant because we think we've seen it. By giving an image a new twist, the artist asks us to take a second look and think about what we see. The contemporary look of the grapes and wheat in the second banner comes from the straight vertical lines for the wheat and separated circles for the grapes.

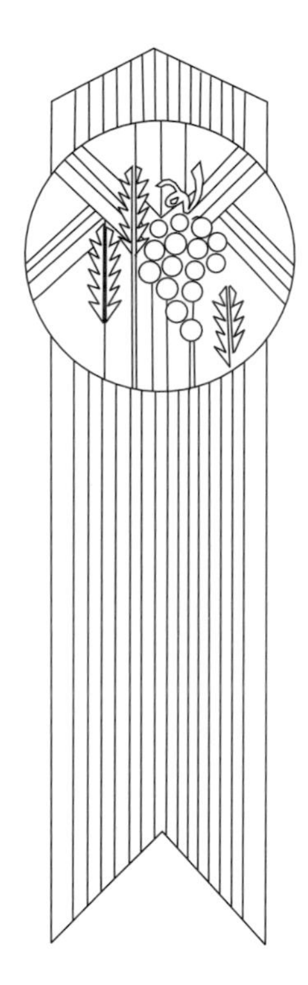

Eucharist.

The pieced top and bottom sections were added to give the banners height, to make them more visible when carried in procession, and to better fit their space when standing in place. Their bright colors and lavish amount of gold might not complement all churches, but they contrast nicely with the dark rough brick of this church. They were sewn and quilted all in one step with a foundation piecing technique, where strips of fabric were pieced on a base of batting on top of a muslin backing. Piecing this way sandwiches the batting between the front and back of the banner and eliminates the need to quilt the layers to hold them together.

To use this technique on the bottom part of the banner, begin with a pile of brightly colored strips, 2½" wide and varying lengths. Arrange these in columns on a flannel wall roughly in the shapes of the top and bottom pieces. Make sure the columns are extra long, and rearrange until a pleasing effect is achieved. Cut the ends of each strip at 45° angles, as in a trapezoid, so that the left end points down in the left-hand columns and the right end points down in the right-hand columns. Then sew together the ends of the strips in each column with quarter-inch seams.

Cut pieces of muslin and batting slightly larger than the bottom piece of the banner. It will help to keep the columns straight if you draw a series of chalked parallel guidelines directly on the batting; draw the first line 5" from the left edge. Lay down the first column right side up and line it up with the first chalk line. Place the second column right sides together over the first, pin it in place, and sew with a ¼" seam along the right edge. Fold out and finger press. For security, pin the second column flat. Continue adding columns until they are all in place, using the chalk lines to maintain straight lines. Repeat this procedure for the top part of the banner.

For both the top and bottom pieces, cut 5" wide strips of gold metallic lamé and sew them to either side with a ¼" seam allowance. Trim the batting and backing so it is even with the lamé and shape the top and bottom edges according to the diagram. Bind the edges in the same gold metallic.

The appliquéd circles are then layered and quilted, and bound in the same gold metallic. Sew the three pieces together by hand so that the circle slightly overlaps the top and bottom.

Our Lady of the Holy Spirit: Using Photo Transfers

It is possible to transfer photographs to fabric using a fairly inexpensive process. The banner Josephine designed for the twenty-fifth anniversary of the parish of Our Lady of the Holy Spirit utilizes this technique in a unique and interesting way: Mary's dress is composed of many individual photographs of parish members, all shot against a blue background. See the photos on page 192.

In the design, Josephine wished to portray the power of the Spirit and the nature of the Spirit's relationship with Mary. Mary does not just receive, but embraces the Spirit, allowing the Spirit to permeate every action of her life. The size of the flame reflects the power of the Spirit. Its diagonal lines curve into shapes suggesting a dove, another of the Spirit's manifestations. Mary's hair is wind-blown as she reaches out in welcome. Her garment is pieced of photos of parishioners at Our Lady of the Holy Spirit parish, showing that the Spirit continues to breathe in our lives and we are called to welcome that Spirit. The photos that did not fit in the garment were pieced into the border.

The process for photo transfers is quite simple, requiring only a laser color copier and a special transfer paper (one brand is Photo Effects by Hues Inc., available from Nancy's Notions). The resultant copy is ironed onto white fabric, which can be then used in sewing. Finely woven fabric best shows the details (Nancy's Notions sells "Southern Belle Broadcloth" specifically for this purpose, as well as a video and booklet explaining the process in greater detail).

To make Mary's garment, Josephine cut the shape from white muslin and appliquéd it to the background in the usual way. Then she had photo transfers made from each page in the parish's photo directory. She cut apart the photo transfers and placed them to fill the space of the garment. She ironed these on to the muslin following the directions on the package of photo transfer paper. It is important to do the appliqué first, as the heat required for fusible webbing would melt the transfers if they were already on the fabric.

The face and hands were appliquéd with warm beige fabric, and details were added with permanent markers (using Pigma Micron Permanent pens, which contain acid-free archival ink that will not bleed or blur. Always test markers on the fabrics with which they will be used, since they can bleed as you use them.). These details could have been added with machine stitching instead, following the instructions in Deidre Scherer's book, *Deidre Scherer: Work in Fabric and Thread* (Lafayette, CA: C & T Publishing, 1998).

Centennial Banner: Using Fabric Markers

Draw the church on a light-colored cotton fabric with a washable blue marking pen (such as Dritz Mark-B-Gone). To draw the shape easily and accurately, project a photograph or architect's drawing of the church onto the cloth with an opaque projector and trace the lines. Write the names of the parishioners with permanent fine-tip fabric markers on all the lines. Fill in the shadows with rows and rows of names. Wash the fabric and the blue lines are gone.

We used this technique for a centennial banner for the St. Louis Province of the School Sisters of Notre Dame. The one-hundred-year-old provincial house is drawn with names of the sisters, all who have ever been members, because all have contributed to the charism and ongoing life of the province. See photo on page 191.

In your parish, including the names of deceased members might make the list entirely too long. However, you could include them by filling in the lining with names. Invite others in the parish to help you, particularly those with good penmanship. Make the writing itself a greater faith experience by starting with prayer and scripture readings. Ask those participating to share stories of the people whose names they are writing.

The concept of the people of God as church might be strengthened even more if each parish member wrote his or her own name on the banner. This mammoth project would require careful scheduling and supervision, but it could be a valuable experience for all. No matter which method you use for writing the names, consider devising a way to add names. You might do so at the time of baptism or confirmation.

CYANOTYPE

The first step in this process is to order the light-sensitive fabric. (Order a minimum of one yard of sensitized cotton fabric from Blueprints-Printables, 1-800-356-0445. Or send $3.00 for a catalog with fabric samples to 1504 Industrial Way #7, Belmont CA 94002.) Next, have a negative transparency made for each photo in the exact size needed. This can be done as a photographic process or by a laser color copier. If you use the laser copier, tell the person handling the copy machine that by "negative" you mean reversing the black and white of the photo and that you want it printed on acetate. You will also need a piece of glass large enough to cover the negative and a board for arranging the materials.

In a darkened room, spread the fabric on the board, place the negative on top, and sandwich it firmly with the glass. Then bring this sandwich outside and expose to sunlight for about eight minutes. (Specific directions on how to experiment to find the correct exposure time are sent with the fabric.) Rinse the fabric thoroughly in running water until all the excess chemicals are washed away. This also stops the image from getting darker. After it has dried, wash it in cool water with a small amount of gentle soap, rinse it thoroughly, and iron it with a hot iron.

The color of the photograph produced with this process is a warm blue close to that of denim. The directions sent with the fabric include a way to turn the color of the cyanotype from blue to brown. This is particularly effective when an antique look is desired, or when it better fits your color scheme.

Combine your photos with other fabrics for a pleasing design. Consider incorporating the blocks into traditional quilt block designs, as shown in the photographs on page 191, bottom. Although made for home use, these samples illustrate how cyanotype photos can be combined with a shoo-fly block and with the double wedding ring.

Latin cross.

Greek cross.

Jerusalem cross.

Cathedral cross.

Anchor cross.

Dove.

Another dove.

Chi-Rho.

Alpha and Omega.

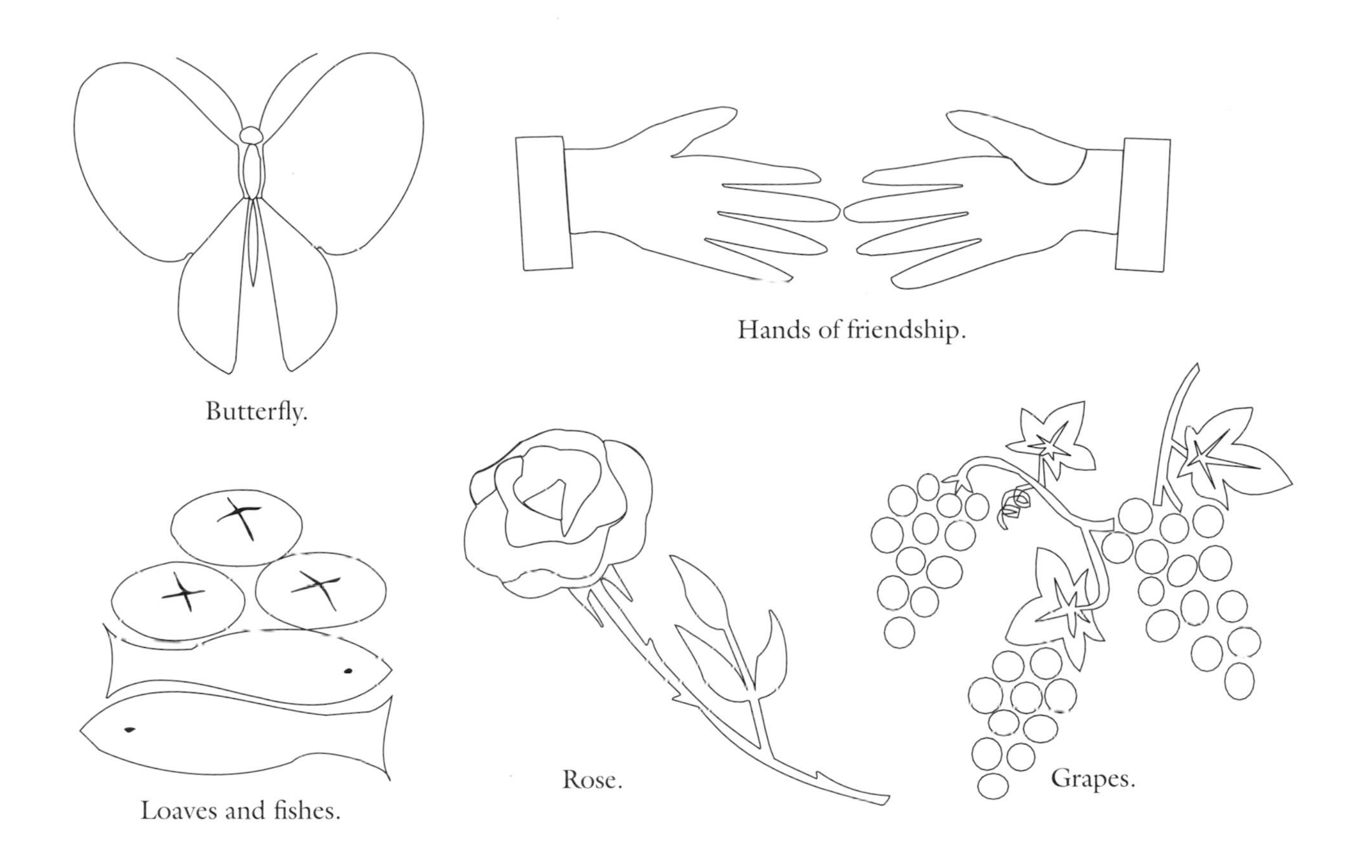

Butterfly.

Hands of friendship.

Loaves and fishes.

Rose.

Grapes.

Sources for Appliqué Designs

Sources for appliqué designs are as varied as your imagination. Look around you and you will see designs you can adapt and sew as machine appliqué banners. To help you on your way, we provide a small library of images that you can use or adapt in designing your own banners. These include several crosses, an alpha and omega, a dove, and bread and fish to fill your pieced basket. Since we drew all of these drawings, you are free to use, combine, and adapt them to suit your personal purposes. Use the general techniques of enlarging to make them the right size. Piecing the background of your appliqué, perhaps using the colorwash technique, will add interest to your banner.

Pieced Pictures

The technique of pieced pictures provides quilters with a versatile tool for sewing a variety of curved shapes without finishing edges. Briefly, you draw a design on a piece of paper the size of the finished banner and use the drawing as a pattern for the shapes in the banner. By adding seam lines in the appropriate places, a great variety of shapes can be pieced and sewn on the sewing machine. If you want to sew by machine and desire flatness and clean edges with no visible lines of thread, pieced pictures may be for you. You can always add decorative stitching later, in the places you want, not where the construction dictates. While you could make any of the designs in this section by using appliqué, we chose to do them by piecing.

You have two options for drawing your cartoon, or pattern: Draw full size, or enlarge a smaller drawing. In either case, start with a piece of paper at least as large as your finished banner and draw the banner's outline on it, using a #2 pencil. Then tape the paper to the wall with either drafting tape or painter's tape.

When you draw full-sized, use your whole arm and sweeping gestures to create free and spontaneous drawings. If you find yourself erasing too much, draw on a chalkboard or whiteboard. Then trace the finished product on tissue paper.

If you prefer to design using smaller sketches, or already have an image you would like to enlarge for your banner (including those in this book), use the directions provided earlier to enlarge the design to the appropriate size.

Design with the sewing in mind, so that you have many long lines. This allows the cartoon to be broken up more easily into sewable sections. Once you have your full-sized cartoon, examine it carefully to find where you might need to add a line to further break down the shapes for ease of piecing, and add these lines now.

Pam prefers to add a line rather than inset a sharp angle. The effect of the seam will be negligible if you use the same fabric on both sides. (For further instruction on drawing cartoons for pieced pictures, see Ruth McDowell's books, *Piecing: Expanding the Basics* and *Pieced Flowers.*)

This will be your master cartoon. Now make a second cartoon to cut up for pattern pieces. This second cartoon is made in reverse of the first, so that your finished banner will look like your master cartoon. Pam uses freezer paper for the second cartoon, since it can be ironed to the fabric for greater accuracy. Tape together the 18" wide freezer paper with masking tape to form a big enough sheet.

To make the freezer-paper cartoon, reverse the master cartoon and tape the freezer paper to it, dull side up. Lay this paper sandwich on a light box or tape it to a window and trace the lines. If you used an overhead projector for your enlargement and have not yet moved it, you could turn over the acetate sheet and project the design on the dull side of the freezer paper. Before cutting your freezer-paper cartoon apart, draw an upward-pointing grain-line arrow on each pattern piece. For some sections, it may also help to code each pattern piece and the corresponding position on the master cartoon to help you remember where each piece goes. Draw hatch marks across each curved seam, 1" or 2" apart; on tight curves, the hatch marks should be 1/2" apart. These registration marks will help you line up the curves later. They do not have to be equally spaced. On any pattern piece that is a closed curve, like a circle, place a double hatch mark to indicate where to start lining up the piece when you are ready to pin. Do not cut the whole freezer-paper cartoon now, but cut out each section as you need it.

The next step is choosing the fabrics for each piece. We do not give yardage requirements for any of the pieces we describe here, since we assume you are working from a stash of fabric. If you need to supplement your stash, buy at least fat quarter yards (18" x 22"), if not half-yards.

"Audition" fabrics by folding several to the approximate size of the pattern pieces and placing them on the cartoon. Once you have decided, cut out the freezer paper pattern piece and lay it on the reverse side of the fabric, dull side up, lining up the arrow with the grain line. Make sure there is about 1/4" of space around the pattern piece. Using a medium hot iron (synthetic setting) and no steam, iron the freezer paper pattern piece to the fabric for about 10 seconds. Trace around the pattern piece with a #2 pencil or a white, silver, or yellow pencil—whatever works. Extend the hatch marks into the seam allowance. Cut around the pattern piece leaving a seam allowance of about 1/4" around all edges.

Leaving the pattern attached, place the piece right side up over the corresponding area of your master cartoon. Continue auditioning fabrics and cutting and placing pieces as you go. Step back occasionally and squint at the cartoon to make sure there is sufficient contrast for the design to be seen from a distance. If you change your mind about a piece, pull off the freezer-paper pattern piece and reuse it on another fabric.

Once you are satisfied with your fabric choices for a section of the banner, determine a logical order for sewing. When you've decided what should be sewn first, a process we will discuss in the context of specific projects, pin those pieces together by carefully inserting pins perpendicularly through the matching points at the ends of the seamlines. When these points are lined up, finish insertisng the pin. Then pin at each hatch mark in between, lining up the penciled seam lines. Sew the seam inside the penciled lines. Press the seam allowances to one side.

You can manipulate the appearance of the piece by the manner in which you press the seams. If you want an element to appear to recede, press the seam away from that element. For example, if you inset an eye, you will want it to appear set in the face, so press the seam away from the eye. To make an element come forward, press toward it. Continue constructing each next logical level of sections until the top is completed.

As you look through the projects in this section, read through all the instructions, even if you do not intend to make the project. The project descriptions are intended to illustrate the basic techniques and to present others that you may find inspiring and useful.

Celtic Cross.

Celtic Cross: Basic Picture with Straight Edges and Round Circles

This project has relatively simple geometry. You could draw the cartoon for this project with not much more than a straight-edge and a yardstick compass, but enlarging the drawing will keep the proportions correct. Some paper piecing is involved, making this a hybrid project.

Inspired by the name of the church, this Celtic Cross was designed by Pam for St. Patrick Church in Farmington, Connecticut, for general use during the year, but particularly for first communion liturgies. The design is fairly simple, containing only straight lines and circular arcs, but it is made elegant through the fabric choices. The background of this banner is natural-colored raw silk, which has a nubby texture and handles nicely. The other fabrics are hand-dyed Bali batiks and African tie-dyes. Cotton floral fabrics might make a nice banner, but here, the unusual, high-quality fabrics make this piece a treasure. See the photo on page 192, bottom.

Begin by making the master cartoon and the freezer-paper pattern, following the general directions. Put hatch marks on all seam lines; put a double hatch mark on the center of the circle so that you know where to begin pinning. Start your selection of fabrics with the background. You might want to wait to actually cut the background pieces until you have made your other fabric selections. Hang the background on the wall or lay it on a flat surface and test your other fabric selections on it.

Since the fabric used in the cross dominates the piece and must work well with the background, choose it next. Pam used a brown Bali batik with blue and golden highlights, which added interest. If your fabric has any kind of stripe pattern in it, cut the arms of the cross so that the stripe goes either widthwise or lengthwise on all four pieces.

Before you begin cutting the freezer-paper pattern, label the four cross arms, the four large circular arcs, the four small circular arcs and the background wedges so you remember how to line them up. Make sure the hatch marks match. Iron the freezer-paper patterns for the cross arms on your chosen fabric and cut around the outside, leaving 1/4" seam allowance. Trace the pattern pieces and transfer any marks.

The large circular arcs are most easily and accurately pieced by paper-piecing each arc, rather than cutting out each segment individually. If you are careful not to let the iron touch the freezer paper, this should work fine. Use a variety of medium to dark blues for the circular arcs. They should be fairly similar in color and value, with enough variation to make it interesting. Once you've selected your fabrics, cut them into strips slightly wider than the width of an individual segment at the outer edge. Arrange the strips into a pleasing pattern and paper-piece the arcs.

Selecting the fabric for the small inner arcs and the central circle presents the most challenge, because here at the center of the banner everything must be in balance. The fabric chosen for the center was a golden yellow, not too intense, but warmly glowing. The arcs had a similar tone, but included more colors. Make sure you put a double hatch mark on the freezer-paper pattern so you know where to begin lining up the marks when you inset the circle.

Assuming you're still satisfied with the background fabric, cut the large piece of background and the four inner background wedges. Begin the construction by piecing the circular arcs (in their proper positions) to the large background piece. Then piece the background wedges to the corresponding arcs. Iron toward the circular arcs.

The cross arms have corners that must be inset, which means sewing each segment of the seam separately. Start by sewing a small circular arc to the end of each cross arm. Begin the sewing of each cross arm to the background with the short seam at the end of the cross. Pin from corner to corner, back-tacking at both ends and sewing only on the pencil line. Carefully clip the background fabric to the stitching line in both corners. Pivot the background fabric so that it lines up along the long edge of the cross arm. Starting at the corner, sew to the seam where the small arc is sewn and the seam turns a slight angle, and lower the needle. Pivot, pin the remainder of the seam, and sew off the end. Iron toward the cross.

The center circle is sewn last. Begin the pinning of the circle by lining up the double hatch mark. As you sew this curved seam, manipulate the background fabric so that it curves outward and lines up with the curve of the circle. Do not try to force both seams to be straight. Iron the seam toward the circle and the top is finished.

The simple quilting of the banner echoes its spare lines. It is stitched in the ditch along each seam-line and then stitched on the background in lines radiating from the center. A variety of colors were used in the ribbons, including metallic gold and dark blue. The darker colors contrast nicely with the background.

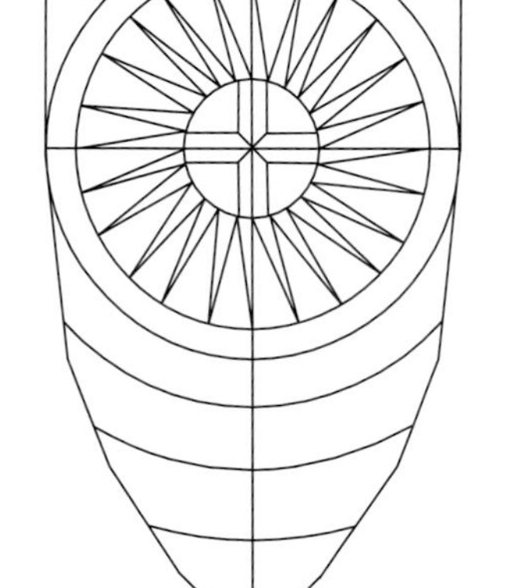

First Communion banners.

First Communion Banners: Piecing Circular Curves and a Simple Gradation

These banners for St Francis Xavier (College) Church at St. Louis University were the first that Pam made. The short amount of time available to make these banners inspired her to adapt a block on which she had been working. A circular sun with a glowing cross in the center, both symbols for Christ, is surrounded by ever-widening circles. One is colored like bread, the other wine. Ten years later, these banners continue to lead the first communion processions and the Holy Thursday processions, where they can be seen in LTP's video "Holy Thursday" in its *Liturgies of the Triduum* series. They even punctuated a visit from the Dalai Lama. (See the photos on page 193.) Pam made the design a second time in fabrics from all over the world for a Christ Our Light banner (collection of David and Lynda Rands) that won an art award. Like the ripples of a pond, this Christ touches every corner of creation.

The design of these banners is somewhat more complex than the Celtic Cross, but still only contains straight lines and circular arcs. It has one long vertical division and one long horizontal division, which should be cut first. Each quadrant then has three components: the inner circle containing the cross, the arcs with the sun's rays, and the unsegmented outer arcs. The cross and the sun ray arcs are all paper pieced. As long as you don't iron directly on the freezer paper, you should be able to use that for the foundation piece. But if your iron slips, the paper should peel off.

Beginning with the arc rays, notice that quadrant of the arc is divided into six sections, each further divided by a diagonal line. The narrow sliver is called the ray and the wider pie is the background. Make three piles of fabric in your chosen color scheme: light, medium, and dark. The mediums are used for the rays in all four quadrants. The backgrounds in two of the quadrants are light, and the other two are dark. After you have arranged your fabrics and are satisfied, paper-piece each arc quadrant, starting at one end and piecing consecutive pieces. Lay them on your master cartoon, alternating light and dark backgrounds.

For the cross, choose a set of solid fabrics that range from light to dark. Arrange them in a graduated progression from light to dark. Stand back and squint to make sure the progression is smooth. Replace fabrics as needed. For the best effect, the gradation should begin with white or cream and end with black or a very dark shade. You can include a metallic in this gradation for sparkle, but be careful with its placement, as metallics tend to read darker than you might think.

Each inner quarter-circle contains two cross sections, one along each of its straight edges. Orient the quarters the same and treat them identically with a straight edge on the left and another on the bottom: Make the vertical cross section progress from light in the center to dark at the edge, and the horizontal section progress from dark to light. After paper-piecing the cross sections, arrange them on your master cartoon. Audition fabrics for the background of the inner circle. The same fabric is used in all four arcs. You will probably find a medium-light fabric will look the best. Finish piecing the quarter-circles. Sew the quarter-circles to the sun ray arcs.

Now audition fabrics for the unbroken outer arcs, following the value placements in the photograph. Note that these alternate in value within a circle. Piece the outer arcs in each quadrant together and sew them to the outer edges of the sun ray arcs. Piece the four quadrants together.

The completed top is finished with a self-edge and quilted. The ribbons are mainly white and off-white. Narrow ribbons in matching colors accent each piece.

Easter Sunrise Banner: Determining an Order for Piecing a Free-form Design

Easter Sunrise banner.

When you construct a pieced picture, certain seams must be sewn in a certain order for the construction to be reasonable. Understanding the stages involved in piecing this design will help you understand how to sew other designs, as well as how to break up a shape in your own drawing. With this Easter Sunrise banner that Josephine made for St. Mark's Church in Indianapolis, we will discuss what kind of seams to look for and how to break up a section for sewing. Notice the exuberantly joyful colors used in this banner. The fuschia, turquoise, and yellow echo the colors of both the central stained glass window in the church and the flowers of Eastertime. See the photo on page 193, bottom right.

This design is composed of three main parts: the sun, the sun's rays, and the background sky and clouds. Notice that long smooth piecing lines delineate each area; the sun is bounded by a simple curved line and the rays by straight lines. These long lines allow you to break up the sewing into manageable sections. When you isolate one section, such as a ray, it becomes more obvious how to piece that section. Each ray has one straight strip and two curved strips. You will need to sew one straight seam and one curved; the order of

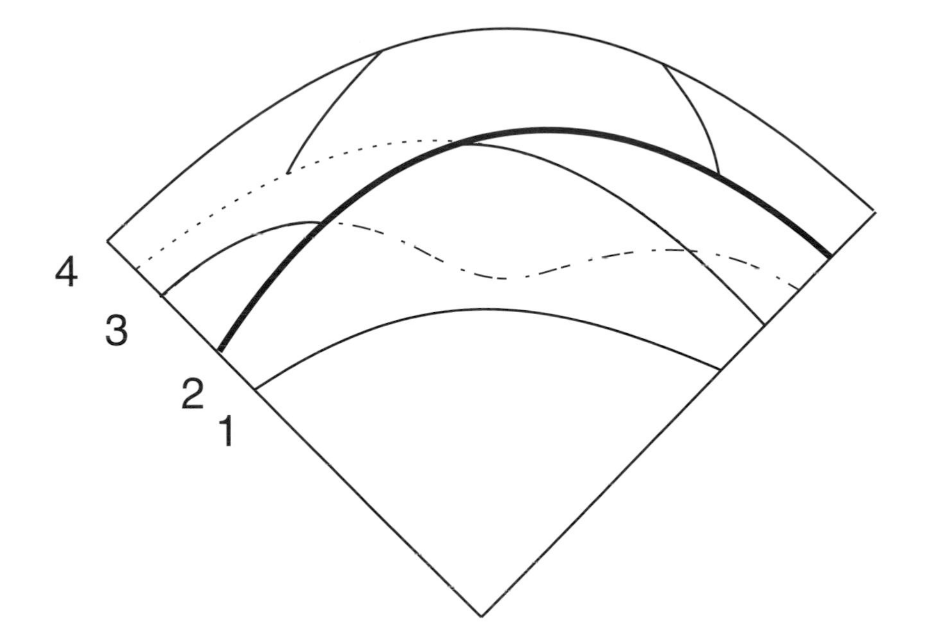

Piecing order for sun in Easter Sunrise.

sewing does not matter. When sewing the curves, line up the beginning and end points, as well as one set of hatch marks in the middle. Then match up the remaining hatch marks and pin. When feeding the seam under the needle, manipulate the top fabric so that it follows the curve of the bottom; do not try to force top and bottom into a straight line. Maintain order by placing each ray on your cartoon as you finish.

The piecing of the background clouds and sky also becomes more clear when you isolate one section of background. Their construction is similar to that of the rays, except that the divisions are horizontal rather than vertical. Again, the order of sewing does not matter. Once you've sewn all the rays and backgrounds, you can piece them together, following the order indicated by the cartoon.

The sun is a more complex unit whose piecing requires further breakdown. To break down a section, look for a smooth line that connects one edge to another and intersects other lines. There are 4 lines that connect one straight edge of the sun to the other (numbered in the drawing above). Number 1 intersects no other lines, so the order of its piecing is irrelevant. Number 3 intersects another line and could be used as a divider. However, this division is uneven, leaving an area nearly as complex as that with which we started.

Number 2 (in bold) neatly separates the sun into two simpler units, an inner pie shape and an outer ring, which we can treat separately. Analyzing the pie shape, we find two lines intersecting, so we need a further division into smaller units (dotted line); note that we could have chosen either line. Sew each of the two smaller sections, then sew the dotted line seam. Add the piece of pie that line 1 separates and you have completed the inner pie shape.

The outer ring also contains an intersection, requiring a further breakdown into smaller units (dotted line). However, this time there is no choice about how the shape can be broken down. Construct the two smaller segments, sew the dotted line seam, and complete the sun by sewing the outer ring to the inner pie shape. Finish by sewing the sun to the rays and background and add the plain border.

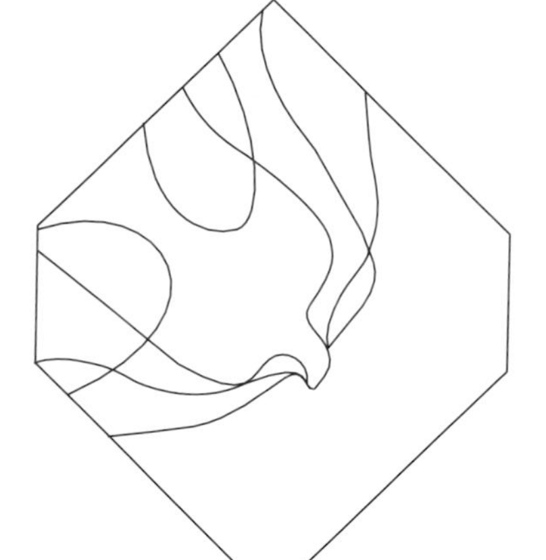

Dove.

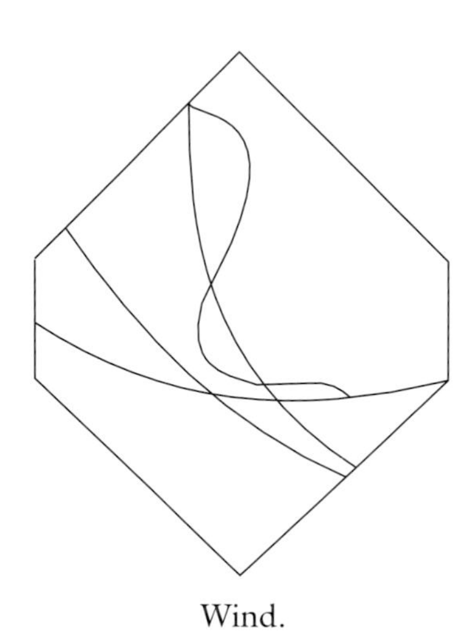

Wind.

PENTECOST DOVE AND WIND BANNERS: SPARE AND ELEGANT DESIGN

Like the Celtic Cross, the Dove and Wind banners rely on spare and elegant design. They are a matching pair of banners designed by Josephine for Webster Groves Presbyterian Church, in Webster Groves, Missouri. During Pentecost, the banners are carried in procession, leading the choir and the ministers into church, and then placed on opposite sides of the chancel. The diagonal lines of the design suggest the strong, powerful movement of the Pentecost wind. This wind was a force that changed lives forever. Scattered, fearful followers became firm and active disciples. See the photos on page 194, top.

The piecing of these two banners requires some analysis for order of construction. The beak of the dove will be the most difficult area to piece, since it is inset. Start your final seam in the middle at the beak, and sew it by hand, if necessary. Then complete the seam on either side.

One of the serendipitous accidents in the construction of the dove banner was the way the yellow section of the dove's wing flowed into the yellow ribbons, effectively extending the wing. Had Josephine realized this at the time, she would have designed the wind banner similarly, so that a yellow section of the wind flowed into yellow ribbons. Try altering the design to get this effect.

If you make this design, you can choose different shades of red. True red is the most commonly used shade for the Holy Spirit, but you could start with a red that harmonizes well with the interior of your church for the dominant color. Find three other colors that look good with this red, one of which is white or off-white. For example, when Josephine made a similar set of banners for Holy Infant Church in Ballwin, Missouri, she felt that the colors should harmonize with the mauve carpet. She started with a dark red and added blue, white, and gray, which complemented the carpet.

The Dove and Wind banners were made with cotton fabrics, but using raw silk or lightweight wool would give these banners a rich look and texture. Hand-dyed fabrics would work well, even if they contain more than one color. Other prints with irregular textures might provide depth and interest.

The Stars Declare His Glory Banner: Using a Gradation of Prints

Pam designed The Stars Declare His Glory banner to accompany a 10' by 7' quilted backdrop for a nativity scene she made for St. Francis Xavier (College) Church in St. Louis for use during the Christmas season. The banner is carried in procession on Christmas and Epiphany, and remains stationary near the ambo throughout the rest of the season. A large star/cross dominates a dark night sky, bringing to mind simultaneously the Star of the Magi and the cross, the beginning and end of Christ's earthly life. For Pam, the image links the crèche and the cross, joining them together to shine through the mystery of the night. See the photo on page 194, bottom.

The design is broken down along the horizontal and vertical straight lines of the star. Three of the quadrants are further broken down for construction along the horizontal and vertical lines of the stars they contain. The piecing of each of these quadrants is fairly simple, the only further breakdown required being that the sections where the falling stars, or white speckles, lie must be pieced first. The difficult aspect of this banner is designing the gradation of prints for the rays of the star. The gradations are not only long, they're uneven; the bottom ray is considerably longer than the other three. Therefore, it must have additional fabrics in it that look consistent with the gradation established in the short rays.

Designing a print gradation is a bit more challenging than using solids or mainly solids. Before attempting this project, practice arranging gradations in solids. Once you have a feeling for how to arrange fabrics from light to dark, move on to prints. It is easiest to work with prints that do not contain large contrasts in value, that is, no black and white checks. In addition, it helps if the prints do not contain large contrasts in color, being mainly one color or a set of harmonious colors similar in value. Bits of a contrasting color can add spice, as long as they are small.

For a gradation to shine most effectively, it must range through the widest possible range of values. Begin with white or cream and end with black or dark navy. In this case, the darkest color of the gradation will also be the dominant color of the background. Thus, the bright white of the star center contrasts sharply with the background and the ray fades into the background as it extends. Use a solid white for greatest contrast with the background.

With white as the center, the gradation progressed with a white-on-cream print, through yellow to orange, each progressively darker in value. At the shift from orange to blue, the value is kept constant, so that only one aspect of the gradation changes at a time. The blues get deeper until the ray merges with the background. Notice that the bands of color, or the strip sizes used in the gradation, get wider as the color gets deeper. This is meant to mimic the effect of light falling off in the darkness; since light grows dimmer with the square of the distance, widening the strips helps the star glow. The shorter arms of the ray have the same progression of prints as the long pole, but stop sooner in the gradation.

Notice that the smaller stars contain gradations with different colors, including peach, reddish purple, and lavender. Varying the star colors, while using the same kind of gradation, makes the piece more interesting. As you work with long print gradations, take the time to stand back and squint. It is not always obvious which is the darker of two fabrics. Practice helps train your eye. Take a break if it seems too hard. Your efforts will add up.

Circle of Friends: Expressing Diversity through Fabric and Design

The Roman liturgical calendar contains eight days called the Octave of Christian Unity. During this week the church prays particularly for the unity of all Christian churches. The Second Vatican Council formally initiated the modern ecumenical movement of working toward Christian unity, and since then various groups have been studying and discussing the doctrinal issues over which rifts developed, separating the churches. A few years ago, officials of the Lutheran and the Roman Catholic churches signed a statement proclaiming that salvation comes through faith, and good works flow naturally from that faith. The significance is tremendous considering that "salvation comes through faith alone" was the basic belief underlying many of Martin Luther's objections to the Catholic church centuries ago.

The attitude of appreciation for diversity applies within a church community, as well as between communities. We are called to love one another, requiring that we reach out to those who differ from us. Age, sex, skin color, ethnic background, physical ability, intelligence, and other human characteristics must not divide the People of God. One way to show that we appreciate and value all members of our community is to make a banner reflecting our differences. Use fabrics or designs from the countries of origin of people living in your area. If you have a "sister" parish, ask them to send you fabric made in their country and use it along with your own. Use a design that expresses a sense of outreach, both within your own

Circle of Friends.

community and to other communities and countries, one that speaks clearly of our desire for unity of Christ's love within our diversity. Use it during the Octave of Christian Unity. Use it when a missionary comes to give an appeal. See the photo on page 195, top left.

Josephine designed the Circle of Friends banner to be used on such occasions. The circle of people can be adapted in many ways, by changing the sizes and proportions of the figures, and the colors of fabric used in the faces. Make some of the people children, some elderly (with white hair), some with handicaps (perhaps with a wheelchair), and use fabric from different countries in the clothing to make it inclusive.

You can also change the orientation of the figures within the circles, perhaps positioning the block on point and adding corner arrows, suggesting compass points. If your banner is very large, with a considerable space in the center, put a globe, or other symbol of the world, in the middle.

As you construct this banner, you may find piecing the heads to be a challenge if they are small. If you think you could not handle them easily in the machine, piece them by hand. Start pinning at the double hatch mark that helps you line up a closed shape, and pin and sew a small segment of the line. Use a small running stitch to sew that segment, and continue pinning and sewing a small segment at a time. Take a single backstitch every so often for strength. Iron the seams toward the head so it stands out from the background. Alternatively, hand-appliqué the heads.

Daniel's Baptism Banner: Using Name Symbols for a Banner Design

When Pam's third son, Daniel Christopher, was born in January, the prospect of a spring baptism sent her to her studio. She would design a banner for the baptism, incorporating imagery of the biblical Daniel, which the family would carry as they walked from their house to the church. She began by drawing the lion, so strongly associated with Daniel. The lamb is a symbol for Christ, as is the cross gently illuminating the morning sky. She added a watery blue-green border at the top, for baptismal imagery. And on that perfect May afternoon, which happened also to be Pentecost, the town was

Symbols for Names

Andrew—saltire, or x-shaped cross, fish, patron of Scotland, fishermen, and sailors

Anne—red dress represents love, green cape represents immortality

Ambrose—beehive, patron of domestic animals and beekeepers

Augustine—heart in hand, heart can be broken or whole, can be aflame

Barbara—tower, peacock feather

Catherine—sword of martyrdom, book for wisdom, Catherine wheel

David—harp, Star of David

Gregory—dove on the shoulder, patron of musicians

Jerome—lion, patron of students

Joan—fleur-de-lis

John—eagle, represents the soaring majesty and inspiration of his writing

Joseph—flowering rod, carpenter's tools

Luke—winged ox

Mark—winged lion

Margaret—dragon, patroness of childbirth

Mary—cape of blue represents constancy, dress of red represents suffering and love, white dress represents purity, purple dress represents royalty, mystical rose, twelve stars around her head represent the Immaculate Conception, one star represents Mary, Star of the Sea

Matthew—winged man or angel, sword or ax, purse

Nicholas—three gold balls or bags of gold

Patrick—shamrock, representing the Trinity

Paul—usually depicted as small, with a long face and straight beard, often with sword or book

Peter—two crossed keys, rooster, patron of butchers, bakers, and clockmakers

Stephen—stone

Thomas—carpenter's rule or square, patron of architects, carpenters, and geometricians

treated to a unique procession, including children waving hand-painted flags and a baby carriage festooned with lilacs, all led by this wonderful banner. See the photo on page 181.

While you may not be up for a parade down your street, a banner with imagery associated with a name is personalized in a unique way. The church's symbolic heritage includes a rich assortment associated with names, a selection of which we provide here. Consider

Meanings of Flowers

Holly	crown of thorns, eternity, red berries suggest blood
Iris	another name is sword lily, prophetic symbol of the crucifixion in pictures of Mary
Laurel	immortality
Lily	purity, innocence, immortality
Myrtle	peace, love
Rose	white: purity, yellow: impossible perfection, red: martyrdom
Violet	humility

using imagery related to a name on baptismal and wedding banners. Since many names used today are not saint's names and would not be on the list, check out a book of baby names to find out whether the name was derived from a saint's name. And don't neglect the middle name in your search for symbols.

The design of Daniel's Baptism banner is rather complex and no line drawing is given. Briefly, the closed curves of the heads form two major sections and the straight arms of the cross two more. Pam sewed both sets of ears into the background before sewing in the face. The lion's head was pieced into the background first, and then the lamb's head. The eyes of both the lion and lamb had a small dot of white paint applied to them after the piecing, which brought the eyes to life. Note the painted ribbons scattered among the solid ribbons. She used blue and green acrylics thinned with water to paint the ribbons.

The realistic quality of this piece results from the careful use of a variety of fabrics. For example, the cross-hatched print near the lion's nose and mouth looks a lot like whiskers and the lion's mane is composed of a number of subtly striped tan and brown fabrics. Hand-dyed fabrics and Bali batiks are invaluable for this kind of piece. The sky fabric was hand-painted and lends an ethereal quality that would be impossible to duplicate with a print.

Queen of Heaven: Strategic Placement of Fabric

Pam designed the Queen of Heaven banner during a summer workshop with Deborah Anderson at the Quilt/Surface Design Symposium in Columbus, Ohio. Here, Mary reigns as the queen of heaven. Her head radiates light, as does her heart. Head and heart, thinking and feeling, balance. She is the one woman who never perceived herself as separated from God. Through her goodness and being, she points the way to her son, himself the Way. See the photo on page 195, top right.

Careful inspection of this banner reveals some interesting uses of fabric. In the crown, note how a number of golds, oranges, and yellows were selected, including a gold lamé. One perceives a single crown because the color values are similar. Yet, the mixture of colors and types of prints provides rich detailing and interest. Note a similar use of reds for the heart and blues for the cloak.

The fabric usage is most notable in the area surrounding the crown points. Here a Bali batik has been carefully cut so that the crown points appear to explode into space. This fabric has a background of navy, with bursts of orange and fuschia. Pam carefully placed the background patterns on these bursts to highlight the crown points. If you carefully study fabrics with large-scale designs, you may find that judicious planning and strategic placement of your pattern pieces produce spectacular results.

Waters of Life: Hand-Painting Fabrics for a Banner

Waters of Life is a baptismal banner in which hand-painted fabric is used extensively. Hand-painted fabric makes possible smooth and imaginative effects that could not be duplicated even by seaming commercially available prints. In fact, the hand-painted fabric Mickey Lawler has been making available to quilters nationally through her company, SkyDyes (83 Richmond Lane, West Hartford, CT 06117, www.skydyes.com), has changed they way many quilters work and think.

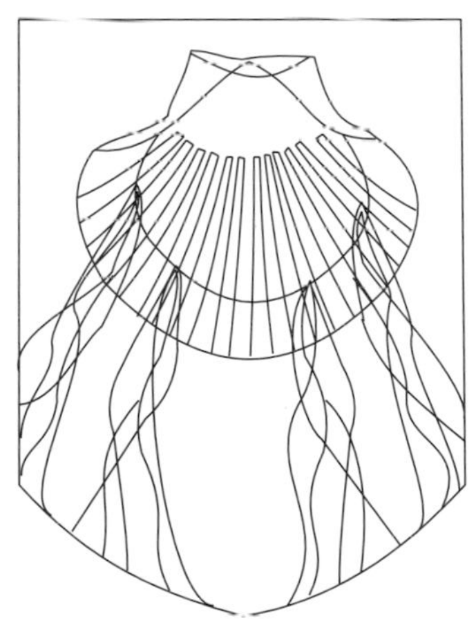

Waters of Life.

Waters of Life is Pam's most recent banner as of this writing, and was designed for a Christian Reformed Church in Ann Arbor, Michigan. It depicts a scallop shell, from which four streams of water flow. While a few more lines in the design and a variety of commercial prints would probably be adequate for the shell, its size and dominance in the design seemed to cry out for special treatment. How could one capture those nuances in the shading of the shell and its pearly quality? Pam chose to paint the fabric specifically for this piece. See the photos on page 195, bottom.

She used commercially available muslin print fabric, which needs no treatment to prepare it for painting. Deka pearlized white and Deka Silk rose and cinnamon brown paints, diluted with water, were used to paint the subtly colored shell. White glitter paint added more sparkle. She painted a dark border on one end of the fabric, and ironed the fabric according to the directions on the paint labels. Then she carefully cut out the shell pieces so that the dark border on the edge of the shell would fall in the right position and sewed the pieces together.

The streams of water were made from fabrics in her stash, which left only the background fabric to be chosen. When the piece of fabric she wanted to use for the sky was too small, fate intervened. After Pam showed the piece to her quilt group, Mickey Lawler volunteered to paint a background during an unforeseen break in the time she had blocked out for painting fabric for sale. The group felt that the top should be darker and the bottom light, which Mickey interpreted in a dappled blue-green water that explodes in foam. Mickey has shared the painting techniques she has developed through years of experience in her book, *SkyDyes: A Visual Guide to Fabric Painting*. Try fabric painting yourself, particularly for any area of a banner where you want a shift in color but feel that seams would detract from the integrity of the piece.

Cleaning and Storage of Banners

To keep your banners looking their best, they should be cleaned periodically and carefully stored in a darkened area with moderate humidity. Since processional banners receive only brief handling, their care is fairly simple. Many problems can be avoided by minimizing exposure to light and moisture during storage.

Besides light and moisture, the main enemies of fabric are dust and skin oils. To remove dust, use an upholstery attachment on your vacuum and adjust the power of the vacuum to be as low as possible. You can place net over the banner to further minimize the impact of the vacuum cleaner. Carefully vacuum both sides of the banner.

Handling the banner as little as possible minimizes the impact of skin oil. After a period of years, you might consider washing it. Should anything be spilled on the banner, you will certainly want to wash it. Assuming you have prewashed all your fabrics, including silk or wool, you should be able to wash the banner in cold water using a soap made specifically for washing quilts, such as Orvus Quilt Soap (available from Clotilde). Remove the ribbons first. Use the spin cycle on the washing machine to remove the excess water. Spread the banner flat on a layer of toweling in a darkened room and allow the banner to dry naturally.

Banners should be stored in a way that protects them from creasing, as well as dust, moisture, and light. Ideally, you will store the banners and ribbons either completely flat or hanging in a darkened closet and protected from dust. If you do not have such a storage facility, the next best option is to roll the banner and ribbons right side out around a muslin-covered tube, inserting acid-free tissue paper between the layers as you roll. Place the rolled banner in a muslin bag and store in a cool, dry, dark place.

Raise Your Banners

We hope that the ideas and banners we've presented have inspired you. If you feel the need to learn a bit more about color and design, look up some of the sources we quote. May your banners help all enter more deeply into the liturgy. May the Spirit of God guide you. Raise *your* banners high!

RESOURCES

BOOKS

Blair, Margot Carter, and Ryan, Cathleen. *Banners & Flags: How to Sew a Celebration,* New York: Harcourt Brace Janovich, 1977.

Cameron, Julia. *The Artist's Way: A Spiritual Path to Higher Creativity.* New York: G. P. Putnam's Sons, 1992.

Chiles, Lynette, and Joan Lewis. *Better Homes and Gardens 501 Quilt Blocks: A Treasury of Patterns for Patchwork & Applique.* Des Moines: Meredith Books, 1994.

Doak, Carol. *Easy Machine Paper Piecing: 65 Quilt Blocks for Foundation Piecing.* Bothell, Wash.: That Patchwork Place, 1994.

Edwards, Betty. *Drawing on the Right Side of the Brain.* Los Angeles: J. P. Tarcher, Inc., 1979.

Environment and Art in Catholic Worship. Washington: United States Catholic Conference, 1978.

Guelzow, Diane. *Banners with Pizazz: A Step by Step Guide.* San Jose, Cal.: Resource Publications, 1992.

Hall, Jane, and Dixie Haywood. *Foundation Quilts.* Paducah, Ky.: American Quilter's Society, 2000.

Hynes, Mary Ellen. *Companion to the Calendar.* Chicago: Liturgy Training Publications, 1993.

Jinzenji, Yoshiko. *Quilt Creation: Develop a New World of Quilted Texture.* Japan: Nihon Vogue-Sha, 1994.

LaLiberte, Norman. *Banners and Hangings.* Place: Reinhold, 1966

Laury, Jean Ray. *Imagery on Fabric.* Lafayette, Cal.: C & T Publishing, 1992.

Laury, Jean Ray. *The Photo Transfer Handbook.* Lafayette, Cal.: C & T Publishing, 1999.

Liddell, Jill. *The Patchwork Pilgrimage:How to Create Vibrant Church Decorations and Vestments with Quilting Techniques.* New York: Viking Studio Books, 1993.

Magaret, Pat Maixner, and Donna Ingram Slusser. *Watercolor Impressions.* Bothell, Wash.: That Patchwork Place, 1995.

Martin, Judy. *The Block Book.* Grinell, Iowa: Crosley-Griffith Publishing Co., Inc., 1998

Martin, Judy. *Scrap Quilts: Techniques Plus Patterns Old and New for Making Quilts from Collected Fabrics.* Wheatridge, Colo.: Moon over the Mountain Publishing Company, 1985.

Mazar, Peter. *To Crown the Year: Decorating the Church through the Seasons.* Chicago: Liturgy Training Publications, 1995.

McDowell, Ruth B. *Pieced Flowers.* Lafayette, Cal.: C & T Publishing, 2000.

McDowell, Ruth B. *Piecing: Expanding the Basics.* Lafayette, Cal: C & T Publishing, 1998.

Scherer, Deirdre. *Deidre Scherer: Work in Fabric and Thread.* Lafayette, Cal.: C & T Publishing, 1998.

Sill, Gertrude Grace. *A Handbook of Symbols in Christian Art.* New York: Collier Books, 1975.

Wolff, Colette. *The Art of Manipulating Fabric.* Radnor, Penn.: Chilton Book Company, 1996.

Wolfrom, Joen. *The Magical Effects of Color.* Lafayette, Cal.: C & T Publishing, 1992.

Journals and Organizations

American Quilter (4 issues per year), American Quilter's Society, 5801 Kentucky Dam Road, P.O. Box 3290, Paducah KY 42002-3290. 1-800-626-5420.

CIVA: Christians in the Visual Arts, P.O. Box 18117, Minneapolis MN 55418-0117. www.civa.org.

E & A: Environment and Art Letter, Liturgy Training Publications, 1800 North Hermitage Avenue, Chicago IL 60622-1101. 1-800-933-4213.

LAG: The Liturgical Art Guild, 501 East Broad Street, Columbus OH 43215.

Ministry and Liturgy (formerly *Modern Liturgy*), Resource Publications, Inc., 160 East Virginia Street, #290, San Jose CA, 95112.

Sources for Materials

American Quilter's Society, 5801 Kentucky Dam Road, P.O. Box 3290, Paducah KY 42002-3290; 1-800-626-5420 (books, computer programs, acid-free tissue paper).

Blueprints-Printables, 1400-A Marsten Road, Burlingame CA 94010-2422; 1-800-356-0445, www.blueprintables.com (cyanotype chemicals, pretreated yardage and print squares).

Clotilde, Inc., B 3000, Louisiana MO 63353-3000; 1-800-772-2891, www.clotilde.com (505 Spray & Fix, Orvus Quilt Soap).

Nancy's Notions, 333 Beichl Avenue, P.O. Box 683, Beaver Dam WI 53916-0683; 1-800-833-0690, www.nancysnotions.com (paper-backed fusible webbing, photo transfer paper, colorfast printer fabric, tracing paper, light table).

Web of Thread, 1410 Broadway, Paducah KY 42001; 1-800-955-8185, www.webofthread.com (100% cotton thread, wide variety of specialty threads).

For Nylon Fabric

Glaser Mills, Inc., 107 Northern Blvd., Great Neck NY 11021; 516-466-4028, www.glasermills.com (color charts for flag nylons and Solarmax nylon, 15-yd. minimum of each color).

Into the Wind, 1408 Pearl Street, Boulder CO 80302-5307; 1-800-541-0314, www.intothewind.com (eight colors of flag and windsock nylon, small minimum, hot gun with tip, fiberglass rods).

For small amounts in a greater variety of colors, check with your local flag manufacturers.

PATTERNS

On the following pages are the pattern pieces for the Amish Cross, Advent and Christmas Star, Festive Cross, Lenten Cross, and Resurrection Rose banners described on pages 111, 113, 116, 119, and 128.

Please feel free to photocopy these pattern pieces for use in your own banners.

For the sake of space, the pieces for the Amish Cross block are shown as if stacked atop each other. In order to use them correctly, photocopy the page twice and cut up the copies. Piece A is the whole square underlying B, C, and D. Piece I is the long trapezoid underlying pieces E and F; E underlies F. Once you have all the paper pattern pieces, proceed as described in the directions.

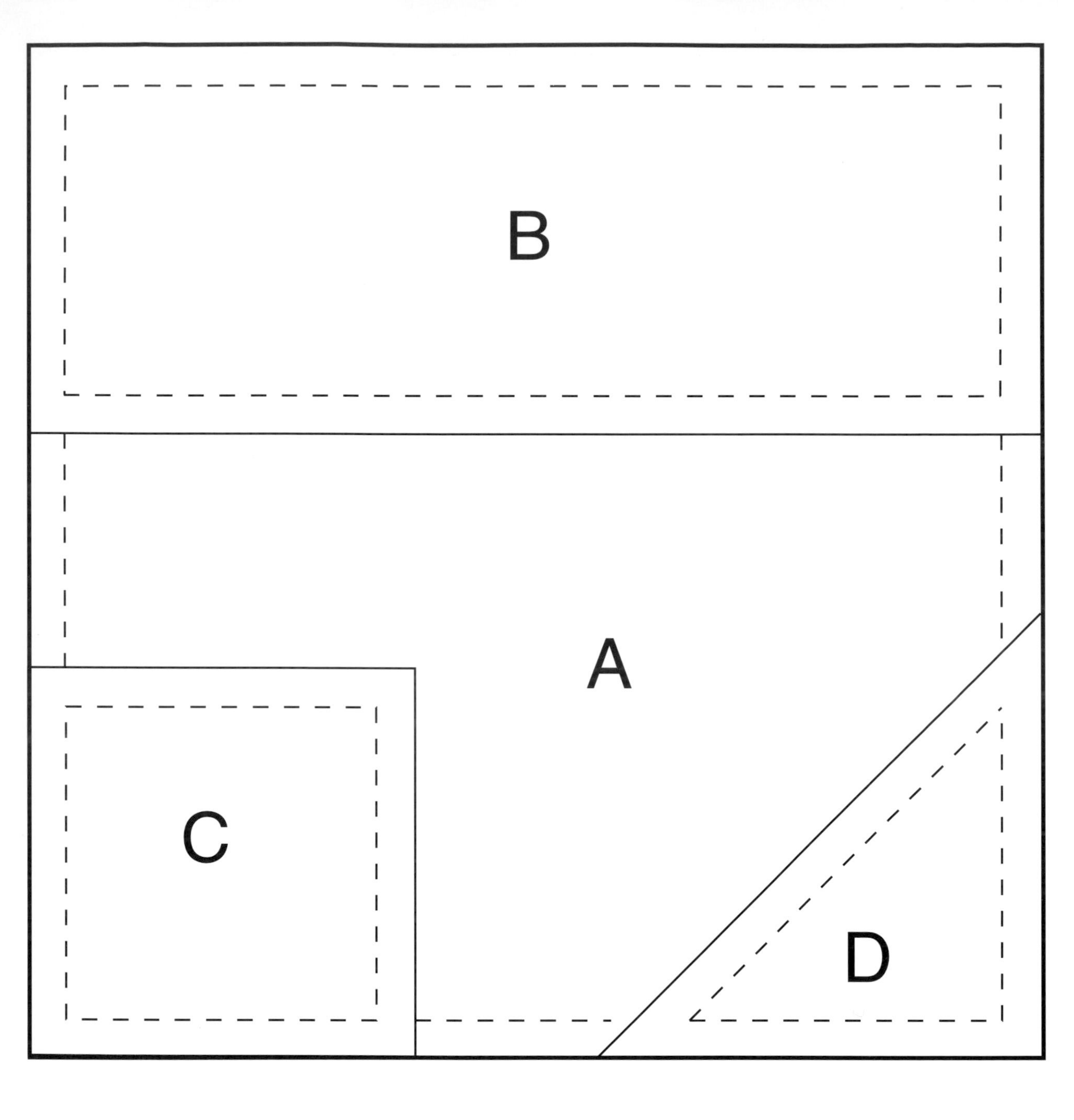

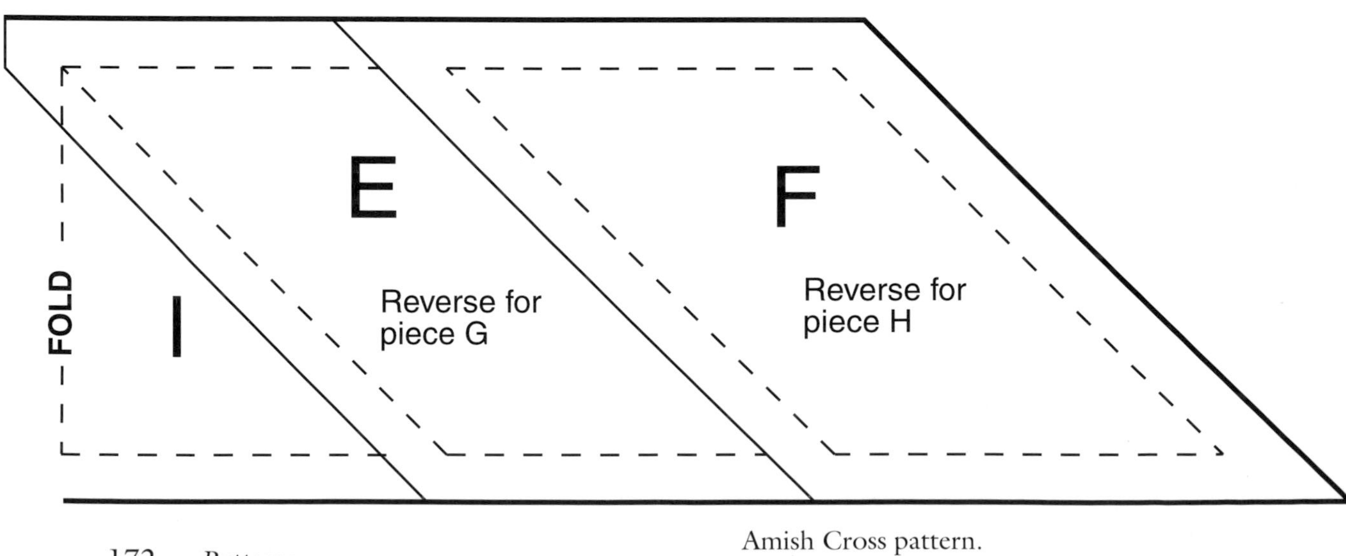

Amish Cross pattern.

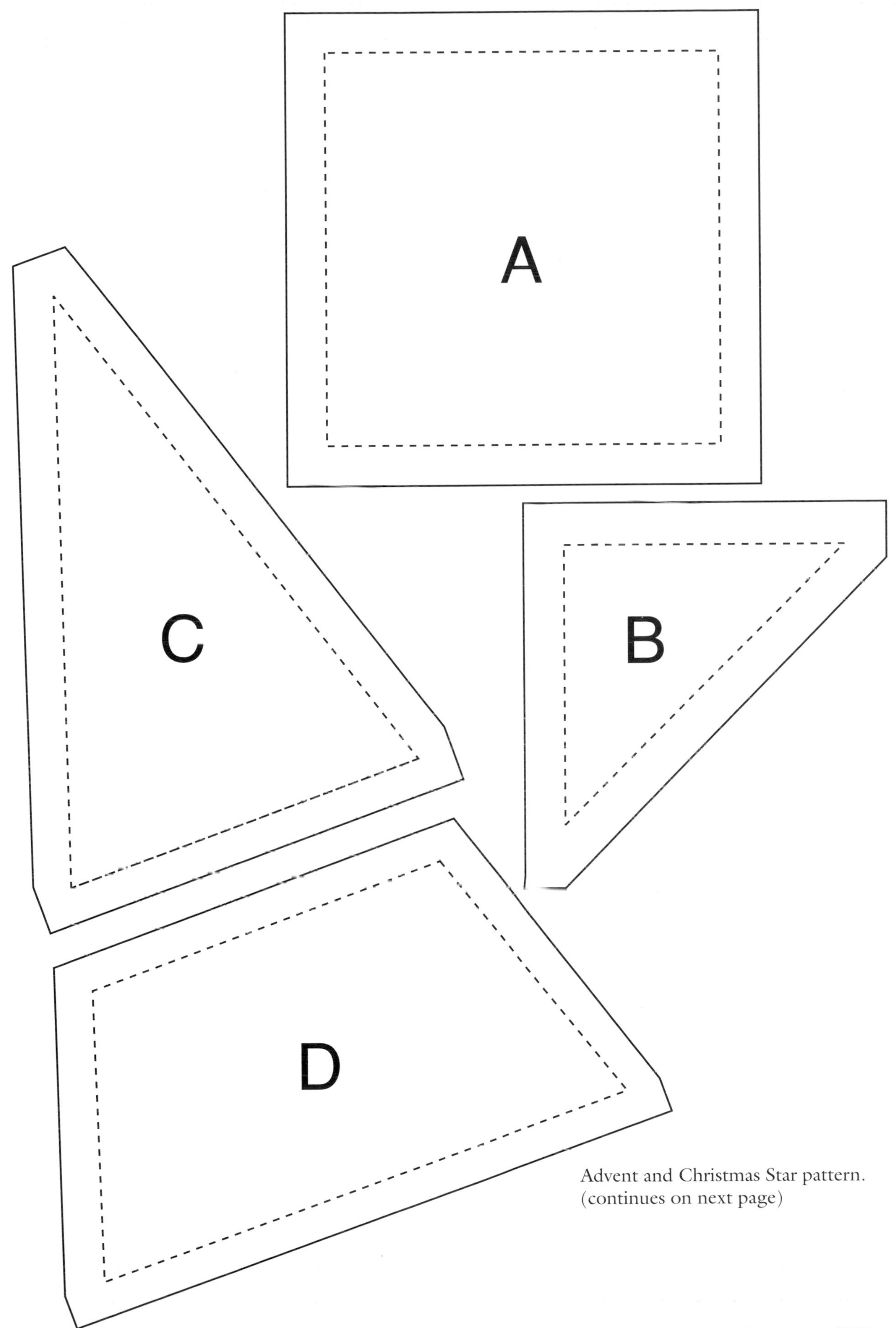

Advent and Christmas Star pattern.
(continues on next page)

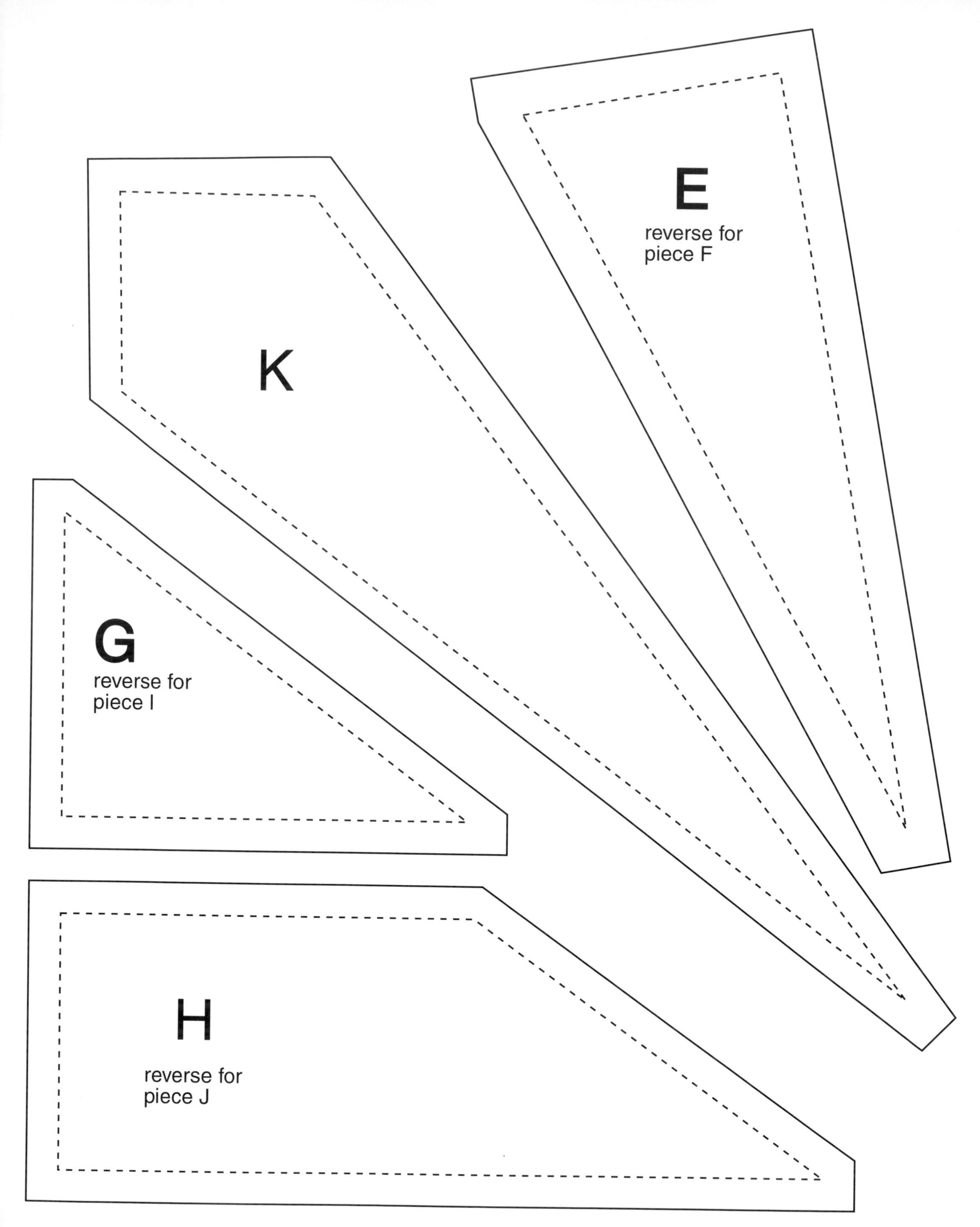

Advent and Christmas Star pattern.
(continued from previous page)

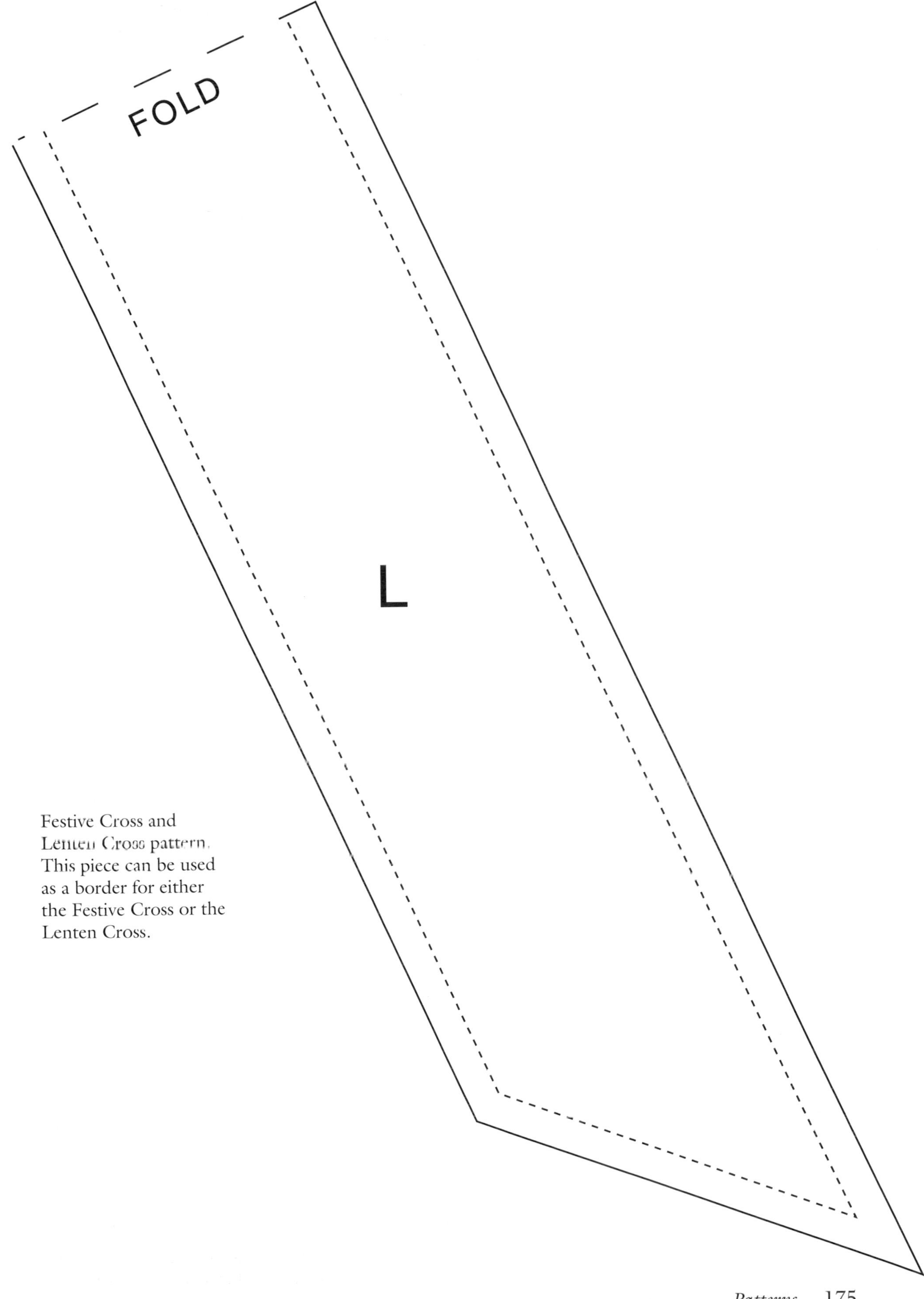

Festive Cross and Lenten Cross pattern. This piece can be used as a border for either the Festive Cross or the Lenten Cross.

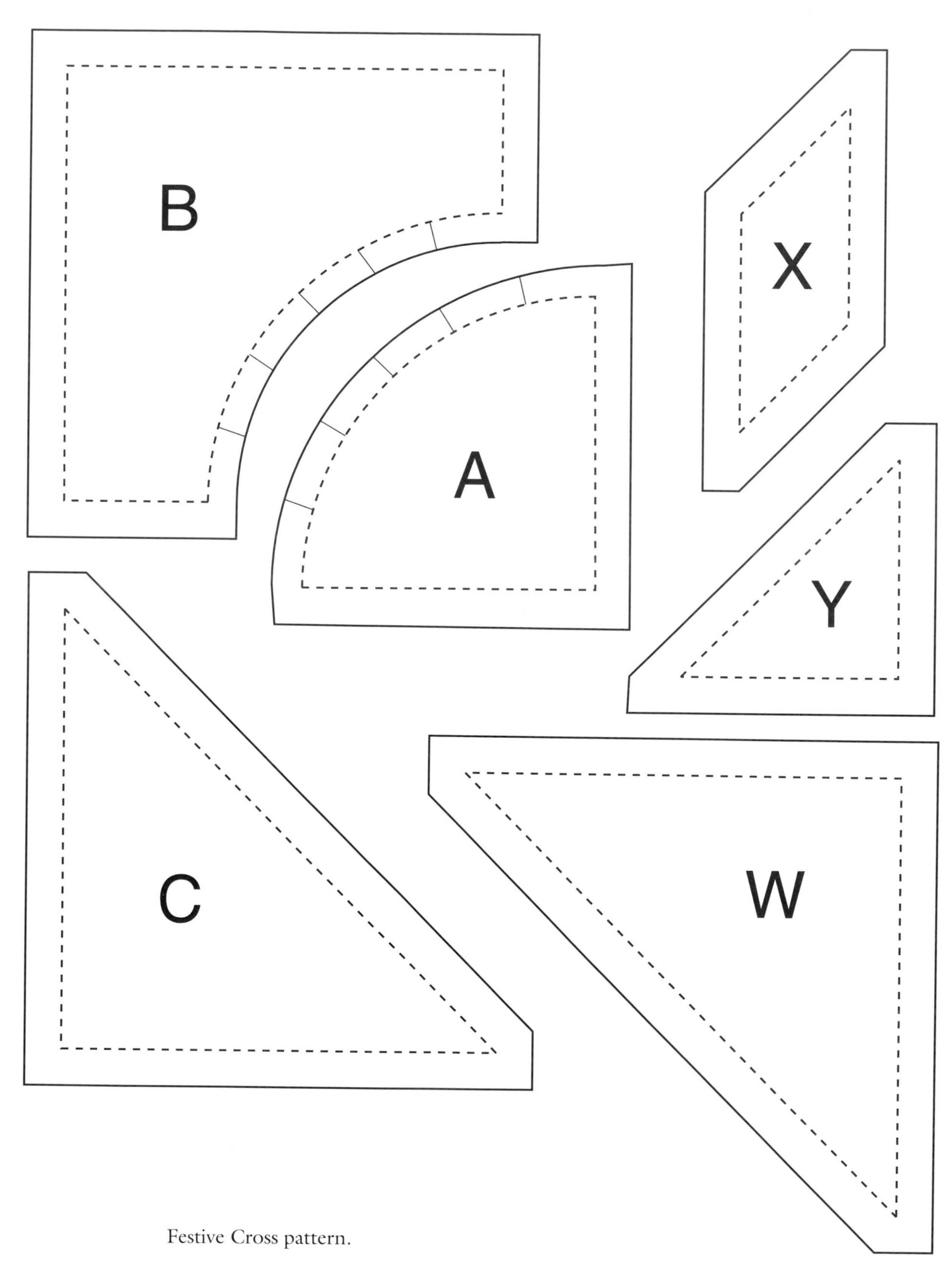

Festive Cross pattern.

Lenten Cross pattern.

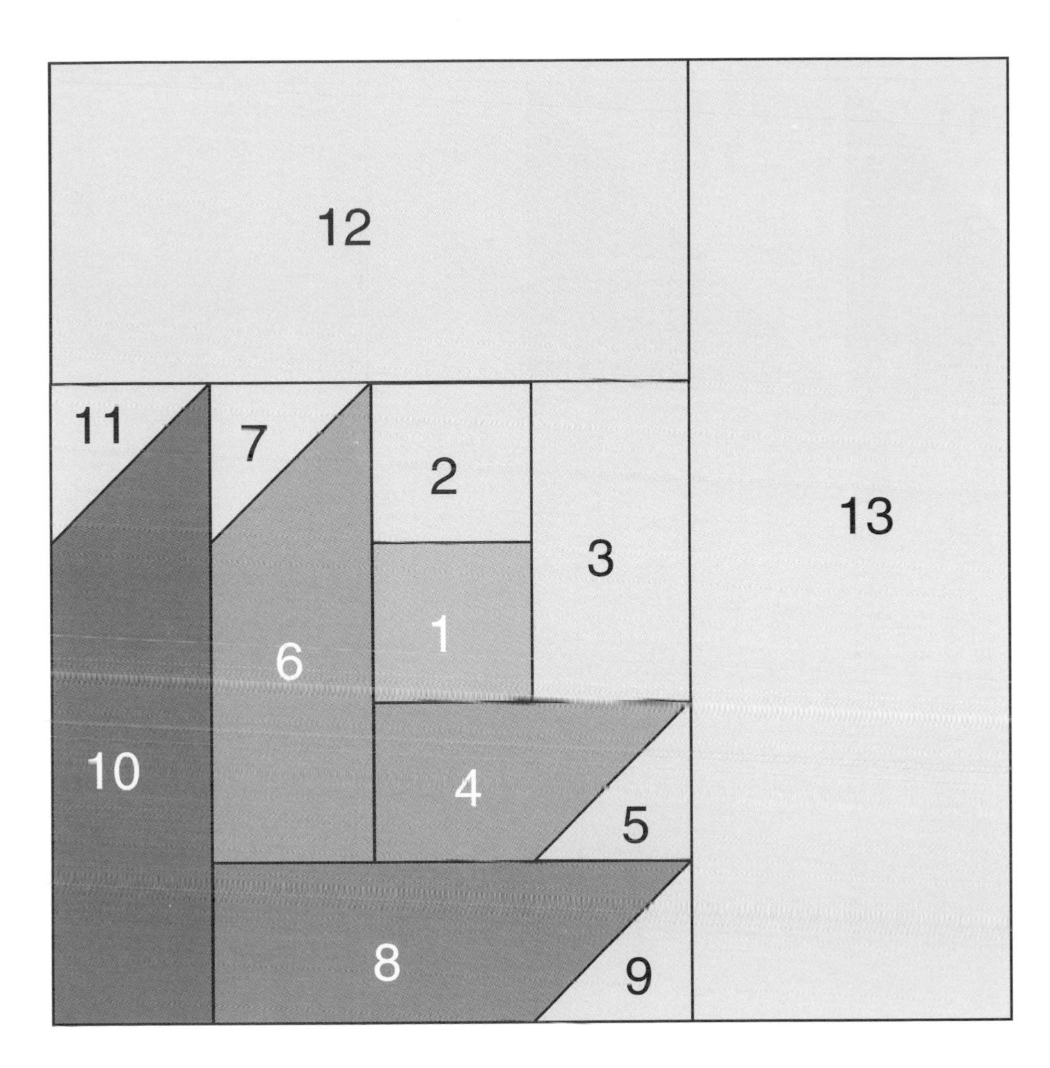

Block A.
Resurrection Rose pattern.

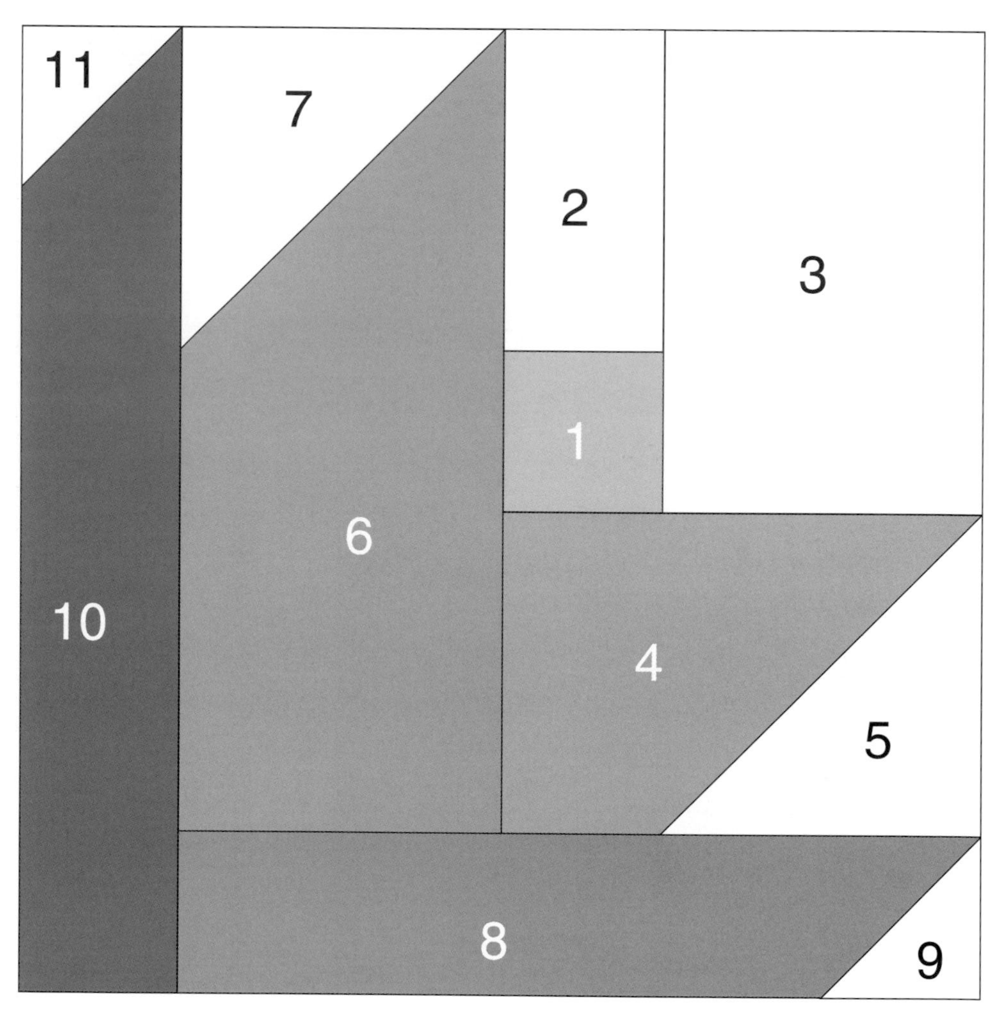

Block B.
Resurrection Rose pattern.

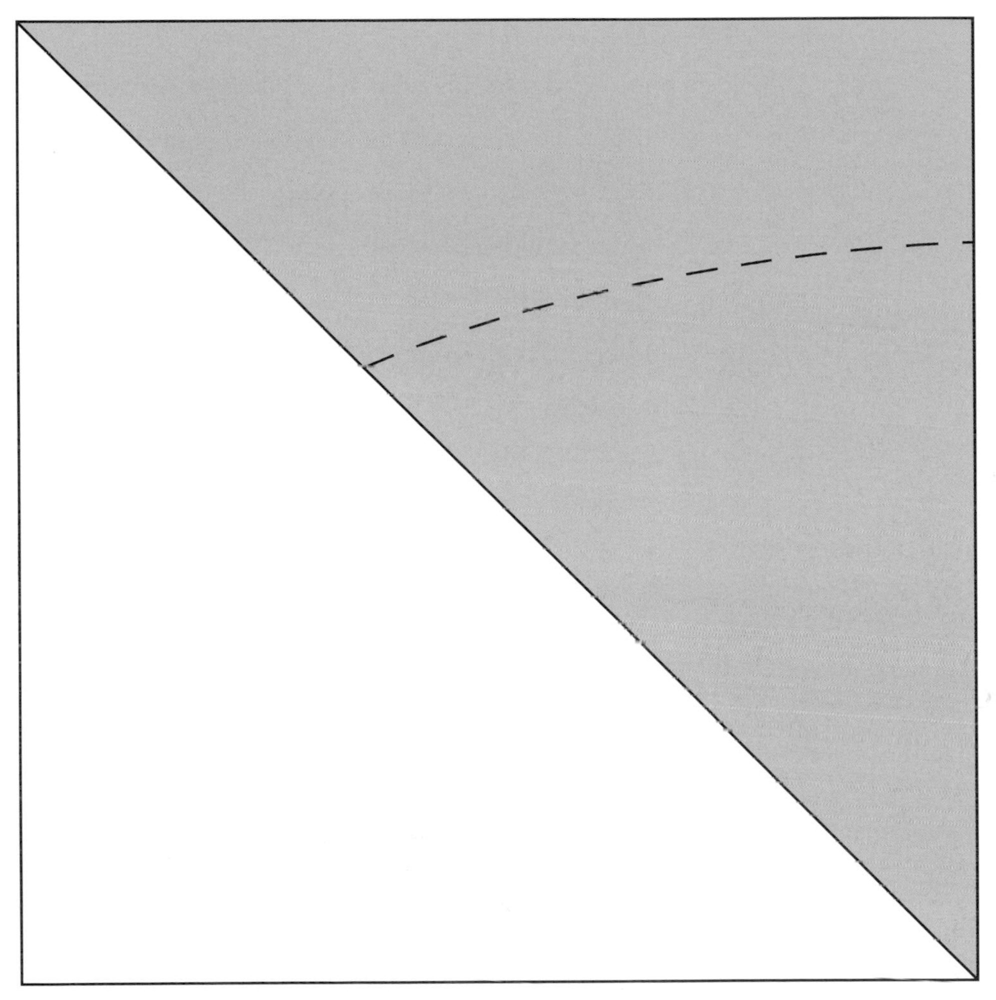

Bock C.
Resurrection Rose pattern.

PHOTOGRAPHS

The photos are arranged according to the chapters in which they are discussed.

All of the photographs in this book were taken by the authors except: front and back cover photos and photo on page 193, bottom left, © 2001 by Matthew Grasse; photo on top of page 181 by Michael Bozza; photo on top of page 184 by the Washington Missourian; the two photos on the bottom of page 191 are by Magudefai; the photo on the top left of page 195 is by Janis M. Brockland.

Chapter 1

Pentecost entrance procession, also celebrating the 50th anniversary of the ordination of Rev. Thomas Quinn, St. Patrick Church, Farmington, Conn. (Pamela T. Hardiman, collection of St. Patrick Church).

Chapter 3

Daniel's Baptism banner (Pamela T. Hardiman, collection of Daniel C. Hardiman, Farmington, Conn.).

Bride's red woven ribbon banner for the wedding of Greg and Julie Rohde (Josephine Niemann, SSND, collection of St. Margaret of Scotland Church, St. Louis).

Funeral banner, Rising to Glory (Josephine Niemann, SSND, Archdiocese of Seattle).

Groom's blue woven ribbon banner for the wedding of Greg and Julie Rohde (Josephine Niemann, SSND, collection of St. Margaret of Scotland Church, St. Louis).

CHAPTER 4

Academy of the Holy Angels banner (Josephine Niemann, SSND, collection of Academy of the Holy Angels, Dermaset, N.J.).

CHAPTER 5

Easter Cross (Josephine Niemann, SSND, collection of Holy Family Church, St. Louis).

Chapter 6

Mighty Waters. Large-scale banners in a large-scale space, a football stadium transformed into a worship space during the pope's 1999 visit to St. Louis. The ten banners are 5' x 6' nylon panels on 12' poles with 30' streamers.

Chapter 7

Amish Cross (Josephine Niemann, SSND, collection of Liturgical Fabric Arts, St. Louis).

Advent and Christmas Star (Josephine Niemann, SSND, collection of Our Lady of Loretto, St. Louis).

Festive Cross banner (Josephine Niemann, SSND, collection of Little Flower Church, Clayton, Mo.).

Lenten Cross banner (Josephine Niemann, SSND, collection of St. Joseph Church in Martinsburg, W.V.).

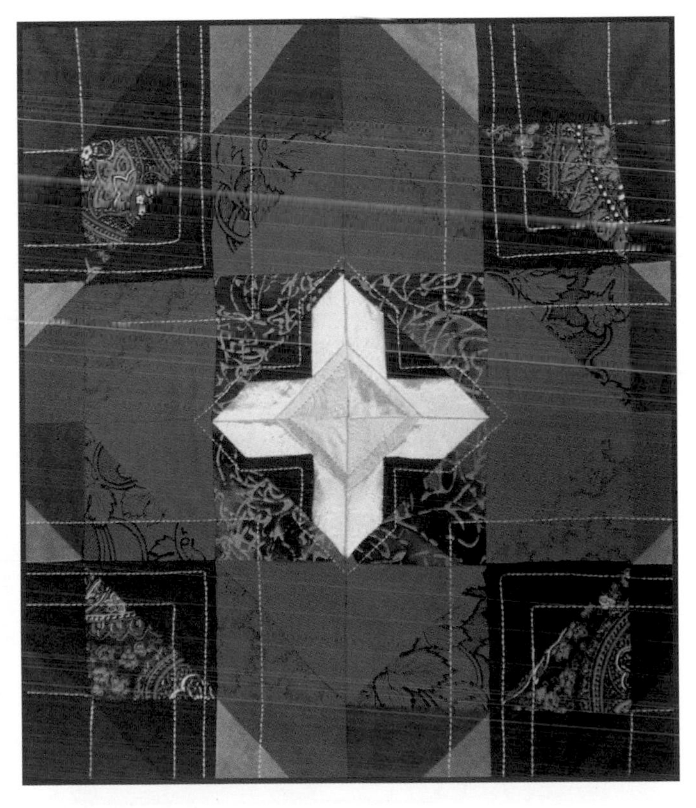

Detail of Lenten Cross (Josephine Niemann, SSND, collection of St. Joseph Church in Martinsburg, W.V.).

Gemstones banner (Josephine Niemann, SSND, collection of Liturgical Fabric Arts, St. Louis).

Easter Cross banner (Josephine Niemann, SSND, collection of the School Sisters of Notre Dame, St. Louis Province).

Resurrection Rose banner (Josephine Niemann, SSND, collection of St. Theresa/St. Elizabeth Ann Seton Church, Morgantown, W. V.).

Ordinary Time Anchor banner (Josephine Niemann, SSND, collection of School Sisters of Notre Dame, St. Louis Province).

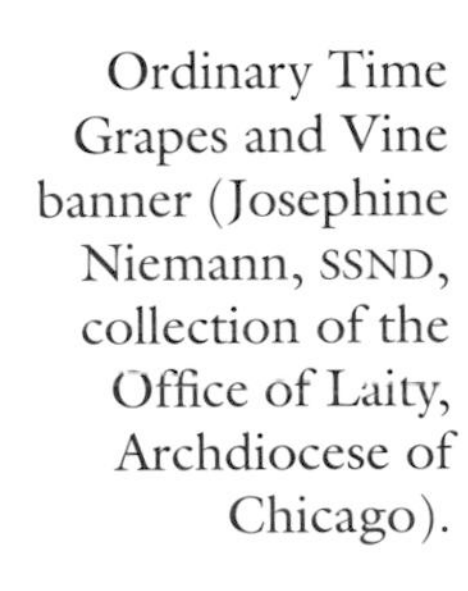

Ordinary Time Grapes and Vine banner (Josephine Niemann, SSND, collection of the Office of Laity, Archdiocese of Chicago).

Detail of Grapes and Vine banner.

Wedding banner (Pamela T. Hardiman, collection of Pamela T. Hardiman, Farmington, Conn.).

Pentecost Fire banner (Josephine Niemann, SSND, collection of School Sisters of Notre Dame, St. Louis Province).

Mighty Waters banner. One of a series of ten made for the visit of Pope John Paul II to St. Louis in January of 1999 (Josephine Niemann, SSND, collection of the Archdiocese of St. Louis).

Harvest banner for Thanksgiving (Josephine Niemann, SSND, collection of Holy Infant Church, Ballwin, Mo.).

Christ the King banner (Josephine Niemann, SSND, collection of Holy Infant Church, Ballwin, Mo.)

Eucharist banner (Josephine Niemann, SSND, collection of St. Margaret Mary Alacoque, St. Louis).

Sacred Heart banner (Josephine Niemann, SSND, collection of St. Margaret Mary Alacoque, St. Louis).

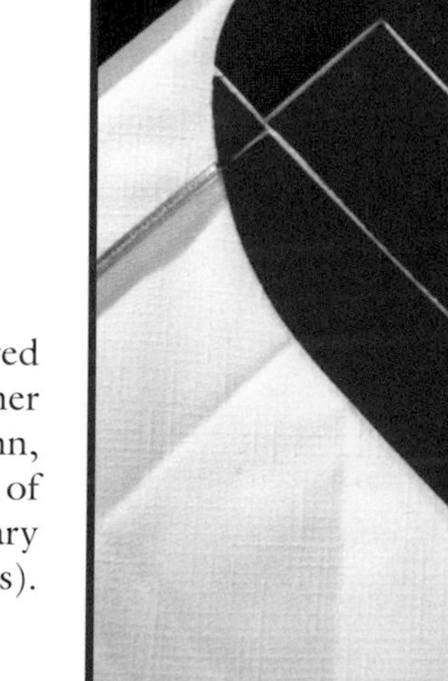

Detail of Sacred Heart banner (Josephine Niemann, SSND, collection of St. Margaret Mary Alacoque, St. Louis).

Detail of Mother Caroline centennial banner, showing the motherhouse of the St. Louis Province of the School Sisters of Notre Dame drawn with the names of all the sisters (Josephine Niemann, SSND, collection of the School Sisters of Notre Dame, St. Louis Province).

Detail of cyanotype (Josephine Niemann, SSND, private collection.).

Cyanotype, "Women's Lib Apron" (Josephine Niemann, SSND, private collection).

Our Lady of the Holy Spirit banner (Josephine Niemann, SSND, collection of Our Lady of the Holy Spirit Church, Mount Zion, Ill.).

Detail of Our Lady of the Holy Spirit banner, showing iron-on transfer faces (Josephine Niemann, SSND, collection of Our Lady of the Holy Spirit Church, Mount Zion, Ill.).

Celtic Cross banner (Pamela T. Hardiman, collection of St. Patrick Church, Farmington, Conn.).

First Communion Bread banner (Pamela T. Hardiman, collection of St. Francis Xavier (College) Church, St. Louis).

First Communion Wine banner (Pamela T. Hardiman, collection of St. Francis Xavier (College) Church, St. Louis).

Christ Our Light banner (Pamela T. Hardiman, collection of David and Lynda Rands, Olney, Ill.).

Easter Sunrise banner (Josephine Niemann, SSND, collection of St. Mark Church, Indianapolis).

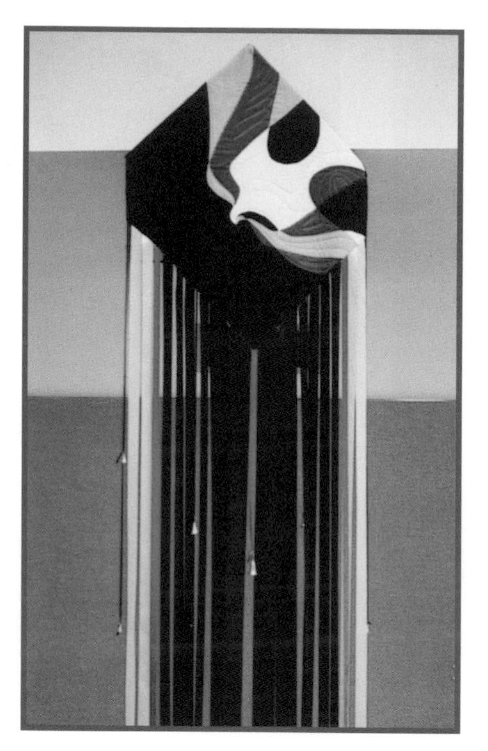

Pentecost Dove banner (Josephine Niemann, SSND, collection of Webster Groves Presbyterian Church, Webster Groves, Mo.).

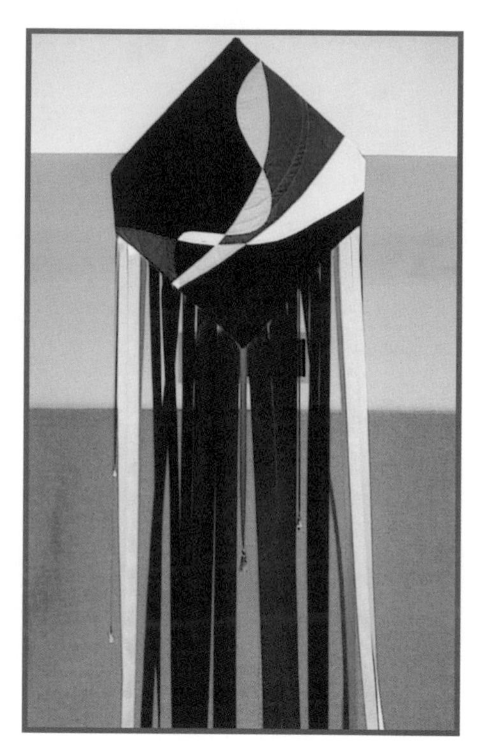

Pentecost Wind banner (Josephine Niemann, SSND, collection of Webster Groves Presbyterian Church, Webster Groves, Mo.).

The Stars Declare His Glory banner (collection of St. Francis Xavier (College) Church, St. Louis).

Unity. Five banners forming a united whole, made for a eucharistic liturgy celebrated in Forest Park, St. Louis (Josephine Niemann, SSND, collection of the Boy Scouts of America).

Queen of Heaven banner (Pamela T. Hardiman, collection of Pamela T. Hardiman, Farmington, Conn.).

Fabric for reverse of Waters of Life banner, prior to cutting and piecing (Mickey Lawler of SkyDyes, collection of Christian Reformed Church, Ann Arbor, Mich.).

Waters of Life banner (Pamela T. Hardiman, collection of Christian Reformed Church, Ann Arbor, Mich.).

About the Authors

Josephine Niemann, SSND, with A Life Woven with Love banner (banner by Josephine Niemann, SSND, collection of St. Theresa/ St. Elizabeth Ann Seton Parish, Morgantown, W.V.).

Josephine Niemann, a School Sister of Notre Dame, currently designs vestments and banners for Liturgical Fabric Arts, a ministry active since 1898 in the community's St. Louis motherhouse. After teaching art in secondary schools for twenty years in Illinois, Iowa, Missouri, and Sierra Leone, Josephine began working full-time as an artist. Having grown up in a family where quilting is a loved tradition, she naturally began to use this medium for her creative expression. Her style ranges from traditional to contemporary, from geometric to pictorial. Her work can be seen in church collections across the country, as well as in numerous books, quilting magazines and liturgical publications. Josephine earned a master's degree in art from the University of Notre Dame.

Pamela T. Hardiman with First Communion banner (banner by Pamela T. Hardiman, collection of St. Francis Xavier (College) Church, St. Louis.

Pamela T. Hardiman is an accomplished quilt artist who was for many years a partner in the much-traveled Double T Quilt Shop. Her award-winning liturgical work includes small- and large-scale wall hangings, processional banners, and vestments. Over the years, she has studied with many nationally and internationally known quilt artists and has published work in books and magazines. Pam is also an assistant director of religious education. She holds a master's degree in mathematics and a doctorate in psychology from the University of Massachusetts. She lives with her husband and three sons in Farmington, Connecticut.